Trans-Allegheny Pioneers

HISTORICAL SKETCHES

OF THE

First White Settlements West of the Alleghenies

1748 AND AFTER

WONDERFUL EXPERIENCES OF HARDSHIP AND HEROISM OF THOSE
WHO FIRST BRAVED THE DANGERS OF THE INHOSPIT-
ABLE WILDERNESS, AND THE SAVAGE TRIBES
THAT THEN INHABITED IT.

By JOHN P. HALE
CHARLESTON, WEST VIRGINIA

CINCINNATI
THE GRAPHIC PRESS, 135 MAIN STREET
1886

ENTERED ACCORDING TO ACT OF CONGRESS, IN THE YEAR 1886,

BY JOHN P. HALE,

IN THE OFFICE OF THE LIBRARIAN OF CONGRESS, AT WASHINGTON, D. C.

Facsimile Reprint

Published 1988 By

HERITAGE BOOKS, INC.
1540E Pointer Ridge Place, Bowie, Maryland 20716
(301)-390-7709

ISBN 1-55613-128-3

SYNOPSIS.

Progressively advancing settlements along the entire Virginia border, from the New River-Kanawha and tributaries, in the southwest, to the Monongahela and tributaries in the northwest, the intervening country to the Ohio River and into Kentucky.

On the above-mentioned first settled western flowing streams, occurred, in after years, the desperate and bloody conflicts of Braddock's Fields and Point Pleasant, for the possession of, and supremacy in, this fair western country.

To the New River-Kanawha, and tributaries, however, more especial attention is here given; all sandwiched throughout with collateral facts and incidents of more or less general or local historical interest.

Draper's Meadows Massacre.—Destruction of the early Greenbriar Settlements.—Tragedies of Burke's Garden and Abb's Valley.—Origin of the American Cotton Trade.—Old time Family Fall Hunt.—Remarkable Clock.—Progressive Changes within a Lifetime.—Davy Crockett and his Wise Motto.

Battle of Point Pleasant.—Brief Outline of Events Leading to It.—The First Blood of the Revolution.—A Pivotal Turning Point in American History.—Short Sketches of Some of Those Who Participated in It.—Brief Review of Lord Dunmore's Relation to It.—Its Influence as a Developing Military High School, etc.

Murder of Cornstalk.—Desperate Fight at Donnally's Fort.—Short Sketch of Daniel Boone's Life in Kanawha Valley.—Chronological Table of Events, of more or less importance or interest, that have occurred along the western border.

Charleston, West Virginia.—Short Sketch of Its Early Settlement and After History.—Dublin, Virginia.—History of Its Name.—Augusta County.—Its Original Vast Extent and Its Subdivisions.

INTRODUCTION.

PIONEER HISTORY does *not* repeat itself. Our country—and especially our great Western trans-allegheny country—has but recently passed through, and is hardly yet entirely emerged, in the far West, from a period of intensely active, exciting and eventful history, which can never be repeated.

The discovery, exploration, conquest, settlement and civilization of a continent, once accomplished in this age, is done for all time; there are no more continents to discover; no more worlds to conquer.

To McCauley's imaginary New Zealander who is to stand upon the broken arches of London Bridge, and speculate on the ruins of St. Paul and of London, the opportunity will never come; the ratchets of steam, electricity and printing, will hold the world from ever again retrograding. The course of civilization is onward and upward, as that of Empire is Westward.

The wilderness, to be settled by the pioneer Ingleses and Drapers, the Harmons and Burkes, the Gists and Tygarts, no longer exists. The occupations of the Boones and Kentons, the Zanes, McCullochs, Bradys and Wetzels, as border settlers and Indian fighters, passed away with them. There is no longer need for the Lewises and Clarkes, as transcontinental explorers. For the Fremonts and Kit Carsons as mountain path finders and path makers. For the Schoolcrafts and Catlins to study and portray, with pen and pencil, unknown races and tribes; the Pontiacs and Cornstalks, the Logans and Tecumsehs, the Black Hawks and the Girtys, have left the stage forever. The Andrew Lewises and Mad Anthony Waynes, the George Rogers Clarkes, and William Henry Harrisons, the daring frontier commanders, would have to mold their swords into pruning hooks and plow shares now. The martyrdoms of the Colonel Crawfords, the Mrs. Moores, and the Flinns, can never occur again. The experiences of captive life and remarkable escapes of the Mary Ingleses, the Bettie Drapers, the Mary Moores, the Hannah Dennises and the Rebecca Davidsons, are, thanks to advancing civilization, the last of their kind, and the Anne Baileys and Bettie Zanes need fear no future rivals for their well-earned laurels.

The history that the hundreds of brave actors—of whom these are but the types and exemplars—made, in their day and generation, by their heroic deeds and sufferings, was a history unparalleled in the past, and that can never be repeated in the future; the conditions no longer exist, and can never exist again.

For the present generation, born and reared in these days of safety, law and order, peace and plenty, ease and luxury, in these days of steam and electricity, of rapid transit, more rapid communication, and all the nameless accompaniments of the latest civilization, it is difficult to look back to the days of our grandfathers, and realize that, in their day, all this vast Western country from the Alleghenies even to the Pacific, now teeming with its many millions of busy, prosperous, and happy people, with their thriv-

ing cities, towns and villages, and productive valleys
and plains, was then one unbroken expanse of wilderness, lying in a state of nature, roamed by herds
of wild animals and tribes of savage men ; unknown,
or but vaguely known to the white man ; never penetrated by white men except by a few exceptionably
adventurous Spanish and French explorers and
traders, accompanied, as usual, by pious Monks and
Jesuit Fathers, tempted by the love of God or gold,
and the hope of gain or glory.

Those who braved the dangers, privations, and
hardships of pioneer life, and participated in the stirring scenes and events that attended the transform-
ation of this wilderness into hives of busy industry,
and homes of comfort and luxury, seldom kept
diaries, or left written records or histories of their
wonderful achievements and thrilling experiences—
the circumstances and surroundings not favoring the
writing or preserving of such records—nor, indeed,
did the tastes of the hardy pioneers run in that direction, and, therefore, as the older generations passed
away, many of them carried with them recollections
and traditions that can never be recovered, and thus
has been lost much of pioneer history probably as
interesting as any that has been preserved

As the histories of these exciting times will, no
doubt, possess deeper interest and be more valued and
prized the farther the period in which the events
occurred recedes adown the stream of time, it should
be the duty of every one who can, to collect and add
whatever he can, from authentic and trustworthy
records and traditions, to the general fund of reliable
history of this interesting period, for permanent
preservation.

The Ingles and Draper families—my maternal ancestors—were pioneers in the then great Western wilderness. The history of these first transalle-gheny settlements is full of interest, and some of their experiences, for daring adventure, terrible suffering, and heroic endurance, are not excelled by anything with which I am acquainted in all the annals of border life.

As I am now one of the oldest surviving descend-ants of those early pioneers, and having taken some pains to collect the family records and vanishing traditions relating to the settlements and the families, I have felt constrained to commit them to print to preserve them from the fate of so many others now lost in oblivion, for lack of timely record, and add them to the many other interesting histories of the period.

In connection with, and following these histories of the Ingles and Draper settlements and families, I shall endeavor to trace, in chronological order, the progressive frontier explorations and settlements along the entire Virginia border, from the Allghanies to the Ohio, from the New River-Kanawha and tributaties in the South-west, where settlements first began, to the Monongahela and tributaries, in the North-west, when they followed, and the intervening country, and along the Ohio, where the frontier line of settlements was last to be advanced, but I shall give more especial attention to the early history of the region of the New River-Kanawha and tributaries, all sandwitched, throughout, with collateral facts and incidents of more or less local or general historical interest.

TRANS-ALLEGHENY PIONEERS.

CHAPTER I.

THE INGLES FAMILY.

THOMAS INGLES, according to family tradition, was descended from a Scotch family, was born and reared in London, lived about 1730 to 1740, in Dublin, Ireland, was a large importing wholesale merchant, was wealthy, owned his own ships and traded with foreign countries, chiefly to the East Indies.

Sir Walter Scott states that in the reign of James I., there was a Sir Thomas Inglis who lived and owned baronial estates on the border of England and Scotland. He was much annoyed by the raids and border forays of those days, and, to escape them, exchanged his border estates called "Branx-Holm," with a Sir William Scott, ancestor of the late Sir Walter, and of the Dukes of Buckcleu, for his Barony of "Murdiestone," in Lanarkshire, to which he removed for greater peace and security. Branx-Holm or Branksome, in Tiviotdale, on the Scottish border, is still owned by the Dukes of Buckcleu. From the close similarity and possible original identity of the names—both very rare—and now only differing from i to e in the spelling, Thomas Ingles of Dublin, may have descended from the Sir Thomas of "Branx-

Holm Hall," but, if so, the present Ingles family
have no record or knowledge of it. They only trace
their line back to the Thomas Ingles of London,
Dublin, and America.

There are two families in America who spell their
names Inglis. The ancestor of one of them emi-
grated from Selkirk, Scotland, to Montreal. Those
of the other branch came from Paisley, Scotland, to
New York. Descendants of the first still live in
Canada, but while they spell their name Inglis, they
pronounce it Ingles, and say it has always, within
their knowledge, been so pronounced. The descendants of the Paisley family live in Philadelphia, Baltimore, South Carolina, and Florida. These two families, and the descendants of the Ingles who came
from London and Dublin, and settled in Virginia,
are the only families in America, so far as I know,
who spell their names either Inglis or Ingles.

In some revolution or political trouble, occurring
during the time of his residence in Dublin, Thomas
Ingles took a prominent and active part, and happened not to be on the right, or, rather, on the winning side, for the winning side is not always the
right side, nor the right side the winning side.

On the failure of the cause he had espoused, his
property was confiscated, and he was lucky to escape
with his life.

He, with his three sons, William, Matthew, and
John—he then being a widower—came to America,
and located for a time in Pennsylvania, about Cham-
bersburg.

Just when they came, and how long they remained
there, is not now accurately known; but in 1744,

according to the tradition, Thomas Ingles and his eldest son, William, then a youth, made an excursion to the wilds of Southwest Virginia, penetrating the wilderness as far as New River.

Of the details of this expedition no record has been preserved. On this trip they probably made the acquaintance of Colonel James Patton, who held a grant for 120,000 acres of land west of the Blue Ridge, and in the valley of Virginia. Colonel Patton, who came from the North of Ireland, about 1735–36, was one of the earliest settlers in the valley, and first located near Staunton. He and his son-in-law, Colonel John Buchanan, located lands on James River, and named the villages which sprang up on opposite sides of the river, Pattonsburg and Buchanan, now in Bottetourt County, Virginia.

It is also probable that the Ingleses, during the trip above mentioned, first made the acquaintance of the Drapers, then living at Pattonsburg, and whose after history and fates were so closely connected and interblended with their own.

George Draper and his young wife, whose maiden name had been Elenor Hardin, came from County Donegal, North of Ireland, in 1729, and settled at the mouth of the Schuylkill River, within the present limits of the City of Philadelphia. Here two children were born to them, John in 1730, and Mary in 1732.

Between 1740 and 1744 they, with their two children, came to Virginia, and located at Colonel Patton's settlement (Pattonsburg), on James River.

Staunton and Pattonsburg, though the valley was but so recently settled, are about the same age as

Richmond and Petersburg. Settlements were begun at the two former about 1738, and at Richmond and Petersburg about 1737–38. The two latter were laid off by Surveyor Mayo, in 1737, for Colonel William Byrd, of Westover. Richmond was organized as a town in 1742—Colonel Byrd had had plantations here as early as 1732.

While the Drapers lived at Pattonsburg, George Draper started out on a game-hunting and land-seeking expedition, westward. He never returned, and was never again heard of by his family; it was supposed that he was killed by the Indians.

There is no account preserved of how far he went, who accompanied him, nor any other details of the trip.

CHAPTER II.

IN 1848 Doctor Thomas Walker, Colonel James
Patton, Colonel John Buchanan, Colonel James
Wood, and Major Charles Campbell, accompanied by
some hunters, of whom John Findley, who afterward,
in 1767, penetrated into Kentucky, and, in 1769,
accompanied Daniel Boone from North Carolina to
Kentucky, was one, made an excursion through
Southwest Virginia and were the first white persons
from this direction to penetrate the then unknown
region of Kentucky. Dr. Walker, the leader of the
expedition, discovered the pass in the mountains, and
gave the name of "Cumberland" to the mountain
range and gap hitherto called by the Indians
"Wasioto;" "Cumberland River" to the stream
hitherto called "Shawanee," or "Pelisipi;" and
"Louisa" to the river called by them "Che-no-ee,"
now Kentucky River. Major Jed Hotchkiss, who,
I believe, has seen the MS. diary of Doctor Walker,
thinks he did not get on to the Kentucky River, and
that the stream he named Louisa was the one now
called Coal River, West Virginia, which heads up in
the big Flat-Top Mountain along which he traveled.
The earliest maps that lay down Coal River—Jeffer-
sons and others—call it Louisa.

The Cumberland Mountains, Gap, and River, were
named after the Duke of Cumberland, and Louisa
River for his wife, the Duchess of Cumberland.

Walker's Creeks (big and little), of New River,

which were explored by Dr. Walker and party on
this expedition, and Walker's Mountains (big and
little), parallel ranges, were named after Dr. Walker.

About this time (1748), probably immediately on
the return of Walker, Patton and others—if, indeed,
they did not accompany the Walker expedition as
far as New River—Thomas Ingles and his three sons,
Mrs. Draper and her son and daughter, Adam Harmon, Henry Lenard, and James Burke " came West
to grow up with the country," and made the first
settlement west of the great Allegheny " divide," the
first on the waters of New River, or Wood's River, as
it was then interchangeably called, and the first on
any waters flowing to the undefined, unknown, mysterious West, whither they knew not.

The name given to this locality and settlement was
" Draper's Meadows."

The first buildings and improvements, which were
built of round logs, as all frontier buildings then
were, stood upon the present sites of the " Virginia
Agricultural and Mechanical College," and "Solitude," the residence of the late Colonel Robert
Preston, near Blacksburg, now Montgomery County,
Virginia.

Even at the present day, when all Southwest Virginia is settled and highly improved, and is known
to excessively abound in grand and beautiful land-
scape scenery, few, if any, scenes surpass this little
" Draper's Meadows" Valley, the original, and at
that day, probably, a hap-hazard settlement, as they
had not sufficiently explored the country to compare
localities and make choice.

Its eastern limit is near the crest of the Allegheny,

here a very low "divide" between the waters of the
Roanoke on the east and New or Woods River on the
west; its western, the beautiful "Horse-Shoe Bend"
of New River; while to the north and south, in the
near distance, are parallel mountain ridges. Between
is a beautiful undulating plain, with rich limestone,
blue-grass soil. There are numerous bold, never-
failing limestone springs, and the drainage is to New
River, through Toms Creek, Straubles Creek, and
Walls Creek.

At the date of this Draper's Meadows settlement
(1748) the entire population of Virginia—which then
extended from the Atlantic to the Mississippi (or, as
claimed, to the Pacific), and embraced the present
States of Virginia, West Virginia, Kentucky, Ohio,
Indiana, Illinois, Michigan, and Wisconsin—was but
eighty-two thousand. All but a few hundred of these
were east of the Blue Ridge; these few hundred were
settled in the Valley of Virginia, so-called, being the
territory lying between the Blue Ridge and the Alle-
ghany Ranges. This valley it is claimed, but erroneously, as we shall hereafter see, was first discovered
by Governor Spottswood and his "Knights of the
Golden Horse-Shoe," in 1716, penetrating the Blue
Ridge at Swift Run Gap, and first settled in 1732 by
Joist Hite, John Lewis, Bowman, Green, Chrisman,
McKay, Stephens, Duff, and others; followed, in
1734, by Morgan, Allen, Moore, Shephard, Harper,
and others, and in 1735 to 1738 by Beverly, Christian,
Patton, Preston, Burden, and others. These colonists
took up lands and made settlements from Harper's
Ferry to the site of Staunton and above. They were
mostly Scotch-Irish families, who had stopped for a

time in Pennsylvania, and found their way from there
into the Valley of Virginia, by way of Harper's Ferry,
taking up the best lands on the waters of the Shenandoah, the James, and the Roanoke Rivers.

The Ingles and Draper families, who were also
Scotch-Irish, and who had also come by way of
Pennsylvania, were the first to press on beyond these,
then frontier settlements, scale the Allegheny, the
then limit and western barrier of civilization and
discovery, and pitch their tents, as above stated, in the
great outside, unknown, and mysterious wilderness
beyond.

The first map of this region to which I have had
access, is a map of 1744, accompanying Rapin de
Thoyers' History of England. This map shows
pretty fair knowledge of the coast lines, but wild
guesses, based upon small information about the
country beyond the mountains. The Tennessee River
called Hogoheegee, empties in the Wabash or "Ouback." The head waters of the Hogoheegee are left
blank—cut square off. The Cumberland, called Pelisipi, empties into the Hogoheegee. The Ohio or
"Hohio," empties into the Ouback on the north,
and the Ouback unites with the Potomac in a lake
common to both, lying south of Lake Erie, and from
which they flow their respective ways east and west.
The Allegheny mountain is laid down with a fair
degree of accuracy as to location and direction. The
next map of this part of Virginia was made by Peter
Fontaine, Surveyor of Halifax County, at the request
of the Governor of Virginia, in 1752. In this map
the Allegheny Mountain is put down as "Mississippi
or Allegheny Ridge." New River is put down as

" New Riv., a branch of Mississippi Riv.," and all the
region west of the Allegheny is left blank, and

FROM RAPIN DE THOYERS' MAP OF 1744.

called " a mountainous tract of land west of the
Blue Ridge," Augusta County, " parts unknown."

The " New River " was first discovered and named
in 1654, by Colonel Abraham Wood, who dwelt at

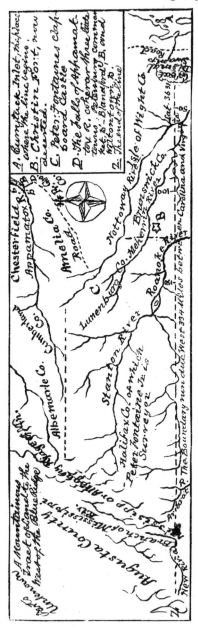

FROM PETER FONTAINE'S MAP OF 1752.

the falls of the Appomatox, now the site of Petersburg, Virginia. Being of an adventurous and speculative turn, he got a concession from the Governor of Virginia to "explore the country and open up trade with the Indians to the west." There is no record as to the particular route he took, but as the line of adventure, exploration, and discovery, was then all east of the mountains, it is probable that he first struck the river not far from the Blue Ridge, and near the present Virginia and North Carolina line.

From the fact that the gap in the Blue Ridge lying between the heads of Smith's River branch of the Dan, in Patrick County, and Little

River branch of New River, in Floyd County, is, to
this day, called "Wood's Gap." I think it highly
probable that this was his route, and that the gap was
named after him; if so, then it is almost certain that
New River was first seen by Colonel Wood, probably
the first white man who ever saw it, at the mouth of
Little River, about a mile and a half above "Ingles'
Ferry," and being to him a *new river*, without a name,
he then and there named it after himself, "Wood's
River."

If this supposition is correct, as I believe it to be,
then Colonel Abraham Wood and his party of hum-
ble hunters and traders, anticipated, by many years,
the famous exploits of the Hon. Governor Spottswood and his Knights of the Golden Horseshoe,
in passing the then limits of western discovery, the
mysterious "Blue Ridge." As a singular example
of the injustice of the Fates: Governor Spottswood
was knighted, immortalized, and had his name perpetuated by a Virginia County for what he *didn't do*
(*first* cross the Blue Ridge), while Colonel Wood,
who *did* do it, is *almost* forgotten.

CAPTAIN HENRY BATTE, BLUE RIDGE.

Even Colonel Wood was not the *only* one, though
the first, who preceeded Governor Spottswood in
crossing the Blue Ridge.

In 1666, twelve years after Colonel Wood, and fifty
years before Governor Spottswood, Governor Sir
William Berkely, says Arthur, despatched an exploring party across the mountains, to the west,
under Captain Henry Batte, with fourteen Virginians

and fourteen Indians. They also started from Appomatox. In seven days they reached the foot of the mountains. After crossing them they came to level, delightful plains, with abundant game, deer, elk, and buffalo, so gentle as not to be frightened by the approach of man. Here they discovered a river flowing westward; having followed it for several days, they came to fields and empty cabins, lately tenanted. Captain Batte left in them some trinkets, in token of friendship.

But here the Indian guides stopped and refused to go any farther, saying that there dwelt near here a tribe of Indians that made salt and sold it to other tribes. This tribe was said to be numerous and powerful, and never let any one escape who ventured into their towns. Captain Batte finding his Indians resolute in their determination not to venture farther, reluctantly abandoned the trip, and returned to the Province. Governor Berkely was so interested in the report that he determined to go and explore the country himself, but other cares and duties occupied him, and he never did. No mention is made here of Colonel Wood's trip, but Captain Batte must have known of it, as it had been but twelve years since Colonel Wood started from, and returned to, the same point. From this meager account, it seems probable that Captain Batte followed the same route that Colonel Wood had traveled, crossed the Blue Ridge at the same point—Wood's Gap—struck New River (Wood's River), which he calls a western flowing river, at or about the same point that Wood had, and followed it downward several days before reaching the territory occupied by the salt makers which, it is highly probable, was in the Kanawha Valley, and the salt made at the old Campbell's Creek Salt Spring. There were abundant remains of ancient Indian pottery about the spring when the country was first settled by the whites.

Colonel Wood when he discovered New River did not know, of course, the extent of the river nor the destination of its waters; but these names (Wood's River and New River) were intended to attach to the whole course of the stream, from its source to its mouth, wherever that might be.

By reference to modern maps, a curious topographical feature in regard to the rivers of this upper New River region will be observed.

Within a radious of a few miles four important rivers take their rise; their head waters interlocking with each other; they, however, soon bid each other a final adieu, and flow their several ways to the four points of the compass.

New River rises in North Carolina, a sea-board State, on the slopes of Grandfather Mountain; but, instead of going down through the sunny South to its natural home in the bosom of the Atlantic, it strikes out defiantly, nearly due north, through Virginia, cutting its way through the Blue Ridge, the Allegheny, and parallel ridges, and, finally, finds its way through the waters of the Ohio and Mississippi into the Gulf of Mexico.

The Yadkin River, on which, not far from here, Squire Boone and family, including the afterward renowned pioneer, Daniel Boone, settled, in 1750, having come from Berks County, Pennsylvania, rises in Virginia; but, instead of " pooling its issues " and joining its fortunes with its close and bold neighbor, New River, it leaves its native State and takes the back track, nearly south, through the Carolinas to the broad Atlantic, through the great Peedee.

The Roanoke River, or the Dan branch of it, rises both in Virginia and North Carolina, along the dividing line, flows nearly east until it joins the Staunton River, forming the true Roanoke, and empties into Albemarle Sound; whilst the Tennessee, or Pelisipi, as the Cherokees called it here, now called the Holston, rising similarly along and on both sides of the Virginia and North Carolina line, and in close interlock with the other streams named, starts out on its long western journey, and, finally, mingles its waters with those of the Ohio and Mississippi, or Me-sa-cha-ce-pe, as the aborigines called it, meaning the Big River, or "Father of Waters," the "Rio Grande" of De Soto.

The dividing line between Virginia and North Carolina, or the part of it which runs through this nest of river heads, was run under commission from the State of Virginia, in 1749, by Colonel Joshua Fry and Peter Jefferson, father of Thomas Jefferson; and continued westward to the Mississippi, in 1780, by Dr. Thomas Walker and Colonel Daniel Smythe commissioners. In 1754 Colonel Fry was the senior officer in command of the Virginia army to the Northwest, and Washington his subordinate (or Lieu-tenant-Colonel).

CHAPTER III.

*A*S so few facts and dates have been preserved in relation to the Ingles-Draper frontier settlement, owing, in great measure, to the fact above stated, that but few records were written in those days, owing to disinclination and the disadvantages under which they labored, and to the additional fact that, a few years later, their houses were burned, and all books, papers, and documents of every sort were destroyed, every collateral fact that helps to fix dates, or throws other light upon the subject becomes of interest.

Such are the following, of which there is record evidence:

In April, 1749, the house of Adam Harmon, one of the party, was raided by the Indians, and his furs and skins stolen. This was the first Indian depredation ever committed on the whites west of the Allegheny. The theft was reported by Henry Lenard to William Harbison, a Justice of the Peace for Augusta County. The names of Adam Harmon and Henry Lenard will appear again farther on.

In 1751 an allowance was made by the State to Colonel Patton for moving a party of Indians from Williamsburg, the then capital, to Reed Creek, in Augusta County. Reed Creek empties into New River a few miles above Ingles Ferry.

In 1753 the Indians stole the skins of George

Hoopaugh and Jacob Harmon, killed their dogs and shot their "critters."

In 1758 the State sent Captain Robert Wade from "Fort Mayo," with thirty-five rangers, to this settlement to "Range for enemy Indians." They came by Goblintown, by Black Water, Pigg River, and Smith's River, branches of the Dan, and crossed over to the head of Little River, through "Wood's Gap," and down Little River to New River. Probably just the route of Colonel Abraham Wood and Captain Henry Batte many years before. Thence they passed down as far as Draper's Meadows and back up to Reed Island Creek.

They fell in with a party of five Indians and one white man, the latter named Dunkleberry. They let the white man escape, but followed and killed the Indians.

The result of the expedition was reported by Captain John Echols, and sworn to before Abraham Maury, a Justice of the Peace for Augusta County.

CHAPTER IV.

ANOTHER adventurous hunter and pioneer had quietly made his appearance in this Draper's Meadows camp. It was the chubby and rosy-cheeked little god of the bow and arrow. He had evidently counted on finding fair and proper game here, and he had not mistaken his reckoning.

William Ingles and Mary Draper had fallen victims to his skillful archery. They had surrendered at discretion, and, early in 1750, they were bound by the silken cords, he being then twenty-one and she eighteen years of age. This was the first white wedding west of the Alleghenies.

Their rose-colored hopes and anticipations of the future, and their youthful dreams of happiness, were not all to be realized, as will soon appear.

Mary Draper, having no sister, had spent much of her time in her girlhood days with her only brother, in his outdoor avocations and sports. They played together, walked together, rode together. She could jump a fence or ditch as readily as he; she could stand and jump straight up nearly as high as her head; could stand on the ground, beside her horse, and leap into the saddle unaided; could stand on the floor and jump over a chair-back, etc., etc. It will soon be seen how invaluable to her such physical training was a few years later. In the long after-years she used to delight in telling over to her grandchildren of her feats of agility in her youthful days.

In 1754, John Draper, finding it not good to be alone, had prevailed upon Miss Bettie Robertson to join him in the search for happiness in this wild wilderness home.

Notwithstanding the isolation of the Draper's Meadows settlement, and its remoteness from civilization and society, the settlers were reasonably happy, prosperous and contented. They were busy clearing out and improving their lands, adding to their herds of stock, building houses, and increasing their comforts. Others, influenced by their favorable reports, were coming in and settling near them, and they were laying, as they hoped and believed, the foundatians of a growing and prosperous community.

CHAPTER V.

SEVERAL times parties of Indians, from north of the Ohio, had passed and repassed this settlement to make raids upon the Catawbas, their enemies, living farther south; but they had made no attack upon the white settlers, nor given them any annoyance or cause for alarm, except the thieving raids to Harmon's and Hoopaugh's above related.

The friendliest relations had existed between the whites and the redskins up to this time, but this happy condition of things was not long to last; indeed, the Indians may already have meditated or determined upon mischief, but disguised their designs by a show of friendship until they had made full observations and matured their plans.

On the 8th of July, 1755, being Sunday, and the day before Braddock's memorable defeat, near Fort Du Quesne, when all was peace, and there was no suspicion of harm or danger, a party of Shawanees, from beyond the Ohio, fell upon the Draper's Meadows settlement and killed, wounded, or captured every soul there present, as follows:

Colonel James Patton, Mrs. George Draper, Casper Barrier and a child of John Draper, killed; Mrs. John Draper, James Cull, wounded; Mrs. William Ingles, Mrs. John Draper, Henry Lenard, prisoners.

Mrs. John Draper, being out of doors, a short distance from the house, first discovered the enemy

approaching, and under circumstances indicating
hostile intent.

She ran into the house to give the alarm and to
get her sleeping infant. Taking the child in her
arms she ran out on the opposite side of the house
and tried to make her escape. The Indians discovered her, however, and fired on her as she ran, breaking her right arm, and causing the child to fall. She
hastily picked it up again with her left hand, and
continued her flight. She was soon overtaken, however, and made a prisoner, and the child brained
against the end of one of the house logs. The other
Indians, meanwhile, were devoting their attention to
other members of the families and camp, with the
results in killed, wounded, and captured, as above
stated.

Colonel James Patton, who had large landed interests hereabout, was here at this time, and with him
his nephew, William Preston.

Whether Colonel Patton was only temporarily
here, or was then making this his home, I do not
know. He had command of the Virginia militia in
this region, and had just brought up a supply of
powder and lead for use of the settlements, which, I
believe, the Indians secured.

Early on the morning of the attack, Colonel Patton had sent young Preston over to the house of Mr.
Philip Lybrook, on Sinking Creek, to get him to
come over and help next day with the harvest,
which was ready to be cut, and this fortunate absence
doubtless saved young Preston's life.

Colonel Patton was sitting at a table writing when
the attack was made, with his broadsword, which he

always kept with him, lying on the table before him. He was a man of large frame (he was six feet four inches in height), and herculean strength. He cut down two of the Indians with his sword, as they rushed upon him, but was, in turn, shot down himself by others out of his reach. He was a widower, sixty-three years of age, and full of health and vigor when he met his untimely death.

The father-in-law of Colonel Patton was Benjamin Burden, who came over as the general agent of Lord Fairfax, and also had large grants of land himself, chiefly in (now) Rockbridge County. He was a man of great business capacity and integrity, meeting all business obligations and engagements with such scrupulous promptness and exactness, that his habits became standards of comparison for others, and his name a synonym of punctuality and reliability. To say of any one that his promise, note, or bond, was as "good as Ben. Burden's bill," was to credit him with the "ne plus ultra" of business solvency and promptness.

This phrase is still currant and common in Virginia to this day, though few, perhaps, now know how it originated.

CHAPTER VI.

HAVING everything in their power after the massacre and capture, the Indians secured all the guns and ammunition on the premises, all the horses and such household valuables as they could carry away.

After loading up their stolen plunder, and putting the women and children on the horses, ready for moving, they set fire to the buildings and consumed everything left.

William Ingles, who was in a grain field, some distance from the houses, received his first notice of the attack through the ascending smoke and flames of the burning buildings. He at once started, instinctively, towards the scene of the tragedy, with the hope of giving aid to his family; but upon approaching near enough to see that there was a large force of well armed Indians, and that, single handed, unarmed resistance would be madness, he turned and sought his own safety in flight; he was seen, however, and pursued by two fleet warriors, each with tamahawk in hand.

He soon got out of the fields and ran down the slope of the hill through the woods and brush, the enemy, meanwhile, gaining on him slowly. In jumping over a fallen tree that lay in his path, he fell, and being concealed by the log and brush, the Indians did not know he had fallen, and passed by him, having run around the upturned roots of the tree, instead of jumping over it as he had done.

Seeing that the Indians had overlooked him and passed on, William Ingles hastily got on his feet, changed his course and succeeded in making his escape.

Ingles and Draper being without arms or horses, and having no near neighbors at hand to aid or join in pursuit, the Indians were enabled to make good their escape with their prisoners, horses, and stolen plunder, unmolested. Captain Buchanan raised a company from the more eastern settlements and despatched them in pursuit, but too much time had been lost, and no tidings of them were gotten.

About half a mile or a mile to the west, on their route, they stopped at the house of Mr. Philip Barger, an old and white haired man, cut his head off, put it in a bag, and took it with them to the house of Philip Lybrook, on Sinking Creek, where they left it, telling Mrs. Lybrook to look in the bag and she would find an acquaintance.

Lybrook and Preston would, probably, have shared the same fate as Barger, if they had been found at Lybrook's house; but they had started back to Draper's Meadows on foot, by a near pathway across the mountain, and thus missed meeting the Indians, and saved their lives.

In 1774, nineteen years later, the family of John Lybrook, son of Philip, was attacked by a party of Indians. John Lybrook himself succeeded in eluding them, by secreting himself in a cave in the cliffs—five of his children were murdered. About the same time, Margaret McKenzie and three Snidow

3

boys were captured in the neighborhood, two of them, Jacob and William soon escaped and returned, but John, a small boy, was taken on to the Indian towns. He was recovered by his family after some years of captivity, during which he had almost forgotten his mother tongue, and meanwhile had acquired so strong a taste for wild, Indian life, that he returned to the Indians and spent his life with them. Margaret McKenzie was recovered after eighteen years of captivity, returned to Giles County, married a Mr. Benjamin Hall, and lived to a very old age, dying about 1850.

The general course of retreat of the Indians with the prisoners and spoils of the Draper's Meadows massacre, was down New River, but there is no record preserved of the exact route, and but few details of the trip down.

It is presumed that the Indians knew and traveled ridge roads and creek routes for much of the distance, where the river route was impracticable for pack-horses.

Terrible as were these experiences generally, they were especially painful and trying to Mrs. Ingles, who was nearly approaching a period of maternity. Neither this, in her case, however, nor a shattered arm in the case of Mrs. Draper, were allowed to stand in the way of their making the trip. They were permitted to ride the horses, carry the children, and make themselves as comfortable as the circumstances allowed, but go they must, whatever the pain and suffering to them.

It was very fortunate for each that the other was along, as their companionship was not only a comfort

and solace to each other in their trying situations,
but they rendered most important services to each
other as nurses, as occasion required

On the night of the third day out, the course of
nature, which waits not upon conveniences nor surroundings, was fulfilled, and Mrs. Ingles, far from
human habitation, in the wide forest, unbounded by
walls, with only the bosom of mother earth for a
couch, and covered by the green trees and the blue
canopy of heaven, with a curtain of black darkness
around her, gave birth to an infant daughter.

Ordinarily, such an occurrence would have been
equivalent to a death warrant to the mother and
child, for if they had not both died, under the stress
of circumstances, the Indians would have tomahawked them, to avoid the trouble and the necessary
delay of their journey; but Mrs. Ingles was an extraordinary woman, and equal to any emergency.
Owing to her perfect physical constitution, health
and training, she seems to have passed through her
trouble with almost as little suffering and loss of
time as one of the wild Indian squaws themselves.
She was next morning able to travel, and did resume
the journey, carrying the little stranger in her arms,
on horseback.

One strong reason—probably the controlling one,
with the Indians—why Mrs. Ingles and infant were
not tomahawked, was that they counted upon getting
a handsome sum for the ransom of herself and her
children. It was not tender humanity, but cold business calculation that prevailed, and induced them to
put up with the small additional trouble and delay
for the hope of future gain.

The particulars of the eventful history of this ill-fated babe I get from a short sketch of Mrs. Ingles' captivity, together with facts relating to the early settlements of the Pattons and Prestons, written by Mrs. Governor John Floyd, nearly half a century ago. Mrs. Floyd was a Preston, born and reared at Smithfield, so that she and Mrs. Ingles were near neighbors, and it is probable that she received the facts related, from Mrs. Ingles direct.

About forty miles down, as Mrs. Ingles afterwards estimated, the party crossed from the east to the west side of the river; this must have been at or about the mouth of Indian Creek; as this creek was then, and afterwards, known to be in the line of the Indian trail, and there is here a practicable ford across New River.

At this point, in 1764, Captain Paul, from Fort Dinwiddie, attacked a party of returning Indians whom he was pursuing; killed several, stampeded the rest, and recovered some prisoners, among whom was Mrs. Catharine Gunn, a neighbor and friend of his.

From the mouth of Indian Creek the Draper's Meadows party came down the river, on the west side, to the mouth of Bluestone River, when they left New River, going up Bluestone a short distance, thence crossing over Flat Top Mountain, and probably following very much the route of the present Giles, Raleigh and Fayette Turnpike, to about the head of Paint Creek, and thence down Paint Creek to Kanawha River.

At some point below the mouth of Paint Creek, probably at Cabin Creek, or Witcher's Creek Shoals, where, in low water, the river was shallow enough to ford or wade, they again crossed over to the northeast side of Kanawha River, and upon reaching the salt spring, just above the mouth of Campbell's Creek, then well-known to the Indians, they stopped and rested, and feasted themselves on the abundance of fat game they killed, as it came to the "Licks" for salt.

Some of the prisoners were treated very roughly on the route down, and suffered very much; but Mrs. Ingles, owing to her delicate condition, and to her having policy and tact enough to simulate a reasonable amount of cheerfulness and contentment under all her trials, and to make herself useful in many ways, was treated with more leniency and respectful consideration than any of the others.

She was permitted to ride and to carry her children. It was made one of her duties, when well enough, as it was also her pleasure, to attend to and aid her wounded sister-in-law, Mrs. Bettie Draper. The Indians instructed her to bathe and poultice the broken arm with the steeped leaves of the wild comphry plant, and to dress the wounds with a salve made from the comphry plant and deer fat.

In searching for this plant in the woods, Mrs. Ingles says she sometimes wandered off some distance from the camps, and felt strongly tempted to try to make her escape; but the thought of leaving her helpless children restrained her. She determined to share their fate, hoping that, by some good fortune, deliverance might come to them all, and that they should be saved together.

CHAPTER VII.

WHILE the Indians hunted, rested and feasted themselves at the salt spring, they put the prisoners to boiling brine and making a supply of salt to take with them to their homes beyond the Ohio.

Mrs. Ingles took part in this salt making; boiling salt water in some of her own pots and kettles, that had been brought along on the pack-horses, and she, together with the other prisoners, were undoubtedly the first white persons who ever made salt, not only in this valley, but anywhere else west of the Alleghanies.

About a hundred years later one of her grandsons, Crockett Ingles, was, for a number of years, a saltmaker almost within sight of the original salt spring; and I, one of her great grandsons, have been a salt manufacturer for more than thirty-five years, within a few hundred yards of where she first made salt in July, 1755.

After several days of resting, feasting, and salt-making, the party again loaded up their pack-horses and resumed their onward march down the Kanawha and down the Ohio to the capital town of the Shawanees, at the mouth of the Sonhioto, or Scioto River, which they reached just one month after leaving the scene of the massacre and capture at Draper's Meadows.

Soon after their arrival at the Indian town there

was a general gathering of old and young to welcome back the raiding party, to congratulate them on their success, to learn the extent of their good fortune, and to celebrate the event by a general jollification.

The prisoners, according to custom, were required to "run the gauntlet," except Mrs. Ingles, whom, on account of her condition, they excused. Mrs. Draper, notwithstanding her lame arm, not yet recovered, was subjected to this painful ordeal, with much suffering.

It was a great comfort to Mrs. Ingles, amidst all the distressing circumstances with which she was surrounded, that her children were left in her own charge, and that she could, in some degree, care for them and promote their comfort. This, however, proved of but short duration. It was but a few days until there was a meeting of the Indians who had made the last raids, to divide out the spoils. The prisoners were all separated, as was the custom, and allotted to different owners, and not again allowed to see or communicate with each other.

It was an agonizing experience to Mrs. Ingles to have her young and helpless children, excepting, of course, the infant, torn from her and from each other, but the Indians and the fates had so decreed, and she had to submit with what grace she could.

Her eldest son, Thomas, named after his grandfather Ingles, now four years old, was taken up to or near Detroit; her youngest son, George, named after his grandfather Draper, now two years old, was taken somewhere in the interior, not now known, and Mrs. Draper went up to the region of Chillicothe. What became of the other prisoners then or afterward I do not know.

Shortly after this division of prisoners, some French traders came into the Indian town for the purpose of trading and bartering with the Indians. They had, among other things, a stock of check shirting, and as check shirts were in great demand among the Indians, and Mrs. Ingles a good sewer, she was put to making check shirts. Her proficiency in this line so increased her value and importance to them that she was treated with unusual leniency and consideration.

When a shirt would be finished and delivered to its owner, the buck would stick it on the end of a pole, and run through the town exhibiting it, and singing the praises of the "heap good white squaw."

The French traders seeing their interest in encouraging the shirt trade, were very kind to Mrs. Ingles, who was so important a factor in the business, and induced the Indians to pay her liberally for the sewing. This, fortunately, enabled her to supplement her own scanty wardrobe, a matter very essential to her personal comfort.

After this trading and shirt making had continued for two or three weeks, a party of Indians with these Frenchmen was made up to go to the "Big Bone Lick" to make salt. Mrs. Ingles and some other prisoners, among them a Dutch woman, but none of her party or acquaintances were taken along.

CHAPTER VIII.

THIS Big Bone Lick is about one hundred and fifty miles below Scioto, and about three and a half miles, by the creek, from the Ohio River, on Big Bone Creek, in (now) Boone County, Kentucky.

Some of the largest mastodon bones ever discovered, and the largest number ever found together, strewed the ground here, or were partially buried beneath the surface.

The Lick seems to have been a swampy morass, some eight or ten acres in area, with the sulpho-saline waters oozing up through it, and when the huge animals waded in to get the coveted mineral water, many mired, and being unable to extricate themselves, so perished, with their legs imbedded in the mud, and their bodies resting on the surface.

Colonel Thomas Bullitt, and other early explorers and surveying parties, here, in after years, used the immense ribs and tusks for tent poles, and the skulls and vertebra for stools and benches. These huge bones, tusks, and teeth, have been taken from here in large numbers, to enrich many museums both in this country and in Europe. Many of the tusks were eight or ten feet long.

Here Mrs. Ingles again assisted in making salt, thus being the first white person to make salt west of Kanawha, as she had been the first there, and while the first white *person* in the Kanawha Valley, she was the first white *woman*, so far as I know, who ever saw the Kanawha or New River, and the first white woman ever within the bounds of Ohio, Indiana or Kentucky, all then, however, still parts of Virginia.

While at the Big Bone Lick, Mrs. Ingles, to escape the ills she suffered, and to fly from others, threatened or feared, formed the desperate resolve to make her escape, and, if possible, find her way home. A more hopeless undertaking, apparently, she could not have conceived, but her condition was so distressing, that even death was preferable, and she determined that, come what would, she would make the attempt.

She confided her secret to the elderly Dutch woman above mentioned, who had been captured in Western Pennsylvania, somewhere in the region of Fort Du Quesne, and who was the only other white female in the camp. She, at first, discouraged the scheme, and tried to dissuade Mrs. Ingles from throwing her life away on so mad and desperate a venture.

Mrs. Ingles was not to be shaken in her resolution, but the Dutch woman, dreading to be left alone with the savages in the wilderness, and dreaming, with freshly stimulated hope, of the comforts and joys of home, listened with more and more favor to the earnest appeals of Mrs. Ingles, and, finally, was completely won over to the desperate scheme, and determined to accompany her.

They had been in the habit of going out daily from the camp at the Lick, ostensibly to hunt wild grapes, walnuts, hickory nuts, etc., which they would take back, and distribute among the Indians, but the more important matter to them was to discuss the question and the ways and means of escape.

When the Dutch woman gave in her adhesion to the scheme, they stood not upon the order of their going, but prepared to start at once.

There was little preparation for the women to make; they could make but little without exciting suspicion.

They had each secreted a blanket for the trip, but took no clothes except what they wore, which were scanty enough. They each started with a tomahawk. Mrs. Ingles says she exchanged hers for a sharper one, just before starting from the camp, with a Frenchman, who was sitting cracking walnuts with his on one of the mammoth bones, since so noted.

Mrs. Ingles had been tried as few women are, but now the supreme moment of her life was upon her. To try to escape, she had determined; but what was to be done with her child? She well knew that if she attempted to take it with her, its cries would betray them both to recapture and death. And, even if she should possibly escape recapture, she knew too well what she would have to encounter and endure to suppose, for a moment, that it was possible to carry the infant and succeed in her effort. Clearly there was but one thing to do, under the circumstances, and that was to abandon the unhappy little sufferer to its hard fate.

Who can conceive of the agony of a young mother compelled to decide such a question, and to act, with such alternatives before her? But Mrs. Ingles was a woman of no ordinary nerve. She did decide and act, and who will say that she did not decide wisely? Certainly, in the light of subsequent events, her decision and action were wise and fortunate.

She nestled the dear little babe as cosily as she could in a little bark cradle, gave it her last parting kisses and baptism of tears, tore herself away, and was gone, never to see it again in this world, and knowing, or having every reason to believe, that it would be murdered so soon as it was known that she was gone.

They started late in the afternoon, and bent their steps toward the Ohio River, to get a known starting point.

There were no roads, no guides; they knew but little of routes, distances, or points of the compass.

Their only chance out of the wilderness was to get to, and keep within sight or striking distance of, the Ohio River, and follow that up, through its long, weary course, to the mouth of Kanawha, which Mrs. Ingles felt that she could recognize, and so on up Kanawha and New Rivers to her far-off and longed-for home and friends.

It is an interesting fact, as shown by census reports, that this Big-Bone Lick, then in an unknown and seemingly interminable wilderness, is now almost exactly the center of population of the United States.

CHAPTER IX.

A WORD about the history, names and signification of the rivers up which these fugitive women
were to travel, as guides to their distant homes, may
not be without interest here.

The first mention of the river now called Ohio is
found, I believe, in an old map of 1672, attributed to
the French explorer, La Salle. In this the Iroquois
name is given as "Oligen-Sipen," "The Beautiful
River."

A map of 1687 calls it "Dono," or "Albacha." A
Dutch map of 1708 calls it "Cubach." A map of
1710 calls it "O-o," and makes the Ohio and Wabash
or Oubache one river. In 1711 it is called "Ochio."
In 1719 it is called "Saboqungo." The Miamis called
it Causisseppione. The Delawares, Kitono-cepe, and
others Alliwegi-Sipe. The Wyandottes called it
"Oheezuh," "The Grand or Beautiful." On the map
accompanying Rapin De Thoyers' History of England
(1744), it is called Hohio, and empties into the Wabash, or "Ouback," on the north side. In some of
the early treaties of the Pennsylvanians with the
Iroquois, they gót the spelling "Oheeo," probably
intending to represent the same sound as the "Oheezuh" above; this Oheeo became changed in accent,
about 1744, by the Virginians, to "Ohio," or "Hohio,"
as on the above-mentioned map.

When, in 1749, the French called the "O-y-o" or

" Ohio," " La Belle Rivere," they were not giving it a new name, but merely rendering into French the numerous Indian designations, most of which were equivalents, and meant " The Beautiful River."

With the later French, as with the Indians, the name included the Allegheny, or Al-le-ge-ning (the impression of feet), which was considered the extension of the main stream, and the Monongahela only a tributary. In addition to all these names, the Ohio, during its early Indian history, was often called the " River of Blood," from their own bloody encounters along its shores.

The present Big Miami was called Mi-ah-me-zah by some of the Indian tribes; Os-we-ne, by the Delawares; La Roque, by the French, meaning the River of Rocks, or Stony River.

Licking River was named from the Big Buffalo Licks on its banks, now the celebrated Blue Lick Springs of Kentucky.

The Little Miami was called by the Delawares Pio-quo-nee, or High Bank River.

The Scioto was called by different tribes Son-hi-o-to, Si-o-tha, Si-o-to-cepe, etc., its signification was said to be " The Unknown."

The Big Sandy gets its name from the prevalence of sand bars in its bed. It has also been called Tatteroi, Chatteroi, and Chatterawha; but I do not know the signification of this variously spelled term; they may, like some others, all mean one thing—The River of Sand Bars, or Sandy River.

The Miamis called it We-pe-po-co-ne-ce-pe-we. The Delawares called it Si-ke-a-ce-pe, Salt River. And Little Sandy was called Tan-ga-te Si-ke-a-ce-pe-we, or Little Salt River.

One of the upper forks of Big Sandy was named Tug River by some of General (then Major) Andrew Lewis' soldiers returning from the Big Sandy expedition of 1756, when they became so straightened for food that they had to boil and eat their rawhide buffalo thongs and tugs to keep from starving.

The La Visee, or Levisa, fork, as commonly called, or Louisa, as sometimes erroneously called, is said to mean the picture, design, or representation. It was so called by·an early French explorer in the region, from Indian pictures or signs, painted on trees, near the head of the stream.

The Guyandotte River is said to have been named after a tribe of that name. The Miamis called it La-ke-we-ke-ton Ce-pe-we. The Delawares called it Se-co-nee, Narrow Bottom River.

The locality of Point Pleasant was called, by the Wyandottes, Tu-edna-wie, the Junction of the Rivers. The present site of Pittsburg, Washington says, was called De-un-da-ga, the Forks of the River.

The Great Kanawha River was called by the Miamis Pi-que-me-ta-mi; by the Delawares, Ken-in-she-ka-cepe, White Stone River.

The Little Kanawha was called by the Delawares, O-nom-go-how-cepe.

The first name given the Great Kanawha from this end, by the whites, so far as I know, was by a French engineer party, under Captain De Celeron, who, on the 18th of August, 1749, planted an engraved leaden plate at the mouth, giving the river the name of Chi-no-da-che-tha, and claiming for the French crown all the territory drained by its waters.

This complicated name is probably Indian, not

French; but what its signification is or was, I do not know.

This leaden plate was unearthed in 1846, by a little nephew of Colonel John Beale, then a resident at the Point, and in 1849, just one hundred years after the French had planted it, James M. Laidley, Esq., then a member of the legislature of Virginia, from Kanawha, took it to Richmond, and with appropriate remarks, submitted it to the Virginia Historical Society, where, I believe, a copy of it is still preserved, but he was required to return the original to the finder, who was afterwards cheated out of it by the fair and false promises of some itinerant sharper—a duplicate copy of the original plate and inscription is preserved among the French National Archives in Paris.

Christopher Gist, agent of the "Ohio Land Company" passed down opposite the mouth of Kanawha, on the Ohio side in 1751. The name of Kanawha was not given to the river until between 1760 and 1770. The name is commonly supposed and stated to signify, in the Indian tongue, "River of the Woods;" but this, I think, is clearly a mistake. The stream had been discovered as a *New* River, at the other end, by Colonel Abraham Wood, long before, as herein above described, and named after him—"Wood's River"—so when the name Kanawha was given to it, it applied to a river that already had a name, which then became an alias, and thus it was called "Kanawha or Wood's River," and *not* "Kanawha, the River of the Woods."

The name Kanawha.was probably derived by evolution from the name of a tribe of Indians (a branch

of the Nanticokes), who dwelt along the Potomac
and westward, to New River. They were variously
called, or spelled by different authors, at different
times, Conoys, Conoise, Canawese, Cohnawas, Cana-
ways and Kanawhas. The spelling of the name has
been very various, in addition to the ways mentioned above, including nearly all practicable methods
commencing with C or K. Wyman's map of the
British Empire, in 1770, calls it " The Great Cono-
way, or Wood's River." The act of legislature of
1789 forming the county spelled it Kenhawa. In an
original report of survey made by Daniel Boone, at
the mouth of the river, in 1791, and now in my possession, he spells it "Conhawway" — the accepted
spelling now is "Kanawha," probably never to be
changed again.

On some of the old maps the river is called "New
River," or "Wood's River" from its source to its
mouth; on others it is Kanawha from its mouth to
its source. Later it was called "New, or Wood's
River," from its source to the mouth of Greenbriar,
and Kanawha thence to its mouth; still later, and at
present, it is Kanawha from its mouth to the mouth
of Gauley, and New River from that up, the name
of Wood's River having become obsolete. The legis-
latures of Virginia and West Virginia ought to, by
joint action, abolish the name of New River, and give
one name to the whole stream from source to mouth,
and that name should be Kanawha.

"Pocatalico," it is said, signifies, in the Indian
tongue, "The River of Fat Doe."

"Cole River," as then spelled (the Louisa of the
early maps), was named in 1756, by Samuel Cole,

4

who with some others of the returning "Big Sandy
Expedition" (General, then Major Andrew Lewis
among them), got over on to, and followed up this
river; their names were cut on a beech tree near the
junction of Marsh and Clearforks, and remained legible until the tree was cut down by some vandal, three
or four years since, to clear his land.

Since the discovery of mineral coal along the river
in such vast quantities, the spelling of the name has
gradually become changed to c-o-a-l. The Miamis
called it Wa-len-de-co-ni-cepe, the Delawares called
it Wal-hon-de-cepe, or Hill Creek. On probably the
earliest map that laid down Coal River at all—that
used at the treaty of peace in 1783—and also on the
map illustrating Jefferson's notes of Virginia, it was
called Louisa, probably so named by Dr. Walker, as
elsewhere stated.

Elk River was called by some of the tribes Tiskelwah, or River of Fat Elk. By the Miamis it was
called Pe-quo-ni-cepe; by the Delawares To-que-
min-cepe, or Walnut River.

Paint Creek was called by the Miamis Mos-coos-
cepe, and by the Delawares Ot-to-we-cepe, or Deer
Creek.

The present name of Paint Creek comes from
painted trees, blazed and stained with red ochrous
earth, by the Indians, to mark their early trail. It
is also said that at a point of crossing of trails, near
the head of the creek, returning raiding parties used
to record on the trees, in this red paint, the number
of scalps taken, and other important events in char-
acters understood by them.

Gauley River was called by the Miamis Chin-que-
ta-na-cepe-we; by the Delawares To-ke-bel-lo-ke, or

Falling Creek. How the stream got the name of Gauley, or what it signifies, I don't know. The earliest spelling of the name that I have seen, in Henning Statutes, was Gawly. In the treaty map of 1783, and also Jefferson's map, the river is not even laid down.

Greenbriar River, according to Colonel John Lewis Payton, was named by Colonel John Lewis, in 1751. He with his son (afterwards General Andrew Lewis), were surveying lands along the river, and were very much scratched and annoyed by the greenbriars. John Lewis told his son to note the name of the stream, on his surveys, as Greenbriar River, which was done, and from the river the county was named. The Miami's name of the river was We-o-to-we-cepe-we. The Delawares called it O-ne-pa-ke-cepe.

Blue Stone River was named by the whites from the deep blue valley limestone over which it flows. Its Miami name was Mec-ce-ne-ke-ke-ce-pe-we. The Delawares called it Mo-mon-ga-sen-eka-ce-pe, or Big Stone Creek.

East River was named by the whites from the direction of its flow. Its Miami name was Nat-weo-ce-pe-we. Its Delaware name Ta-le-mo-te-no-ce-pe.

Wolf Creek was so named from the many wolves trapped or killed on it, by the early settlers. Walker's Creek, as hereinbefore stated, was named after Dr. Walker.

Many of the foregoing river names are from a list of Indian names and equivalents, compiled by Colonel William Preston, of the Draper's Meadows-Smithfield settlements. The suffix of ce-pe or ce-pe-we, to these various names, means, in the Indian tongue, *water* or river.

CHAPTER X.

BUT to return to the fugitive women and their daring, desperate, and apparently hopeless undertaking. There were hundreds of miles of wilderness before them. The savage Indians and wild animals would alike seek their blood. Pursuit, exposure, privation, and, possibly, starvation were staring them in the face, but they flinched not; they had determined to start, and start they did.

Against all these tremendous odds, it looked like flying in the face of Providence and the Fates that they trusted to help them through, but hope led on, and despair lay behind; they followed the one, and fled from the other.

They had not gotten far from the camp at Big Bone Lick before the sun went down and the shades of night gathered around them.

They selected an obscure place, raked some leaves into it for a bed, and, with the aid of their blankets, got such rest and sleep as they could; but there was not, as may be supposed, much sleep for them that night.

When they failed to return to the camp at or later than the usual time, the Indians became uneasy, thinking they had strayed too far and lost their way, or else had been killed by wild beasts.

Some of the Indians went some distance in the direction they had started, but which course they

had reversed so soon as out of sight, and fired guns
to attract their attention if they should be lost. They
gave up the search that night, however, and did not
renew it the next day.

Their conclusion was that the women had been
destroyed by wild beasts, and gave themselves no
farther concern about them. They did not at all
suspect that the women had attempted an escape.

These facts were learned by William Ingles, from
the Indians, many years after, at an Indian treaty, or
conference, held at Point Pleasant not long after the
battle of the Point, when they (the Indians) learned
for the first time what had become of the missing
women so long before.

The next morning, not having the trouble of
making their toilets, nor cooking nor eating their
breakfasts, they made an early start, from a point
near the mouth of Big Bone Creek, fifteen miles
below the mouth of the Big Miami, which De Celeron
had called "La Roque," and about forty miles below
the present site of Cincinnati.

They kept the Ohio River in view, and tramped
and toiled their weary way up its course, cheered by
the knowledge that every mile they made took them
one mile nearer their far, oh! how far-off homes!

Without any special misadventure, after days and
days of toil, and nights of uneasy rest, having passed
Licking River, the sites of the present cities of Cov-
ington and Newport, and of the proud city of Cincinnati, just opposite, first called Losantiville; all
then an untrodden wilderness. This is a curious
patchwork name invented by the cranky pedagogue
and historian, John Filson, as a suitable name for

the town when first started. L is for Licking; os, the mouth; anti, opposite; and ville, the village; all meaning (L-os-anti-ville) the village or town opposite the mouth of Licking. Having passed the sites of Foster, Augusta, Maysville, first called Limestone, Concord, Vanceburg, etc., they at last reached the point opposite, or nearly opposite the Shawnee town at the mouth of the Scioto. The main Shawnee town in those days was not above the mouth, where Portsmouth now stands, but a short distance below.

This was their chief or capital town. Their council house, built of logs, was ninety feet long and covered with bark.

A few years later (1763 to 1765) a very extreme, if not unprecedented flood in the rivers swept off the greater part of the town, and it was never rebuilt at that place; but the tribe moved their head-quarters to the upper Little Miami, and up the Scioto, and built up, successively, the old and the new Chillicothe, or Che-le-co-the, towns.

There remained a Shawnee village at the mouth of Scioto, which was then built upon the upper side, the present site of the city of Portsmouth. During the existence of the main Indian town just below the mouth of the Scioto, there was another prominent settlement at the mouth of a creek about four miles above the mouth of Kanawha. This town was also abandoned about the same time as the Scioto town; whether from the same cause, or for what reason, I do not know. The creek, at the mouth of which the town stood, is still known as " Old Town Creek."

When Mrs. Ingles and her companion reached the point opposite the Scioto Shawnee town, they were weary and worn, and almost famished with hunger. They had subsisted, thus far, on walnuts, hickory-nuts, grapes, and paw-paws; here they found a corn-patch and an isolated, untenanted cabin.

As it was about dark when they reached it, they slept in the cabin—seeing no sign of any one about it—and enjoyed a hearty supper and breakfast of corn.

Some nineteen years later Colonel John Floyd (father of the afterward Governor John Floyd, of Virginia, and grandfather of Governor John B. Floyd), then deputy surveyor under Colonel William Preston, of Draper's Meadows, or Smithford, father of the afterward Governor James Preston, of Virginia, accompanied by Hancock Taylor, uncle of President Zachary Taylor, located and surveyed for Patrick Henry, afterward Governor of Virginia, two hundred acres of land at this place, binding one and an eighth miles on the river, covering the site of this cabin, corn-patch, and Indian settlement opposite the late site of the main town across the river.

Next morning the women discovered an old horse, with a tinkling bell on its neck, grazing about, loose. They "appropriated" this horse, muffled the bell clapper with leaves and rags to prevent its sounding, gathered what corn they could manage to carry, and getting away from the neighborhood of the settlement as quietly and quickly as they could, resumed their onward movement.

They could plainly see the town and Indians on the opposite side, but managed to keep themselves unseen.

The horse was a most valuable acquisition, and a

great comfort to them. Sometimes they rode him on
the "ride and lead" plan, alternating, and sometimes
both would have to walk and lead, depending upon
the nature of the ground and route, whether rough
or smooth, etc.

This day they had a great fright and narrow escape. A party of Indian hunters passed very near
them, but they secreted themselves and horse as best
they could among the underbrush, to avoid being
seen, and waited until the hunters passed out of
range, when they again moved on.

After several days of travel, having passed the
sites of the future towns of Greenup, Riverton, Ash-
land and Catlettsburg, they reached a stream (the
Big Sandy), which they were unable to cross near its
mouth, and they traveled up it a long distance before
they could cross. At length they came to a lodg-
ment of driftwood, extending clear across the stream.

They tried it and found it would bear their weight,
but what should be done with the horse?

Mrs. Ingles doubted whether he could be gotten
over on the drift, but the Dutch woman insisted that
he could, and in this case she prevailed, at least to
make the effort. They were already a long way up
the stream; they did not know how much farther
they might have to go before they could ford or wade
it; they thought they might get the horse over (the
wish being, no doubt, parent to the thought), and
they tried it.

They had gotten but a short distance from the
shore, however, when his legs slipped down through
the drift, and there he stood, with his feet hanging
down in the water, and his body resting on the logs
above, unable to extricate himself or to move.

It was a sad case. The loss of the horse was most serious, and in their feeble, footsore, and famished condition, might be fatal to them. They were touched with pity to have to leave the poor creature in this sorry and helpless plight; but there was no help for it. There was no choice but to abandon him to his hapless fate, and try to save themselves.

They each took a little corn from what was left of their scanty stock, and the old woman, who seems to have had a very practical and provident turn of mind, took the bell off the horse, and carried it through all the after troubles and trials of the journey. This point of crossing of the river was probably about the forks, and near the site of the present town of Louisa, where fifteen years later, according to Collins, Colonel George Washington located, for John Fry, 2,084 acres of land, the first survey ever made in Kentucky. The first settlement made on the Big Sandy was by Charles Vancouver, at this point in 1789, but the settlement was soon after broken up by the Indians.

They now started down the upper or east side of Big Sandy, and retraced, with weary steps, the distance to the Ohio again, and thence up it, sometimes along the river bank, and sometimes along the ridges, with the river in sight.

As they did with the Big Sandy, so they had to do with every stream they came to, from first to last. When they could not wade the stream at the mouth, they had to go up it until they could, and many of the streams required days and days of weary travel up to a point of practicable crossing, and back again to the main stream, their only guide, thus increasing

very greatly the distance traveled, perhaps nearly
doubling a direct river line.

Fortunately for them, it was at a season of the year
when the waters were comparatively low, or this
difficulty, serious as it now was, would have been
insurmountable.

Frequently, in going up or down these side streams,
they could see that the stream made a large bend,
and, to save distance, they would go across the ridge,
having to pull themselves up the steep hills by the
bushes and sods, until they reached the top, when,
from fatigue and exhaustion, they would more slide
than walk down, bruising and scratching themselves
severely as they went.

Since the loss of the horse, the old woman had
become greatly disheartened and discouraged. She
became very illnatured to Mrs. Ingles, blaming her
for having pursuaded her to leave the Indians, to
starve and perish in the wilderness.

In her desperation she threatened to kill Mrs. Ingles, and even attempted violence. The old woman
was, physically, much larger and stronger than Mrs.
Ingles, but the latter was younger and more active,
and managed to keep out of reach, though both were
so exhausted from hunger and fatigue that they
could little more than walk. By gentleness, kind
talk, and delicate little attentions to the old woman,
Mrs. Ingles succeeded, at length, in getting her paci-
fied, and to some extent reconciled, and on they
trudged together again.

The weather was getting cold, and they suffered
greatly from exposure. They had long since worn
out their shoes or moccasins, and their clothes were

worn and torn to shreads and rags by the bushes, briars, etc. At nights they slept under shelving rocks or in hollow logs, on leaves, moss, or such stuff as they could rake together.

When they failed to find nuts and berries enough to sustain them, they were often driven by hunger to pull up small shrubs or plants, and chew such as had tender bark on their roots, without the slightest idea of what they were, or what their effects might be; the cravings of hunger must be appeased by whatever they could chew and swallow. On one occasion they found, on the drift, in some stream, a deer's head, probably cut off and thrown away by the Indians. This they made a meal of, though it was considerably advanced in decomposition, and strongly odorous.

They protected their feet, as best they could, by wrapping them with strips torn from what was left of their dresses, and tied on with strings made from the soft, flexible bark of the young leather-wood shrub.

CHAPTER XI.

TOILING along in this sorry plight day after day, having passed the present sites of Huntington and Guyandotte, and crossed Guyandotte River, passed Green Bottom, where Thomas Hannon, in 1796, made the first white settlement within the present limits of Cabell County, the first on the Ohio River from the Kanawha to the Big Sandy, opposite the site of Gallipolis, and under the noted cliff over which Ben. Eulin, years after, made his famous fifty-three feet leap, when pursued by Indians, and was saved from death by falling in the tops of paw-paw bushes and grape vines, they at length reached the mouth of the Kanawha River, not then so called, but New River, or Wood's River, as they knew it, or the "Chinodachetha" as the French had then recently named it.

This point was well remembered by Mrs. Ingles, and the sight of it again, under such circumstances, after her terrible experiences and sufferings for the past few months, stirred within her breast a flood of painful recollections and reflections, and a terrible struggle between hope and despair. Here, at last, after all she had gone through on this desperate effort to regain her liberty and home, was the river that led on to that home and the friends from whom she had been torn by savage hands.

These waters came down from them, but brought her no tidings.

If she could but follow up the stream, it would lead her to them, if, indeed, they still survived; but could she ever get there? It seemed impossible, weary and worn as she was by toil and anxiety, reduced as she was by exposure, cold and starvation, and her companion, instead of being an aid and comfort to her, had now become a source of danger and dread; but her situation was too horrible to let her mind dwell upon it. She dared not count the odds or weigh the chances too closely. She knew that these odds and chances were largely against her. She knew that there was constant danger from savage Indians, for this was a favorite route for their raids into the Virginia settlements, danger from wild beasts, from starvation, cold, exposure and sickness, and danger from her companion. To give up, or delay, was certain death; to press on was, at least, going in the direction of relief, and of home and friends. She summoned to her aid all her resolution for another effort, and again the toilsome journey was resumed.

Day after day they dragged their weary limbs along, suffering and starving; night after night they shivered, starved and suffered, crawling into hollow logs or hollow trees as a partial protection from the increasing cold, and thus they traversed this now beautiful valley, then an unbroken wilderness, never penetrated by foot of white person, until Mrs. Ingles and others passed through it, a few months before, as prisoners.

In those days herds of buffalo and elk roamed through these valleys and over the hills. There were well beaten paths where they passed through the low gaps, between the hills, on their way to and from the

Salt Licks or Springs, traces of which were visible to
within recent years.

The last buffalo killed in this valley was by Archibald Price, on the waters of Little Sandy Creek of
Elk River, about twelve miles from Charleston, in
1815. The last elk killed in the valley, and probably
the last east of the Ohio River, was by Billy Young,
on Two Mile Creek of Elk River, about five and a
half miles from Charleston, in 1820. One of our
venerable citizens, Mr. John Slack, Sr., then a small
boy, still alive and vigorous, remembers this elk and
its huge horns between which a man could walk up-
right, and ate a part of the game.

It is said that vast herds of buffalo summered in
the Kanawha Valley, "in an early day," within
reach of the Salt Spring, or "Big Buffalo Lick," as
it was called, and in the fall, went to the grass regions
of Ohio and Kentucky, and the cane brakes of the
Kentucky streams. Their routes were—for Kentucky,
down through Teays' Valley, and for Ohio, down
Kanawha to Thirteen Mile Creek, and over to Letart,
where they crossed the Ohio River. Colonel Croghan,
who came down the Ohio in a boat in 1765, encountered a vast migrating heard crossing at Letart.

TENANTS OF THE FOREST.

It is curious to note what changes occurred in the
tenantry of the forest upon the advent of the white
man. The Indians, after a bloody and desperate resistance, were driven back. The buffalo, deer, elk,
bears and panthers, probably feeling themselves
unequal to the contest, tamely submitted to the
inevitable, and passed on. Wolves were extremely

numerous "in an early day," but soon became almost
extinct. Dr. Doddridge, one of the most observant
of the early pioneers, thinks this was occasioned,
more than all other causes put together, by hydro-
phobia. Probably this was introduced among them
by the dogs of the white man. Carnivorous birds,
as eagles and buzzards, were very numerous, but
rapidly diminished in numbers. Wild turkeys were
extremely abundant, but were soon "cleaned out."
Venomous snakes were numerous, and held their
own with some tenacity.

Gray and black squirrels were very numerous, and,
for a time, seemed rather to increase than diminish,
and were very destructive to the early corn fields.
Every few years, moved by one of the inexplicable
instincts of animals, they migrated, in countless
numbers, from west to east.

There were no crows nor black birds in the wilderness, and no song birds, but they soon followed in
the wake of the white man. There were no rats,
but they soon followed. 'Possoms were later coming, and the fox squirrels still later. There were no
wild honey bees, but they came in with the whites,
keeping a little in advance.

The famishing women daily saw plenty of game
and wild animals, but only to be tantalized by them.
They could make no use of them. They were only
too glad to be let alone by the frightful beasts.

As they passed the mouth of Kanawha, they passed
in sight of the afterwards bloody battle ground of
Point Pleasant, which will be treated of at length in
a separate chapter.

About eighteen years later (in 1773) there was

much discussion in the country in reference to establishing a separate colony in the west, with the seat of government at the mouth of Kanawha.

General Washington, who owned tracts containing about 30,000 acres of land on the Kanawha and Ohio Rivers, among them a tract of over 10,000 acres on both sides of the Kanawha, commencing a short distance above the mouth, in advertising to sell or lease the latter, in 1773, says, in conclusion :

" And it may not be amiss, further to observe, that if the scheme for establishing a new government on the Ohio, in the manner talked of, should ever be effected, these must be among the most valuable lands in it, not only on account of the goodness of the soil and other advantages above mentioned, but from their contiguity to the seat of government which, it is more than probable, will be fixed at the mouth of the Great Kanawha.   " GEORGE WASHINGTON."

A few years earlier, Washington and the Lee's, says Payton, were figuring on a gigantic land scheme in the west. They formed a land company called " The Mississippi Company," and they modestly asked George III. for a grant of two and a half million acres in the West. The company was composed of George Washington, F. L. Lee, R. H. Lee and Arthur Lee. From about 1767 to 1769 or 1770, Washington had Colonel Crawford through the west, off and on, examining and making notes of the best bodies of lands. In 1769, Arthur Lee went over to urge the claims of the Mississippi Company, in person, before George III. and the parliament.

The grant was not made, and the scheme was finally

abandoned. But suppose it had succeeded, how different might have been the history of our country! Washington and the Lees might have been the ruling spirits in a great Western Republic, with the seat of government at Point Pleasant.

The country west of the Ohio was then sometimes called the "State of Washington." In 1787, the Legislature of Virginia, in granting a ferry franchise across the Ohio River, says, from lands of so and so, in Ohio County, Virginia, to lands of so and so, in the "State of Washington."

From Point Pleasant the fugitives passed up on the lower or west side of Kanawha, passing opposite the present towns of Leon, Buffalo, Red House and Raymond City, all now built up on the east side, passed by Tackett's Knob, and the famous pine tree to which Tackett was tied by the Indians, in after years; over the site of Winfield, the present county seat of Putnam County, etc.

In passing the mouth of Scary Creek, where the Chesapeake & Ohio Railway now leaves the river, they passsed the site of the first, or one of the very first, battles fought between the Federals and Confederates in the late civil war, being on the 17th of July, 1861, and one week before the first battle of "Bull Run." The Federals were commanded by Colonel Norton, and the Confederates were under the immediate command of Captain (afterwards Colonel) George S. Patton. Both commanders were wounded; twelve Federals were killed, and three Confederates. General Henry A. Wise was then in supreme command of the Kanawha forces, with Colonel C. Q. Tompkins next in command.

At the mouth of Coal River the fugitives passed, on the lower side, the future site of Fort Tackett, one of the first forts built in the valley, when the white settlements began, and the scene of a bloody tragedy and capture of the fort by the Indians. In after years (1788), from this fort, under cover of darkness, John Young escaped, taking in his arms his young wife with a babe of one day old, and the bed or pallet on which she lay, put them in a canoe, and, during the night, through a drenching rainstorm, poled the canoe up to the fort where Charleston now stands. Neither father, mother, nor babe suffered from the exposure, the mother lived to be about ninety, and the babe lived to be over ninety, dying but a few years since, leaving a large family of worthy descendants in this valley.

Above the mouth of Coal River the fugitive women passed the site of the present town of St. Albans, a Chesapeake & Ohio Railway station.

They had to go up Coal River until they could wade it, as they had done with Licking, Little Sandy, Big Sandy, Guyandotte, Twelve Pole, and other streams. Twelve miles above Coal River, they passed opposite the mouth of Elk River, two miles up which, Simon Kenton, the afterwards renowned pioneer and Indian fighter, and two companions, Yeager and Strader, sixteen years later (1771), built a cabin, and occupied it; engaged in hunting and trapping until the spring of 1773, when they were attacked by Indians. Yeager was killed, and Kenton and Strader both wounded, though they made their escape to a hunting camp at the mouth of the Kanawha.

So far as known, Simon Kenton and companions

were the first white men who ever built a cabin or camp and lived in the valley. Mrs. Ingles and companions having been the first white persons ever here, as above stated.

Immediately above the mouth of Elk River, they passed opposite the site of the present city of Charleston, the capitol of West Virginia, and where I now write. Here, Fort Clendenin was afterwards saved from Indian capture by the heroism of a brave little woman, Ann Bailey, who rode her black pony, called "Liverpool," to the fort at Lewisburg, called Camp Union or Fort Savannah, one hundred miles distant, through a wilderness, and back, alone, bringing the besieged a supply of powder, etc.

Between four and five miles above here, they passed the spot where, thirty odd years later, that prince of pioneers and frontiersmen, Daniel Boone, built a cabin and lived for ten or twelve years. See chapter on Boone.

Opposite this, and just above the mouth of Campbell's Creek, was the Salt Spring where Mrs. Ingles and her companions and captors had stopped to rest and make salt, as they passed down, some months before, as above stated.

For many years after the settlement of the country, this locality was the chief source of supply of salt for the great West, until the Pomeroy salt region, and afterwards Saginaw, Michigan, were developed. For full history of the salt interest of Kanawha, see a paper by the author, published by the State, in "Resources of West Virginia."

Ten miles further up the river, having passed opposite the afterwards noted Burning Spring, first

located and owned by Generals Washington and
Lewis, in 1775. General Washington in his will, in
speaking of this tract says: "The tract of which
the 125 acres is a moiety, was taken up by General
Andrew Lewis and myself, for and on account of a
bituminous spring which it contains, of so inflam-
mable a nature as to burn as freely as spirits, and is
nearly as difficult to extinguish." General Washington gave, or intended to give, to the public forever,
as a great natural curiosity, two acres of land embracing the Burning Spring, and a right of way to the
river; but from oversight, or other reason not now
known, the grant was never put on record, and Dr.
Lawrence Washington, nephew of his uncle, and to
whom it descended, sold it to Messrs. Dickinson &
Shrewsberry, who, in 1843, bored on it, striking the
largest yield of natural gas ever tapped in the valley.

BURNING SPRING.

While on the subject of this spring, I will mention
a curious and interesting fact that occurred here in
1831 or 1832. Three men who had but recently come
to the neighborhood, and were employed at a salt
furnace, close by, were standing around the wonderful
spring, watching with amazement and awe the bubbling and boiling of the water, and the gasseous
flames leaping up from its surface, when, suddenly,
there came, from a passing cloud, a flash of lightning,
and an electrical stroke, or discharge, right into the
spring. The shock instantly prostrating the three
men standing around it. One, who was least stunned,
soon got up and ran to the furnace and gave the
alarm. A second one, after a little time, was able to

hobble off without help; but the third had to be carried home on a stretcher, and was so seriously shocked that he never entirely recovered from the effects of it. One of our elderly citizens, Mr. Silas Ruffner, was present, and a witness of the facts related.

It may be well to explain, for those who do not understand it, that the Burning Spring was not actually a spring of flowing water, but simply a pool, or puddle, up through which issued a stream of natural gas, keeping the water in bubbling motion, resembling boiling, and the gas, upon being lighted, would burn 'til put out by rain, or blown out by the wind.

Having passed the mouths of Rush, Lens, Fields and Slaughters Creeks, they (the escaping women) next passed the mouth of Cabin Creek, where, about twenty years later, the family of John Flinn, one of the earliest settlers, was in part killed, and the remainder captured by the Indians, for more particulars of which, see chapter on Boone.

Four miles above here they passed the mouth of Kelly's Creek, where, in 1773, Walter Kelly made the first family settlement in the valley, and where, in the following year, he lost his life, as elsewhere related. At this place William Morris founded a permanent settlement soon after Kelly's death, and built Fort Morris, the first in the valley. The Kelly cabin stood near a ravine, a few rods above, and the Morris Fort on the creek, about 150 yards below the present Tomkins brick church. About the same time his brother, Leonard Morris, made a settlement at the mouth of Slaughters Creek, and not long after, Henry Morris, another brother, settled on Peters Creek of Gauley.

Three miles above Kellys Creek, the fugitives passed the mouth of Paint Creek, the route of the Indian trail down which Mrs. Ingles and her captors came, some months before.

About the mouth of Paint Creek there seems to have been a large and very ancient aboriginal settlement. There are still remains of extensive stone fortifications on the high hill above the creek, and similar and larger ones, acres in extent, on the high mountain between Armstrong and Loup Creeks, and from an old burying ground, at the river, about the town of Clifton, are still unearthed, from time to time, interesting relics of the "Stone age," or Moundbuilder period.

Fourteen miles above Paint Creek, having passed the present sites of Coal Valley and Cannelton, Morris, Armstrong and Loup Creeks, they passed the Falls of the Great Kanawha—over "Van Bibber's Rock," where, in 1773, John and Peter Van Bibber, Mathiew Arbuckle and Joseph Alderson spent a night under a shelving rock near the water's edge, just under the Falls, to secrete themselves from a party of Indians, whose sign they had discovered, and where John Van Bibber pecked his name in the rock with the pole of his tomahawk. This fact is related by David Van Bibber, "nephew of his uncle," still living, and about ninety.

FALLS OF THE GREAT KANAWHA.

NEW RIVER CANON.

CHAPTER XII.

TWO miles above the Falls, the fugitives passed, on the opposite side, the mouth of Gauley River, and thence out of the Kanawha Valley proper, and entered the grand canyon of New River.

How did they ever get through it? Can the Railroad Engineers who located the C. & O. Road, or the contractors and others who built it, or any body who ever looked down into that awful chasm from the cliffs and precipitous mountains, 1,000 to 1,500 feet above, or ever looked out at it from the windows of a Chesapeake & Ohio Railway car—can any of these, looking back, in imagination, to the time when all this wild scene was in a state of nature, tell how these destitute and famished, but heroic women ever made the passage of this terrible gorge from Gauley to Greenbriar? Or conceive of the amount of daring and desperation it required to nerve them to the effort? The how can not now be told in full detail, but the simple and comprehensive answer is: They did it and survived.

They passed up by Penitentiary Rocks, the Little Falls, Cotton Hill, the Blue Hole, the Pope's Nose, the Short Tunnel, the Lovers' Leap, the Hawk's Nest, Sewell, Quimemout, War Ridge, Fire Creek, Stone Cliff, Castle Rock, Stretcher's Neck, Piney, Glade Creek, New River Falls, etc., etc.—all nameless then.

They walked, climbed, crept and crawled, through
brush and thorns, vines and briars, over and around
the huge rocks that have tumbled down from the
towering cliffs above, and the avalanches of debris
that followed their crushing courses—climbed under
or over fallen timber, over slippery banks and inse-
cure footings, wading creeks that had to be crossed,
wading around cliffs and steep banks that jutted out
into the main stream, and when this was impossible,
as was sometimes the case, they had to climb over or
around the obstruction, however high, however difficult, however tedious, however dangerous, looking
down from the dizzy heights upon the rushing, roaring
torrents of New River below, madly dashing against
the huge rocks and bowlders that obstruct its course,
and lashing the bases of the cliffs and the tortuous
shores as it furiously rushes on.

Suppose, in this terrible struggle, these poor, leg-
weary and foot-sore women had, in their unrestful
slumbers, on couches of leaves or bare earth, in caves
or hollow logs, dreamed that their great-grandchil-
dren would now be gliding through this wild canyon,
the roughest this side of the Rocky Mountains, in
luxurious Pullman Palace Cars, at the rate of forty
miles an hour—outspeeding the wind—and that time
and distance should be annihilated in sending mes-
sages through it to far away friends! They probably
did not, in their wildest flights, even dream anything
so seemingly impossible; and yet, how strangely
true it is!

VIEW OF HAWK'S NEST, FROM BOWLDER ROCKS.

VIEW OF NEW RIVER, FROM THE HAWK'S NEST.

NEW RIVER FALLS.

C. & O. SCENERY.

SCENE NEAR HINTON.

JUNCTION OF NEW AND GREENBRIAR RIVERS.

CHAPTER ·XIII.

*A*S they progressed, the way became a little less
rough, the mountains a little less precipitous,
and the river began to be fringed, here and there,
with little, narrow margins of bottoms. They seemed
to have passed the worst portion of the New River
gorge. They had passed opposite the site of the
present town of Hinton and the mouth of Greenbriar
River, where the Chesapeake & Ohio Railway leaves
New River, and passed the butte of the Big Flat Top
Mountain.

They next came to the mouth of Blue Stone River,
which was a land-mark and remembered point to
Mrs. Ingles. Here she and her captors had left the
New River on the down trip, and taken the Blue
Stone Paint Creek Indian trail.

She experienced a strong sense of relief on again
reaching this point. She knew about how long it
had taken her to reach here on her down trip, and
she began to count the weary days that it might take
to retrace those steps; if, indeed, she could hold out
to accomplish it at all.

When she came down she had health and vigor;
now she was hardly able to walk, and scarcely more
than the shadow of her former self; but, however
desperate her condition, there was no help for it but
in pushing forward. If there was relief in any
direction, it was up New River. Hope beckoned up

New River, and up New River they struggled on, still
following up the west bank.

They had passed Flat Top Mountain, Blue Stone
River, Indian Creek, etc., and were about the mouth
of East River, up which the New River branch of
the Norfolk & Western Railroad now runs, when
the old woman again became desperate, and this time
more dangerous than ever. In the extremity of her
suffering from starvation and exhaustion she threatened to kill Mrs. Ingles with cannibalistic intent.
Mrs. Ingles tried temporizing, by proposing to "draw
cuts" to determine which one should be the victim;
to this the old woman consented. The lot fell to
Mrs. Ingles; she then appealed to the old woman's
cupidity by offering her large rewards when they got
home, if she would spare her; but the pangs of present hunger were more potent than the hope of future
gain, and she undertook, then and there, to immolate
her victim. She succeeded in getting Mrs. Ingles in
her grasp, and it became a struggle for life or death.

How sad that these poor women, after all they had
suffered and endured together, should now, in that
vast solitude, alone, with no eye to see, nor hand to
save or aid, be engaged in a hand to hand, life or
death struggle!

The old woman, to prevent death by starvation,
would kill her companion for food, while Mrs. Ingles
was trying to save her life from the murderous hand
of her companion, probably to die a lingering death
from starvation; the choice seemed worth but little.

If they had had more strength, the result might
have been more serious; or, possibly, fatal to one or
both. But both were so feeble that neither had done

the other much hurt until Mrs. Ingles, being much
the younger (she was then but 23), and, by comparison, still somewhat more active, succeeded in escaping
from the clutches of her adversary, and started on up
the river, leaving the old woman greatly exhausted
by the struggle.

When well out of sight, she slipped under the
river bank and secreted herself until the old woman
had recovered breath and passed on, supposing that
Mrs. Ingles was still in advance.

This scene occurred late in the evening, between
sundown and dark.

When Mrs. Ingles emerged from her concealment,
the moon was up and shining brightly, and by its light
she discovered, near at hand, a canoe at the river
bank, half full of leaves blown into it by the wind ;
but there was no paddle, oar or pole; as a sub-
stitute, she picked up, after some search, a small
slab or sliver from a shattered tree, blown down by
storm.

She had never before undertaken, literally, to
" paddle her own canoe," and found much difficulty,
at first, in guiding it; but, persevering patiently,
she caught the knack of steering it, and as the river
was low, and not much current at the place, she
succeeded in making her way safely across.

Here, to her great relief, she found a cabin or
camp that had been built by some hunters from the
settlements above, and a patch where they had
attempted to raise some corn. Seeing no one about—
the place being deserted—she crept into the cabin
and spent the night.

Next morning she searched the patch for some

corn, but was sadly disappointed to find that the buffalo, bears, and other wild animals, had utterly destroyed it; she discovered in the ground, however, two small turnips which the animals had failed to find, and on these she made a sumptuous breakfast.

Resuming her now solitary journey, she had gone but a short distance when she discovered her late companion on the opposite shore. They halted and held a parley. The old woman professed great remorse and penitence, made all sorts of fair promises for the future, and begged piteously to be brought over, or that Mrs. Ingles would come back to her, that they might continue their journey together.

With Mrs. Ingles it was a question between sympathy and safety, but a wise discretion prevailed. After all that had occurred, she concluded that it would be safer to keep the river between them, and, accordingly, each went her way on opposite sides.

CHAPTER XIV.

FROM the best reckoning Mrs. Ingles could make, she concluded that she must now be within about thirty miles of her home; but much of the remainder of the way was extremely rough, the weather was growing colder, and, worse than all, her physical exhaustion was now so extreme that it seemed impossible that she could continue the struggle much longer. She feared that, after all she had suffered and borne, she would at last have to succumb to hunger, exposure and fatigue, and perish in the wilderness, alone.

As her physical strength waned, however, her strong will power bore her up and on, and Hope sustained her as wearily and painfully she made mile after mile, eating what she could find in the forest, if anything; sleeping when and where she could, if at all.

She had passed up through the "New River Narrows," the great rift where New River has cut its way through the solid "Peter's Mountain" (so named at the eastern end for Peter Wright, a famous old hunter and pioneer, but here named after a pioneer family named Peters). It is one of the wildest scenes in the State. She had passed the butte of Wolf Mountain and the mouth of Wolf Creek. Near here Peterstown, on the east side, has since been built. She had passed near the present site of Giles

C. H., and nearly under the shadows of the towering "Angel's Rest" Mountain, on the west side (so named by General Cloyd), 4,000 feet high, with its rock-ribbed sides and castellated towers, said to strongly resemble Mount Sinai, but it brought no rest nor peace to her.

She had passed the cliff near Giles C. H., had crawled around or over the huge cliffs just below the mouth of Stony Creek. She had by some means gotten beyond that grand wall of cliff jutting into the river for two miles, extending from opposite Walker's Creek to Doe Creek, and, two miles above this, another seemingly impassable cliff had been scaled. She had gotten about two miles beyond these last-named cliffs, and was near the base of the "Salt Pond Mountain," with its beautiful lake near its summit, 4,000 feet above tide, and one of the greatest natural curiosities of the State; but her mind was not occupied with the grandeur of the scenery, nor the beauty of these then nameless localities she was passing; she only knew that each one passed put her that much nearer home—sweet home!

Night was approaching; snow had fallen, and it was bitterly cold (it was now about the last of November); just before her she was confronted by still another gigantic cliff, hundreds of feet high, the base in the water and the crown overhanging. At last her progress seemed utterly barred; there were no ledges, no shelving rocks, no foot-holds of any kind to climb around on. The only chance left, it seemed, was to wade around the base, as she had done in other cases; this she tried, but found that, to her, it was an unfathomable gulf.

Her heart sank within her; night was now upon her; cold before, she was now wet and colder still. She had nothing to eat; she could find no soft couch of leaves, no friendly cave or hollow log.

In despair, she threw herself down on the bare ground and rocks, and there lay in that pitiable condition, more dead than alive, until next morning.

With the dawning of the day there was a feeble revival of hope—for while we live we will hope. She thought of the only possible remaining way of passing this gigantic barrier; this was to climb around and over the top of it, but in attempting to rise she found that her limbs were so stiff, and swollen, and sore from the wet, cold and exposure that she could scarcely stand, much less walk or climb. Still, there was no choice; if she could she must, so again she tried.

Slowly, as the effort and exercise relieved her somewhat from the paralyzing chill, she wound her devious, tedious and painful way, hour after hour, getting a little higher, and a little higher. So feeble and faint from hunger, such soreness and pain from her lacerated feet and swollen limbs, that from time to time she looked down from her dizzy heights, almost tempted, from sheer exhaustion and suffering, to let go and tumble down to sudden relief and everlasting rest.

Climbing and resting, resting and climbing, she at last reached the summit, and the day was far spent.

While resting here, her thoughts had wandered on up the river to her home and friends. She knew that she must now be within twelve or fifteen miles of that home. "So near and yet so far." If she had strength, how quickly she would fly to it; but; alas! in her now desperate and deplorable condition the chance of reaching it seemed fainter, even, than when she left Big Bone Lick with strength, hope and resolution. Now, she did not know what hour her powers might utterly fail; what minute nature might yield and she would be lost.

As long as she lived, Mrs. Ingles always referred to this as the most terrible day of her eventful life.

ANVIL CLIFF.

CÆSAR'S ARCH.

CHAPTER XV.

$\mathcal{A}$ROUSING herself again to the necessities of the hour, she started on her painful and perilous descent; crawling, falling, slipping and sliding, she at length reached the bottom as the day was about departing.

I have talked with a friend of mine, born and reared in this neighborhood, and who is perfectly familiar with all this part of New River. He tells me that this cliff is 280 feet high to the top, measured, the first 100 feet overhanging, and that the water in the pool at the base has never been fathomed. He had often tried it in his youth, with long poles and with weighted lines, but never got bottom. There is, he says, a whirl-pool, or sort of maelstrom, here, down into which, when the river is high, logs, driftwood, etc., are drawn, coming up again some distance below. No wonder Mrs. Ingles could not wade around the cliff; no wonder it took her a whole day, in her exhausted condition, to climb over it.

The highest point of this front cliff, from some real or fancied resemblance to a huge anvil, is called "Anvil Rock." Just across the river, in a corresponding cliff—all of the blue limestone—is a natural arch, which is called "Cæsar's Arch." and near it a natural column called "Pompey's Pillar."

"Sinking Creek," a considerable stream, which, in low water, loses itself under ground some miles in the rear, finds its cavernous way under the mountains and into the river, below the surface, in the deep pool at the base of Anvil Rock cliff. In freshets, the surplus water finds its way to the river three-fourths of a mile below.

Mrs. Ingles, after getting to the bottom of the cliff, had gone but a short distance when, to her joyful surprise, she discovered, just before her, a patch of corn. She approached it as rapidly as she could move her painful limbs along.

She saw no one, but there were evident signs of persons about. She hallooed; at first there was no response, but relief was near at hand. She was about to be saved, and just in time.

She had been heard by Adam Harmon and his two sons, whose patch it was, and who were in it gathering their corn.

Suspecting, upon hearing a voice, that there might be an intended attack by Indians, they grabbed their rifles, always kept close at hand, and listened attentively.

Mrs. Ingles hallooed again. They came out of the corn and towards her, cautiously, rifles in hand. When near enough to distinguish the voice—Mrs. Ingles still hallooing—Adam Harmon remarked to his sons: "Surely, that must be Mrs. Ingles' voice." Just then she, too, recognized Harmon, when she was overwhelmed with emotions of joy and relief— poor, overtaxed nature gave way, and she swooned and fell, insensible, to the ground.

They picked her up tenderly and conveyed her to to their little cabin, near at hand, where there was protection from the storm, a rousing fire and substantial comfort.

Mrs. Ingles soon revived, and the Harmons were unremitting in their kind attentions and efforts to promote her comfort.

They had in their cabin a stock of fresh venison and bear meat; they set to work to cook and make a soup of some of this, and, with excellent judgment, would permit their patient to take but little at a time, in her famished condition.

While answering her hurried questions as to what they knew about her home and friends, they warmed some water in their skillet and bathed her stiff and swollen feet and limbs, after which they wrapped her in their blankets and stowed her away tenderly on their pallet in the corner, which to her, by comparison, was "soft as downy pillows are," and a degree of luxury she had not experienced since she was torn from her own home by ruthless savages, more than four months before.

Under these new and favoring conditions of safety and comfort, it is no wonder that "nature's sweet restorer" soon came to her relief and bathed her wearied senses and aching limbs in balmy, restful and refreshing sleep.

CHAPTER XVI.

MRS. INGLES had not seen a fire for forty days
(since leaving Big Bone Lick); she had not
tasted food, except nuts, corn and berries, for forty
days; she had not known shelter, except caves, or
hollow logs, or deserted camps, for forty days;
she had not known a bed, except the bare earth, or
leaves or moss, for forty days. She had been constantly exposed to the danger of recapture and death
by the savages; danger from wild beasts, from sickness, accident, exposure and starvation, and danger
from her companion. Yet, notwithstanding all these,
she had, within these forty days, run, walked, crawled,
climbed and waded seven or eight hundred miles, including detours up and down side streams, through
a howling wilderness, and was saved at last.

Dr. Tanner's forty days' fast, the conditions and
circumstances considered, dwindles into insignifi-
cance compared with this. Indeed, I do not know,
in all history, the record of a more wonderful and
heroic performance than that of this brave little
woman, all things considered.

It is said to be as heroic to endure as to dare; then
Mrs. Ingles was doubly heroic, for she dared and
endured all that human can.

The immortal "Six Hundred" who "rode into the
gates of death and the jaws of hell" were soldiers,
under military discipline. When commanded, they

knew only to obey; they were accustomed to deeds of daring and death. They knew their duty and they did it—grandly, nobly, heroically. When ordered to charge, they nerved themselves for the shock, which could last but a few minutes. Death might come to them within these few minutes; indeed, probably would; but if it came, would be sudden and almost painless, and if they escaped, the strain would soon be over, and glory awaited them.

Not so with Mrs. Ingles. This delicate woman, reared in comfort and ease, and unaccustomed to hardships, being in the hands of savages, in a vast wilderness, beyond civilization and beyond human aid, coolly and deliberately resolved to attempt her escape, knowing that the odds were overwhelmingly against her; knowing that if recaptured, she would suffer death by torture, and if she escaped recapture it would probably be to suffer a lingering death by exposure, fatigue and starvation; but her resolution was fixed; she nerved herself, not for the struggle of a few minutes only, but they were strung to a tension that must be sustained at the highest pitch, by heroic fortitude, for weeks—possibly for months—of mental anxiety and physical suffering, whether she finally escaped or perished.

But, to return to the Harmon cabin.

Mrs. Ingles awoke next morning greatly rested and refreshed. She called to Harmon and told him of her experience with the old woman, her companion, and begged him to send his boys back down the river in search of her, but the boys, having heard Mrs. Ingles relate the story of her adventure with the old woman, and, very naturally, feeling outraged and indignant at her conduct, refused to go, and Harmon, sharing their feelings, declined to compel them; so the old woman was left, for the present, to make her own way, as best she could.

Harmon and his sons had been neighbors of Mrs. Ingles at Draper's Meadows, before her capture, and before they came down here to make this new clearing and settlement. As neighbors on a frontier, where neighbors are scarce, they had known each other well.

Harmon considered no attention, labor or pains too great to testify his friendship for Mrs. Ingles and tender regard for her distressful condition. He had brought to this new camp, when he came, two horses and a few cattle to range on the rich wild pea vine which grew here luxuriantly.

He had heard in his time, and it impressed itself upon his memory, that beef tea was the best of all nourishing and strengthening diets and restoratives for persons in a famished and exhausted condition; so, although he had, as before stated, plenty of nice, fresh game meat in his cabin, he took his rifle, and, against the protests of Mrs. Ingles, went out, hunted up and shot down a nice, fat beef, to get a little piece as big as his hand, to boil in his tin cup, to make her some beef tea, and make it he did, feeding her, first with the tea alone, and then with tea and beef, until within a couple of days, thanks to her naturally robust constitution and health, she was sufficiently recovered, rested and strengthened to travel; when he put her on one of his horses, himself taking the other, and started with her to her home at Draper's Meadows, some ten or twelve miles dis-

tant, up the river; but when they arrived at the
settlement there was an Indian alarm, and all the
neighbors had congregated at a fort at "Dunkard
Bottom," on the west side of the river, a short distance above "Ingles' Ferry," so they went on to this
place, arriving about night, and Mrs. Ingles had,
with glad surprise, a joyful meeting with such of
her friends as were present in the fort.

CHAPTER XVII.

THE next morning, after arriving at the Fort, Mrs. Ingles again begged Harmon, now that he had restored her to her friends, to comfort and safety, to go back and hunt for the poor old woman, and, if still alive, to bring her in. This he now consented to do, and started promptly, down the west bank of the river.

A few miles after she and Mrs. Ingles had parted company the old woman met with a genuine piece of good luck. She came upon a hunters' camp, just abandoned, apparently precipitately, for what reason she could not tell—possibly from an Indian alarm—but they had left on the fire a kettle of meat, cooking, to which she addressed herself assiduously.

She remained here two or three days, resting, eating and recuperating her strength. The hunters had left at the camp an old pair of leather breeches; these the old woman appropriated to her own personal use and adornment, being by no means fastidious about the fit, or the lastest style of cut, or fashion, her own clothes being almost entirely gone.

An old horse had also been left by the supposed hunters, loose about the camp, but no sign of saddle or bridle.

The old woman remained at the camp, its sole occupant (no one putting in an appearance while she was there) until she had consumed all the meat in

the pot; she then made a sort of bridle or halter of
leatherwood bark, caught the old horse, put on him
that same bell which was found on the horse captured opposite Scioto, and taken off by the practical-
minded old woman when that horse had been abandoned to his fate among the drift logs in Big Sandy,
and carried through all her terrible struggles and
suffering to this place.

Having taken the wrapper from around the clapper, and so hung the bell on the horse's neck that it
would tinkle as he went, as, being so near the settlement, she now hoped to meet settlers or hunters, she
mounted him, riding in the style best adapted to her
newly acquired dress of leather unmentionables, and
again started up the river on her way to the then
frontier settlement.

Thus slowly jogging along, hallooing from time to
time to attract the attention of any one who might
be within hearing, she was met in this plight, about
the "Horse Shoe," or mouth of Back Creek, opposite "Buchanan's Bottom," by Adam Harmon, in
search of her, and taken on to the Fort.

The meeting between Mrs. Ingles and the old
woman was very affecting.

Their last parting had been in a hand to hand
struggle for life or death—not instigated by malice
or vindictiveness, but by that first great law of
nature, self-preservation, that recognizes no human
law; but now that they were both saved, this little
episode was tacitly considered as forgotten. Remembering only the common dangers they had braved,
and the common sufferings they had endured together in the inhospitable wilderness, they fell upon

each other's necks and wept, and all was reconciliation and peace.

The old woman remained here for a time, awaiting an opportunity to get to her own home and friends in Pennsylvania. Finding, before long, an opportunity of getting as far as Winchester, by wagon, she availed herself of it, and from there, with her precious bell, the sole trophy of her terrible travels and travails, it was hoped and believed that she soon got safely home, though I can not learn that she was ever afterwards heard of in the New River settlement.

I regret that not even her name has been preserved. In the traditions of the Ingles family she is known and remembered only as "the old Dutch woman."

Adam Harmon, having accomplished his mission of mercy, and improved the unexpected opportunity of a social reunion with his late neighbors and friends, took an affectionate leave of Mrs. Ingles and her and his friends, and returned to his new camp and clearing down the river.

This settlement of Harmon's was at a point on the east bank of New River, now the site of that well known place of summer resort, the "New River White Sulphur," or "Chapman's," or "Eggleston's Springs," which, for grandeur and beauty of scenery, is probably not excelled by any of the beautiful watering places of the Virginia Mountains. The New River branch of the Norfolk & Western Railroad runs along the opposite shore of the river, the station for this place being called "Ripple Mead."

The formidable cliff described above, the climbing over which occupied Mrs. Ingles one whole day, the most terrible of her life, is immediately below the springs, is a part of the springs estate, and well known to the frequenters of that popular resort.

The little cove immediately above the cliff, and the then site of the Harmon cabin and corn patch, is now, as I am informed, called "Clover Nook."

I regret that I do not know the after-history of Adam Harmon and sons, the pioneer settlers of this beautiful place; but from every descendant of Mrs. Ingles, now and forever, I bespeak proper appreciation and grateful remembrance of the brave, tender-hearted, sympathetic, noble Adam Harmon.

Twenty or thirty years later there was a family of Harmons—Henry and his sons, George and Matthias—who distinguished themselves for their coolness and bravery as Indian fighters in the Clinch settlements of Tazewell. I presume they were of the same Harmon stock, but just what relation to Adam I do not know.

I stated above that Mrs. Ingles, on her arrival at the Fort, had a joyful meeting with such of her friends as she found there; but the two of all others whom she had hoped and expected to find there— the two for whom her heart had yearned with deepest love, and the hope of again seeing whom had sustained her in her captivity and nerved her to her desperate exertions in her escape—her husband and her brother—were not there.

They had gone, some weeks before, down to the Cherokee Nation in the Tennessee and Georgia region, to see if they could get any tidings of their

lost families, and, if so, to try, through the Cherokees—they then being friendly with the whites and
also with the Indian tribes north of the Ohio—to
ransom and recover them; but their expedition had
been fruitless, and they were returning, sad, discon-
solate, despairing, almost hopeless.

On the night that Mrs. Ingles had reached the
Fort, William Ingles and John Draper stayed within
a few miles of it, and about where the town of Newbern, Pulaski County, now stands.

Next morning they made a daylight start and arrived at the Fort to breakfast, and to find, to their
inexpressible joy and surprise, that Mrs. Ingles had
arrived the night before.

Such a meeting, under such circumstances, and
after all that had occurred since they last parted,
nearly five months before, may be imagined, but can
not be described. I shall not attempt it.

There is probably no happiness in this life without
alloy; no sweet without its bitter; no rose without
its thorn. Though William and Mary Ingles were
inexpressibly rejoiced to be restored to each other,
their happiness was saddened by the bitter thought
that their helpless little children were still in the
hands of savages; and while John Draper was over-
joyed to have his sister return, he could not banish
the ever-present and harrowing thought that his wife
was still in the far-off wilderness—in the hands of
savages, and her fate unknown.

CHAPTER XVIII.

THE danger of an Indian attack, which had lately been threatening this Fort, now seemed more imminent, and as Mrs. Ingles became very uneasy, her husband took her to another and stronger Fort, called "Vass' Fort," about twenty miles farther east, where the settlers from the headwaters of the Roanoke had gathered for safety.

William Ingles and his wife had been here but a few days when Mrs. Ingles claimed to have a strong presentiment that the Fort was about to be attacked, and prevailed upon her husband to take her to another Fort, or place of safety, down below the Blue Ridge, and not far from the "Peaks of Otter." The very day they left Vass' Fort the presentiment and prediction of Mrs. Ingles was fully realized. The Fort was attacked by a party of Indians and overcome, and every one in it killed or taken prisoner.

John and Matthew Ingles, the younger brothers of William Ingles, were at this Fort. John was a bachelor. Matthew had a wife and one child. Before the attack was made, but after the Fort was surrounded, an Indian climbed a tall poplar tree, which commanded a view of the interior, to take an observation. He was discovered and fired on from the Fort, and it is the tradition that it was the rifle of John Ingles that brought him down.

Matthew Ingles was out hunting when the attack was made; hearing the firing, he hastened back, and tried to force his way into the Fort, to his wife and child; he shot one Indian with the load in his gun, then clubbed others with the butt until he broke the stock off; by this time the gun-barrel was wrenched from his hands, when he seized a frying-pan that happened to be lying near, and, breaking off the bowl or pan with his foot, he belabored them with the iron handle, right and left, until he was knocked down, overpowered and badly wounded. The tradition says that he killed two Indians with the frying-pan handle.

His bravery and desperate fighting had so excited the admiration of the Indians that they would not kill him, but carried him off as prisoner. He was either released or made his escape some time after, and returned to the settlement, but never entirely recovered from his wounds. He died at Ingles' Ferry a few months later. His wife and child were murdered in the Fort, as was also his brother John.

When the land about the site of this Fort was cleared, the poplar tree from which the Indian was shot was preserved. I have often seen it and the remains of the old Fort, when I was a boy, forty-five to fifty years ago. The tree was blown down by a storm, thirty to forty years ago.

This Fort, the remains of which are probably still visible, was on the headwaters of the Roanoke River, about ten miles west of where Christiansburg now stands, about two or three miles east of the present town of Lafayette, and near the residence of the late Captain Jacob Kent. The Fort that was destroyed

was, I believe, a small private Fort, built by the
neighbors for their protection; after which the State,
under the superintendence of Captain Peter Hogg,
built a stronger Fort, and Colonel Washington, then
in command of the Virginia forces, came up to see
and advise about it.

Kercheval, the historian, gives, on the authority of
Mrs. Elizabeth Madison, who resided on the Roanoke, an interesting anecdote relating to this Vass'
Fort. About the time indicated, it was known that
Colonel Washington was to be up to inspect the
Fort. Seven Indians waylaid the road, intending to
kill him. After waiting until long beyond the time
at which the party was expected, the Chief in command of the Indians went across a mountain to a
nearly parallel road, about a mile distant, to see if
Washington and party had passed that way, leaving
with the other six positive orders not to fire a gun,
under any circumstances, in his absence. He had
not been long gone when Colonel Washington, Major
Andrew Lewis and Captain William Preston rode
safely by, the Indians obeying their Chief's instruc-
tions to the letter, though it lost them their game.

At the same time (1756), the State erected a Stockade Fort at Draper's Meadows, under the direction
of Captain Stalnaker.

In March of this year (1756), the Big Sandy expedition, under General (then Major) Lewis, was sent
out, with Captains Preston, Paul Alexander, Hogg,
Smith, Breckenridge, Woodson and Overton; also,
the volunteer companies of Captains Montgomery
and Dunlap, and a company of Cherokees, under
Captain Paris.

They rendezvoued at Camp Frederick, and went thence by way of Clinch River, Bear Garden, Burk's Garden, over Tug Mountain and down the Tug Fork of Big Sandy; but the expedition was unsuccessful and returned, or was recalled, before reaching the Ohio. Partly in retaliation for the raid on Vass' Fort, and others, and to prevent a recurrence of such, a second Big Sandy expedition was contemplated, and preparations for it partly made, but it was afterwards abandoned.

Mrs. Ingles remained in the settlement below the Blue Ridge until there seemed a better prospect of peace and security at the frontier; she then returned to New River, where her husband and she permanently established themselves at "Ingles' Ferry."

William Ingles built here a Fort for the security of his own family and others who were now settling about him, and several times afterwards the neighbors were gathered in this Fort for safety and common defense, when Indian attacks were made or threatened.

Once, when there was no one at the house or Fort but William Ingles and his wife, she discovered, stealthily approaching the house, nine armed warriors in their war paint. She gave the alarm, and William Ingles at once posted himself in a position of defense, but discovered that he had but one bullet, and that in his gun. Mrs. Ingles soon got the lead and the ladle, however, and molded bullets as fast as he fired.

Having failed to take the place by surprise, as they had evidently expected, the Indians, after a few rounds, fired without effect, abandoned the attack and left.

About this time, William Ingles and a companion, named John Shilling, were on Meadow Creek, a branch of Little River. They were fired on by several Indians; all took to trees—white men and Indians—and fought Indian-fashion. The result was that Ingles and Shilling killed two Indians, and the others fled.

William Ingles came near having an eye put out by bark from the tree behind which he stood. Just as he started to look round, at one time, to get a shot, an Indian fired at him; the ball struck the tree and glanced, missing him, but dashed the bark into his face and eyes with great force and painful effect.

About 1760, a party of eight or ten Indians passed Ingles' Ferry and went up Little River and over to a settlement on the head of Smith's River, east of the Blue Ridge, where they murdered some defenceless settlers, took some women and children prisoners, caught their horses, loaded them with stolen plunder, and were returning by way of the New River settlement.

Some one from the Ingles' Ferry Fort had gone out in search of some strayed horses, and discovered the Indian camp, at night, about six miles from the Fort. He returned at once and reported what he had seen.

William Ingles got together, as speedily as possible, fifteen or eighteen men, then at or near the Fort, and, piloted by the man who had made the discovery, they started for the locality, intending to make an attack at daylight next morning. They were a little late, however, and the Indians were up

7

and preparing to cook their breakfast when the party reached the camp. At a concerted signal the attack was made; the Indians flew to their arms and made fight, but they were taken at a disadvantage and seven of the party shot down; the others fled and made their escape. One white man from the Fort was killed. The prisoners, horses and plunder were all recovered.

This was the last Indian engagement at or near this settlement; thenceforth they were undisturbed; peace prevailed, and the country began to settle up rapidly.

CHAPTER XIX.

MRS. BETTIE DRAPER was still a prisoner among the Indians. When separated from Mrs. Ingles at Scioto, she was taken up to about the Chillicothe settlement, where she was adopted into the family of an old Chief (name not mentioned) who had recently lost a daughter. Although kindly treated, she, not long after, made an attempt to escape. She was recaptured and condemned to death by burning (the usual penalty in such cases); but the old Chief concealed her for a time, and by his authority and influence at length secured her pardon.

Finding escape impossible, she set to work earnestly to secure the favor and regard of the family and the tribe, so as to render her terrible fate as tolerable as possible.

She taught them to sew and to cook, and was ever willing and ready to nurse the sick or the wounded, and was regarded as a "heap good medicine squaw." By these means she soon acquired the good will and confidence of the tribe, and secured for herself very kind and considerate treatment.

Thus six weary years had passed since her capture, and since her involuntary parting from Mrs. Ingles at Scioto. During this time John Draper had personally made several trips, and as often sent agents to try to find and ransom her, but all without effect, until, in 1761, a treaty between the whites and In-

dians was held somewhere on the border, about the
close of the Cherokee war, the locality and particulars of which are not now known. John Draper
attended this treaty, met the old Chief in whose
family his wife was living, and, after much negotiation and a heavy ransom paid, he succeeded in effect-
ing her release and restoration to him, when the
once more happy couple set out on their return to
their home at Draper's Meadows.

In 1761, William Preston married Miss Susanna
Smith, of Hanover County, and first settled at Staunton; afterwards, when Bottetourt County was cut off
from Augusta (1770), he was made County Surveyor,
in those days a most lucrative position, and moved
to an estate he called "Greenfield," situated near Am-
sterdam; still later, when Fincastle County was
formed (1772), and he made its Surveyor, he, in 1773,
acquired the Draper's Meadows estate, and, in 1774,
moved his family there, changing the name, probably in honor of his wife, to "Smithfield," which
name it still bears, and it is still the seat of the Preston family in the third and fourth generation from
Colonel William.

The Preston family residence was not built upon
the site of the original Ingles-Draper settlement
and massacre, but a mile or so distant, nearly south.

From this point (Draper's Meadows or Smithfield),
this remarkable family, and its descendants and connections, radiated over the State, and to all parts of
the South and West; and for talent displayed, for
honorable and commanding positions occupied, and
for exalted character and worth, I know of no other
family connection in the whole country which has,

within the last century and a quarter, produced so many distinguished members. Among them may be counted the Pattons, the Prestons, Buchanans, Thompsons, Madisons, Breckenridges, Peytons, McDowells, Floyds, Bowyers, Harts, Crittendens, Bentons, Paynes, Smiths, Andersons, Campbells, Browns, Blairs, Gambles, Wattses, Carringtons, Hamptons, Johnsons, Lewises, Woodvilles, Logans, Edmunstons, Alexanders, Wooleys, Wickliffs, Marshalls, and very many others.

When Colonel Preston moved to Smithfield, there came with him a young man named Joseph Cloyd, only son of a widow Cloyd, a near neighbor of Preston's at Greenfield, and who had recently been murdered by the Indians.

This Joseph Cloyd settled on the west side of New River, on "Back Creek," at the foot of Brush or Cloyd's Mountain, now Pulaski County. He afterwards became the father of General Gordon Cloyd, David and Thomas Cloyd, whom I remember as intelligent, wealthy and prominent citizens of that region more than half a century ago, and the grandfather of the late aged and venerable Colonel Joseph Cloyd, who, with his family, possessed and enjoyed till his death, recently, a portion of the paternal acres on Back Creek, near which was faught the "battle of Cloyd's Mountain," in 1864.

This Draper's-Meadows-Ingles'-Ferry settlement was an outlying, advanced post of civilization, on the edge of the then great Western wilderness, and soon became a place of rendezvous and point of departure, for individuals, families and parties bent on Western adventure, exploration, emigration, or speculation.

This way passed Dr. Thomas Walker and his first party of explorers, in 1748, and, also, his second expedition, in 1750.

From here, in 1754, started out the first four or five family settlements that are known to have been made, that early, west of New River. James Burke went to Burke's Garden, in (now) Tazwell County; whether accompanied by others or not I do not know. There were two families (names unknown to me) settled on Back Creek, now the Cloyd settlement, in Pulaski County; Ingles' Ferry, on both sides; Reed at Dublin, McCorkle at Dunkard's Bottom, two families on Cripple Creek, another tributary of New River, now in Wythe County, and near this, just over the divide, one or two families on the headwaters of the Holston, now in Smythe County.

From here started, in 1770, a party of hunters and explorers, reinforced at the then Holston and Clinch settlements, under Lieutenant (afterwards Colonel) Knox. They penetrated into Kentucky, were on Cumberland, Green and Kentucky Rivers, and, from the long time they were gone, have ever since been known in border history as "the long hunters."

From here, in 1773, a surveying party, composed of James, George and Robert. McAfee, James McCown, Jr., Hancock Taylor and Samuel Adams, started for Kentucky. They came down New River, and were joined on the Kanawha by Colonel Thomas Bullitt and party. Colonel Bullitt, for military services in the Braddock and Forbes wars, having just located the big bottom survey on which the city of Charleston now stands; they went by canoes down the Kanawha and down the Ohio Rivers to the mouth of Kentucky River, where the party separated. The McAfees and Hancock Taylor went up the Kentucky River, and on the 16th of July, 1773, surveyed six hundred acres where the city of Frankfort now stands, being the first survey ever made on that river.

This river, like most other Western streams, has had a variety of names and spellings before settling down to its present one; thus it has been Milewa-keme-cepewe, Kan-tuck-kee, Che-no-ee, Cut-ta-wa, Louisa and now Kentucky. It is generally believed that Dr. Walker named it Louisa, but this may be a mistake, as elsewhere shown.

Bullitt and others stopped at Big Bone Lick and made a survey of land, July 5th; they then went on to the Falls of the Ohio, called by the Miamis "Lewekeomi," where they surveyed, in August, 1773, a body of land at the mouth of "Bear Grass Creek," the site of the present city of Louisville; so that this surveying party located, on this trip, and within a few weeks of each other, the sites of the now capital cities of two States—West Virginia and Kentucky—and one of the largest commercial cities of the Ohio Valley—Louisville.

The surveyors returned overland through Kentucky, by way of Powell's Valley and Gap, and, after experiencing extraordinary privation and suffering, made their way back to the New River settlement.

From here started, the following year (1774), the surveying parties under John Floyd, Hancock Taylor, Douglas, and others, who were in the wilds of Kentucky when the border troubles commenced, which finally culminated in the battle of Point Pleasant;

and to notify whom of the Indian dangers, and pilot them safely back, Governor Dunmore dispatched Daniel Boone, then at the Clinch settlement. Boone's mission was successful; the surveyors (except Hancock Taylor, who was killed), and some colonists, were found, notified, and the surveyors and Boone returned overland, by way of the Clinch settlement; Boone having made eight hundred miles on foot, going and returning, in sixty-two days.

From this New River settlement went many of the early, enterprising settlers of Kentucky, whose descendants have since made honorable records in the history of the State and the Nation, among whom may be mentioned the Pattons, Prestons, Breckenridges, Floyds, Triggs, Taylors, Todds, Campbells, Overtons, McAfees, etc., etc.

CHAPTER XX.

IN 1765, John Draper exchanged his interests at Draper's Meadows for land about twenty miles west of Ingles' Ferry, and near the present dividing line between Pulaski and Wythe Counties. This land had been originally granted to Colonel James Patton, in 1753, one of the earliest grants in this region.

It is described as lying "west of Woods River," and near the "Peaked Mountain," now called "Draper's Mountain," and the end, "Peak Knob." John Draper called this settlement "Draper's Valley," which name it still retains.

Here John Draper and Bettie, his wife, and, after her, his second wife, Jane, passed the remainder of their lives, and here their descendants, prominent, honored and influential citizens, have lived ever since, John S. Draper, a great-grandson, being the present owner and occupant of this beautiful and valuable estate.

And so with Ingles' Ferry, a locality so full of family and general historical associations; it is still owned and occupied by the descendants of William and Mary Ingles, of the third and fourth generation, and after a century and a third of time.

Seven children—four sons and three daughters— were born to John and Bettie Draper, after her return from captivity; the sons were George, James, John and Silas; the names of the daughters I do not know.

I remember Silas Draper, an eccentric old bachelor, very fond of his cups. He was still alive about fifty years ago. I remember a quaint way he had of expressing his contempt for the understanding of any one who was so unfortunate as to differ from him in opinion. Of such an one he would say : "He is a connection of Solomon—a *distant* connection of Solomon—a *very* distant connection of Solomon." And, seeming to think that this bit of irony was sufficient to settle the status of his unfortunate adversary, he would leave him to his fate.

Mrs. Bettie Draper died in 1774, aged forty-two. John Draper married again, in 1776, a widow, Mrs. Jane Crockett. The issue of this marriage was two daughters, Alice and Rhoda.

John Draper lived to the great age of ninety-four. He died at Draper's Valley, April 18, 1824. John Draper was a Lieutenant in one of the companies—probably Russell's or Herbert's—at Point Pleasant, in 1774. His commission, signed by Governor Dunmore, is now in possession of his great-grandson, John S. Draper, of Draper's Valley.

In 1770, Virginia formed from Augusta a new county, covering all this western region, and called it Bottetourt, after Governor Lord Bottetourt; and, two years later (1772), another county was formed from part of Bottetourt, extending from the headwaters of the Roanoke northwest to the Ohio River, and west to the Mississippi. This county was named "Fincastle," from the seat of Lord Bottetourt in England—"Fin-Castle."

The county seat of this county was at "Fort Chiswell," now in Wythe County, and the seat of the McGavock family.

The Fort was built by the State in 1758, under the direction and superintendence of the third Colonel William Boyd, and named by him after his friend, Colonel John Chiswell, the owner and operator of the "New River Lead Mines," then but recently discovered by him, a few miles distant.

Colonel Chiswell was a Tory in the Revolutionary troubles, and his property was confiscated. He was, also, so unfortunate as to kill a man in a personal encounter, and died in Cumberland County Jail, awaiting trial. A son of his successor, Colonel Stephen Austin, who was born here, was the founder of the city of Austin, Texas. The town of Austinville, at the Lead Mines, in Wythe, also took its name from the family.

These mines were the chief source of supply of lead, not only for the Indian border wars, but for the Continental Army during the Revolution, and for the Confederate Army in the late civil war.

Fincastle County did not long continue. In 1776, the territory covered by it was divided up into three new counties—Montgomery, Washington and Kentucky—and Fincastle County abolished.

This Washington County was the first in the United States named after the illustrious George Washington. Now, almost every State in the Union has its Washington County.

The first town in America named after the Father of his Country was Washington, Georgia. Now, they are so numerous as to be confusing.

About this time (1774–75–76), before the boundary line between Virginia and Pennsylvania had been definitely settled, the Ohio River, the Monongahela and the Youghiogheny, in the region of Fort Pitt, where considerable settlements had been made, were supposed to be parts of Virginia territory, and, as such, parts of Augusta County, or "West Augusta." So remote were these settlements from the county seat at Staunton that the State of Virginia provided for the holding of courts for Augusta County at both places—Staunton and Fort Pitt—and for some time they were so held, adjourning from one place to the other, alternately.

On the return of the expedition of Walker, Patton, and others, in 1748, they organized the "Loyal Land Company," based on a grant of 800,000 acres of land, to lie north of the North Carolina line, and west of the mountains, and incorporated their company in June, 1749.

CHAPTER XXI.

WILLIAM INGLES purchased the land at and about Ingles' Ferry from the Loyal Land Company—Dr. Thomas Walker, agent.

In establishing himself at this point, he foresaw that it would be an important crossing place for Western emigrants, and, so soon as practicable, in order to enhance the value of his property, he located and marked out a line of road from the settlements east of him to the west, on towards Tennessee—no doubt following, in the main, the route he and John Draper had traveled in going down to the Cherokee Nation, in 1755, as above related; and they were, probably, the first white Americans to traverse this route, or this region, throughout.

The exploring parties of Dr. Thomas Walker, in their two trips, traveled up and down Walker's Creek, Wolf Creek, East River and Blue-Stone, streams emptying into New River below here; and by way of Upper New River, Cripple Creek and Reed Creek, above here.

It is claimed by Dr. Bickley, historian of Tazwell County, that as early as 1540, more than two hundred years before Dr. Walker and party, or Ingles and Draper, the distinguished Spanish explorer and adventurer, Hernando De Soto, visited or passed through a portion of this region of Southwest Virginia. Dr. Bickley, who seems to have examined the subject with care, satisfied himself, from the official reports of the historian of the expedition, that De Soto, after landing, about Tampa Bay, Florida, in 1739, came, first by Mobile Bay, thence up through what is now Georgia, South and North Carolina, East Tennessee and Southwest Virginia. He found a strong and important tribe of Indians settled on the Upper Tennessee, with their capital or head-quarters town, called "Cafitachiqui." They were governed by a Queen. In that part of Southwest Virginia, now Washington and Smythe, Russell and Tazwell Counties—according to the Doctor's theory—was another province, called Xuala, inhabited by a peaceable, quiet and hospitable race. They were afterwards driven out or exterminated by the Cherokees, who then held the country until they, in turn, were driven out by the English.

From here, De Soto went on westward, to discover for his country the great Mississippi River, or "Rio Grande," as he called it, and, for himself, a watery grave beneath its turbid waters.

The mistake of Dr. Bickley, probably, was in bringing the De Soto expedition too far North. Instead of coming by way of Knoxville and Southwest Virginia, his route is believed, by other authorities, to have been by way of the present sites of Atlanta, Georgia, and Chattanooga, Tennessee, and that the tribes he encountered were on that route, and not in East Tennessee and Southwest Virginia.

Nearly all the emigration that populated Southwest Virginia, Tennessee, Southern and Middle Kentucky, and parts of Northern Georgia, Alabama and Mississippi, passed over this route.

THE WILDERNESS ROAD.

Colonel Thos. Speed, of Louisville, Ky., through the "Filson Historical Club," has recently issued, under the above title, a valuable and exceedingly interesting contribution to the history of the early routes of travel of the first emigrants to Kentucky. He describes two principal routes—one overland by way of New River, Fort Chiswell, Cumberland Gap and the Boone trace, and the other by the Braddock trail to Red Stone, or to Fort Pitt, and thence down the Ohio River, by boat.

I think a third and mixed route, partly by land and partly by water, passing down through this (Kanawha) valley, deserves to be mentioned, as it was traveled by a good many, "in an early day." They came from the settlements along the border, or from farther East, by way of the frontier settlements, to this river, by land, and went from here by water; the mouths of Kelly's Creek and Hughes' Creek, where boats were built, being the usual points of embarcation, by the earlier voyagers. This way went the McAfees, James McCown, Samuel Adams, Hancock Taylor, Colonel Thomas Bullitt, Douglas, John May, Jacob Skyles, Charles Johnson, John Flinn, John Floyd, Volney, and others. And many of the officers and men of Lewis' army, who afterwards went to Kentucky, followed this route, having learned it in their trip to Point Pleasant.

A little later, when settlements began north of the Ohio River, Eastern Virginia and North Carolina sent a very large emigration by this route.

The large early travel by way of Ingles' Ferry

made it one of the most valuable properties in that
region; and long after, when thriving villages, towns
and cities had been built up in this prosperous country, their supplies of dry goods, groceries, hardware,
etc., were hauled over this route, first from Baltimore, via Winchester, and afterwards from Richmond
and Lynchburg, to, finally, as far West as Nashville,
in those picturesque land schooners, or "Tennessee
ships of the line"—the Connestoga wagons, with
their high-bowed and well-racked canvas covers, and
six-horse teams, many of them with the jingling
bells that made lively music as they went.

I well remember, between fifty and sixty years ago,
the long droves of these wagons, going and returning, and how the arches of tinkling bells and red
flannel rosettes, swinging gracefully over the horses'
shoulders, excited my boyish admiration.

The drivers of these teams were a peculiar class;
they were a hardy, honest, jolly, good-natured set,
who knew and were known by everybody on the
route for hundreds of miles. They were greatly
trusted by their employers, and were popular all
along the road.

ORIGIN OF THE COTTON TRADE OF AMERICA.

I will mention here, as an interesting historical
fact—on the authority of the late John W. Garrett,
the distinguished President of the B. & O. R. R.—
that the beginning of the cotton trade of America
was over this road, and in these same Connestoga
wagons.

The Southern and Southwestern emigrants had
begun to raise a little cotton, at their new homes, for

domestic uses. Their little surpluses were saved up
and traded to their merchants to help pay for their
groceries and other family supplies, and the country
merchant sent a few bags of it, now and then, together with feathers, pelts, dried fruits and other
country commodities, by these wagons, to their
wholesale merchants in Baltimore, who took the cotton to encourage trade; but, as there were then no
cotton mills in America, they did not know what to
do with it. It began to accumulate on their hands,
however, and it became necessary to find some use
for it.

A meeting was called of the prominent merchants,
who traded in this direction, to discuss the matter.
After a consideration of the subject, no other sug-
gestion having met with favor, an old gentleman
present, named Brown, a successful Scotch-Irish
linen draper, proposed that, if the merchants would
all contribute to the expense, he would send his son,
"Jamie," to England, to see if it could not be disposed of there. This proposition was agreed to, and
Jamie went, taking with him samples of the cotton.
On his return, he reported that he had not only easily
disposed of all they then had on hand, but had made
satisfactory arrangements for all they might get in
the future.

Jamie was so impressed with the belief that there
was "money in it," that he and his brothers formed
a copartnership, under the name and style of "Brown
Brothers," to buy, and ship, and trade in cotton.

The business rapidly grew to large proportions,
and their wealth increased as rapidy, until they
established branch banking houses at several of the

8

principal commercial centers on both sides of the
water, and the honored names of "Brown Brothers,"
"Brown Brothers & Company," and "Brown, Shipley
& Company," are known, to this day, all over the
commercial world. They are, probably, worth their
millions of dollars, and the cotton trade has grown
to millions of bales per year. So much for small
beginnings.

About 1840, the State of Virginia, to facilitate and
encourage the vast overland traffic of this route,
macadamized the road from Buchanan, the head of
canal navigation oñ the James River, to the Tennessee
line; and Thomas Ingles, the then owner of Ingles'
Ferry, and grandson of William and Mary Ingles,
built a fine bridge over New River (the first to cross
New River or Kanawha), which was afterward destroyed, during the late war.

The progressive spirit of the age, however, was
working a change in all this; the days of the overland schooners were soon to be numbered—their occupation gone—and the values of Ingles' Ferry and
Bridge numbered with the things that were past.

About 1855, the "Virginia & Tennessee Railroad,"
then so called, now known, with its connections, as
the "Norfolk & Western," was completed and
opened. The iron steed and winged lightning came
to the front to fulfill their missions, and the old
methods, with Connestogas and stage-coaches, van-
ished into the misty realms of the forgotten past.

The railroad, for better grade, crosses New River
two or three miles below the old Ingles' Ferry route
and macadam road.

CHAPTER XXII.

TO return to the story of William and Mary Ingles and their lost children. These "babes in the wood" were the "skeletons in their closet." However otherwise happy and prosperous, here was an abiding and ever-present sorrow that marred every pleasure of their lives.

The first thing heard from the children was that George, the youngest boy, had died not long after he was taken from the tender care of his mother, at Scioto. This information first came, I believe, through Mrs. Draper, on her return from captivity. Some years later, and after many ineffectual efforts had been made to recover, or even hear from the elder boy, Thomas, they met with a man named Baker, who had recently returned from a captivity among the Shawanees, in the Scioto country.

It is believed that this was the William Baker who passed here in 1766 with Colonel James Smith, on his way to explore the then unknown region between the Tennessee and Cumberland Rivers.

It turned out that Baker had lived in the same village with the Indian who had last adopted the boy as his son, and knew them both.

William Ingles at once bargained with Baker to go back to the Indian country and ransom his boy and bring him home.

Baker went down the Valley of Virginia by Staun-

ton to Winchester, across by Fort Cumberland (the
site of an old Indian town called Cucuvatuc) to Fort
Pitt, and thence down the Ohio to the Scioto. He
found the Indian and made known his mission. After
much negotiation, he succeeded in purchasing the
boy, and paid about one hundred dollars for his ransom; but the boy was not at all pleased with the
arrangement; he knew nothing of the white parents
they told him about, in the far-off country; he knew
only his Indian father and mother, brothers and sisters, and playmates, and, last but not least, his sweet-
hearts, the pretty little squaws, and he did not want
to be sent away from them.

Partly by coaxing and fair promises, however, and
partly by force, Baker got him started, but kept him
bound until they got forty to.fifty miles from the Indian village. As they passed along, the dusky little
maidens, as they got a chance to talk, would try to
persuade him not to go, or beg him to come back to
them. The little fellow could not withstand their
appeals unmoved, and determined to escape; but, as
the surest means of doing so, he feigned contentment
and perfect willingness to go, until Baker ceased to
bind him at night, as he at first did, but only took
him in his arms when they went to sleep, thinking
the boy could not get out of his embrace without
awakening him. When he awoke one morning,
however, he found, to his surprise and chagrin, that
the boy was missing.

Fearing to go home and report his carelessness and
the loss of the boy to his parents, Baker went all the
way back to Indian village to try to recover him;
but the squaws had concealed him and would not

give him up, and Baker had, at last, to go home
without him.

This was a sad disappointment and blow to Mr.
and Mrs. Ingles, especially to the mother, whose
womanly heart had been so strongly yearning for
her long lost boy.

They had found him now, however, and must recover him. William Ingles determined to go for
him, himself, and hired Baker to go back with him.
They started, and pursued the same circuitous and
tedious route, but when they arrived at Fort Pitt
they found that hostilities had broken out between
the Indians and the frontier white settlements, and
it was impossible, then, to prosecute the journey.

With deep reluctance, they abandoned the trip, for
the time, and returned to their homes, to await the
restoration of peace.

It proved to be more than a year before it was considered safe to renew the effort. William Ingles
then again employed Baker to accompany him, and
started out over the same circuitous route, by Pattonsburg, Staunton, Winchester, Fort Cumberland,
Fort Pitt, and down the Ohio.

When they arrived at the Indian town, they found
that a party of Indians, the father of the boy and
the boy included, had gone to Detroit, and would
not return for several weeks. This was a great disappointment, but there was no help for it; they could
but wait.

A very unwise move on the part of William Ingles,
during this delay, came very near costing him his
life. Knowing the fondness of the Indians for strong
drink, he had taken with him a keg of the " fire-

water," in addition to some money, and goods and trinkets, for trading, hoping, by one or other, or all of these, to induce the Indian father to sell him his boy.

While waiting the return of the absentees, he was trying to make "fair weather" with the Indians at Scioto, and, thinking to conciliate them, he gave some of them some of his rum. He very soon saw the mistake he had committed, but it was too late to correct it.

The Indians, having their appetites inflamed by the small allowance, determined to have more. They seized his rum, drank it all, and were soon wildly and uproariously drunk. They threatened to kill him, and were about to put their threats into execution, but this time the squaws came to his relief, and, no doubt, saved him from a terrible death. They secreted him and kept him secreted until the Indians got over their drunken debauch, and came to their sober senses.

When the Detroit party returned, the Indian father and the boy came home with them, as expected. Much to the gratification and relief of the white father, the boy took to him kindly at once.

The mysterious influence of "blood" and the instinct of filial love asserted themselves, and the boy promised, freely and without reserve, to accompany his father whenever and wherever he pleased.

The terms of his surrender were then negotiated with his Indian father, and the ransom—this time about the equivalent of one hundred and fifty dollars—again paid. All these negotiations and conferences were conducted through Baker, as interpretor; the boy had lost all recollection of his mother tongue, his Indian father could not speak English, and William Ingles did not speak Indian.

Arrangements being completed, there was a general leave-taking, with good feeling all round. The boy bade a long farewell to his old, and started with his new-found father, and Baker, to the far-off home. After weeks of tedious travel, they at last arrived safely at Ingles' Ferry, and the long-lost boy, his mother's first-born, was again in her arms and smothered with a mother's loving kisses. This was in 1768. He found here, too, four other little relatives to give him affectionate greeting. Mrs. Ingles, since her return from captivity, had borne three daughters and one son. Thomas was absorbed into this family circle, and was a sharer of the family affections.

He was very much of a wild Indian in his habits and training when he first returned. He was now in his seventeenth year, and had been among the Indians thirteen years. He was dressed in Indian style. He changed his savage dress for that of civilized life with much reluctance; his bow and arrow he would not give up, but carried them with him wherever he went.

Notwithstanding he was petted, humored and caressed at home, a wild fit would overcome him now and then, and he would wander off alone in the wilderness, with his bow and arrow, and stay for days at a time, and, when he returned, would give no account of himself, nor explanation of his conduct.

These freaks disturbed his mother very much; she feared that he would some day take a notion to return to his Indian friends and wild life, and that she should never see him again.

He learned pretty rapidly to speak English, but very slowly to read and write.

He used often to interest the family and others by relating incidents of his Indian life. Once, when quite young, and learning to use the bow and arrow, he tried to shoot a red-headed woodpecker from a tree near the camp. He became so interested in what he was doing that, while looking up at the woodpecker and walking backwards, to get in range, he stepped into a fire of coals the Indians had to cook their dinner on, and so burned his bare feet that they never grew to quite their natural size.

When a little older, but still quite young, his Indian father and another Indian went to the wilderness, forty or fifty miles distant from the settlement, to kill a supply of game, as was their wont, and they took the boy along to teach him to hunt and to make himself useful.

Not long after they had been in camp his Indian father was taken very sick. The other Indian provided some food, and wood for fire, instructed the boy how to cook and serve the food to his sick father, and what else to do for his comfort, while he went back to the town to get assistance to take the sick man home.

The very day after he left, the sick Indian died, and the boy was left alone to watch him until the other Indian returned with help. A heavy snow fell, and the weather became very cold. The boy, to keep warm at night, lay close to the old Indian, and covered with part of his blanket.

After some days, decomposition had so far progressed that the odor from the old Indian attracted the wolves. They came, howling, to the camp, and the boy could only keep them back by throwing fire-brands at them.

Up to that time the boy had never fired a gun, but his Indian father's gun was standing there, loaded, and he concluded to try what he could do with it. The first thing he saw to practice on was some wild pigeons. Not being able to hold the gun "off-hand," he fixed a rest, took aim and fired, and, much to his delight, he killed his pigeon.

This gave him confidence in himself, and he now concluded that he could safely defend himself and father from the wolves.

Having reloaded the gun, he cut a forked stick with his father's tomahawk, and drove it in the ground in such position that he could rest the gun in the fork and get the proper range for the wolves. Sure enough, they came back again that night. He was ready for them, and, when they came within proper distance, he fired, and again had the proud satisfaction of killing his game.

The other wolves fled, and he was not again disturbed by them.

The messenger Indian soon after returned with assistance, and, having buried his dead father, took him (the boy) back to the town, where he was adopted into the family of another Indian.

CHAPTER XXIII.

*A*FTER acquiring, at home, some preliminary and rudimentary foundation for an education, his father sent him to the care of his old friend, Dr. Thomas Walker, of "Castle Hill," Albermarle County (the present seat of the Rives family, who are descendants of Dr. Walker), to see what could be done in the way of educating him. There was a school for young men at or near Dr. Walker's residence, Castle Hill.

While in Albermarle, he made some progress in his studies; but books were not to his taste, and study was very irksome to him.

While prosecuting his studies here, some three or four years in all, his remarkable history attracted attention, and he made many acquaintances, some of whom were afterwards very distinguished people. Among them were Madison, Monroe, Jefferson, Patrick Henry, William Wirt, etc.

His friend, Dr. Walker, had been the guardian of young Jefferson, during his minority, after his father's death. Young Ingles used to relate that he and Jefferson, both being musically inclined, took lessons on the violin together, from the same instructor.

About this time, young Jefferson was appointed, and for a time acted, as Surveyor of Albermarle County, a position which his father had occupied in his lifetime.

In after years, Jefferson, when Governor of Virginia, gave him (Ingles) a commission of Colonel of militia.

He formed here another acquaintance, who made a deeper and more lasting impression on his after life. It was that of a young lady who had captured his wild heart.

Soon after leaving Albermarle, he volunteered with the forces then being raised to go with General Lewis' army to Point Pleasant, in 1774. He was made Lieutenant in his company, which was part of Colonel Christian's regiment. Young Ingles was in one of the companies left to garrison the Fort at Point Pleasant during the following winter.

When relieved at the Point, he met some of his old Indian friends from Scioto, and, at their earnest solicitation, went home with them, and spent some time in a social, friendly visit.

Shortly after his return from this visit—in 1775— he married Miss Eleanor Grills, the Albermarle sweetheart of his schoolboy days. Being disposed to settle down, but determined to be in the wilderness, his father gave him a tract of land on Wolf Creek, a tributary of New River, in (now) Giles County. He remained here a few years, and had made fair progress in clearing out a farm, when he determined to move to what was then called Absalom's Valley, now Abb's Valley, on the Upper Blue Stone, also a branch of New River, some distance below. This stream is called " Blue Stone " from the deep blue valley limestone over which it flows, and which gives such fertility to the beautiful valley.

The same experience was repeated here. After

one or two years in opening up a farm, he concluded
he was too convenient to the Indian Blue Stone trail,
for safety, as parties were frequently passing over
this route, to make depredations on the settlements
farther south.

He next located in "Burke's Garden," in (now)
Tazewell County—a rich and beautiful little limestone valley, or oval basin, about ten miles by seven,
almost surrounded by high mountains, and one of
the most charming spots in the State. It is drained
by Wolf Creek, on which, lower down, he had lived
some years earlier. I have a copy of an old document showing that William Ingles had "taken up"
the Burke's Garden lands, under "Loyal Land Company" authority, as early as 1753. James Burke,
who came here, from Ingles' Ferry, in 1754, was the
first settler, as elsewhere stated, and gave the place
his name and his life.

Thomas Ingles had but one neighbor in Burke's
Garden—Joseph Hix, by name, a bachelor, who
lived within two miles. Ingles lived here, in peace
and apparent contentment, until April, 1782, when a
large party of Indians, led by the noted warrior,
"Black Wolf," surrounded his house, while he was
out on the farm, and, after taking his wife, three
children and a negro man and woman prisoners, and
taking as much as they could carry of whatever they
found useful, loading the negro man and woman as
well, they burned the house and everything that was
left in it.

When his attention was attracted by the smoke
and fire, and the noise, Thomas Ingles started to his
house; but, being unarmed and seeing so large a

force, he knew he could do no good, so he ran back to where he and a negro man were plowing, unhitched the horses, and, each mounting one, they started to the nearest settlement for help. This settlement was in the "Rich Valley," or "Rich Patch," on the North Fork of the Holston, and the present site of the "Washington Salt Works," about twenty miles distant.

It happened to be a muster day, and most of the settlers round about were congregated here for drill. The messengers arrived about noon, and, so soon as the facts were made known, fifteen or twenty men volunteered to go in pursuit of the Indians. They soon made their preparations and started back, arriving at the site of Ingles' home early next morning; but there was nothing left but a pile of ashes.

It so happened that Mr. Hix and his negro man were on their way to Thomas Ingles' house the morning before, when they discovered that the Indians had attacked and were destroying it. They at once started, on foot, across the mountain, to a small settlement, six or seven miles distant. Here they got five or six volunteers and returned, reaching Burke's Garden about the same time that Thomas Ingles' party got there. They united their forces and started in pursuit.

It was expected that the route of the Indians would be through or near the Clinch settlement, and it was about here that the whites first struck their trail. There was a company of militia stationed here for the protection of settlers on the frontier. Some of these joined the pursuing party, and Captain Maxwell was put in command of the whole.

The pursuit was made very cautiously, to prevent alarming the Indians and causing them to murder the prisoners. On the fifth day after the capture, some scouts, sent in advance by the whites, discovered the Indians where they had camped for the night, in a gap of Tug Mountain.

The pursuers held a consultation and decided that Captain Maxwell should take half the company, flank the Indians, and get round to their front and as near them as practicable, and that Thomas Ingles, with the other half, should remain in the rear, getting as close as possible, and at daylight the attack should be made simultaneously by both parties.

Unfortunately, the night being very dark and the ground very rough and brushy, Captain Maxwell missed his way, got too far to one side, and did not get back within reach of the Indians by daylight.

After waiting for Maxwell beyond the appointed time, and as the Indians began to stir, Thomas Ingles and his party determined to make the attack alone.

So soon as a shot was fired, some of the Indians began to tomahawk the prisoners, while others fought and fled. Thomas Ingles rushed in and seized his wife just as she had received a terrible blow on the head with a tomahawk. She fell, covering the infant of a few months old, which she held in her arms. The Indians had no time to devote to it. They had tomahawked his little five-year-old daughter, named Mary, after his mother, and his little three-year-old son, named William, after his father. His negro servants, a man and woman, captured with his family, escaped without injury.

In making their escape, the Indians ran close to

Captain Maxwell and party, and, firing on them, killed Captain Maxwell, who was conspicuous from wearing a white hunting shirt. He was the only one of the pursuers killed.

The whites remained on the ground until late in the evening, burying Captain Maxwell, who was killed outright, and Thomas Ingles' little son, who died from his wounds during the day. Mrs. Ingles and the little girl were still alive though badly wounded.

It was supposed that several Indians were killed in this engagement, but it was not certainly known. While the whites remained on the ground they heard the groans of apparently dying persons, but, as the sounds came from dense laurel thickets, they did not find them.

This mountain pass through Tug Ridge has ever since been known as "Maxwell's Gap," after the unfortunate Captain Maxwell who lost his life here.

When the dead had been buried, and the wounds of Mrs. Ingles and her little daughter had been dressed as well as practicable under the circumstances, the party started on their return to the settlements. Although only about twenty miles, it took four days to travel it, on account of the critical condition of Mrs. Ingles and her little girl.

News of the capture of Thomas Ingles' family and the pursuit had reached the settlement at New River, and his father, William Ingles, had started out to Burke's Garden to see if he could render any assistance, and, very thoughtfully, took with him the best surgeon he could get.

He met the returning party at the Clinch settlement. The little girl was beyond the skill of the doctor; she died from her wounds the next morning; but he rendered invaluable service to Mrs. Ingles, probably saving her life. He extracted several pieces of broken bone from her skull, dressed her wounds and attended her carefully until able to travel safely, when she and her husband and infant returned with William Ingles, to Ingles' Ferry, and remained there until next season. Mrs. Ingles, in the meantime, entirely recovered from her terrible wound.

It is difficult now to appreciate the constant dangers which beset the early pioneers, or realize the readiness and cheerfulness with which they accepted the dangers, hardships, self-denials and privations incident to such a life.

Probably the fullest and truest description of the conditions of border-life and the state of society existing along the Western frontiers, about the time the first settlements began, was written by Rev. Dr. Joseph Doddridge, who was himself reared on the Western border, on the Upper Ohio, and was an unusually close and intelligent observer. His minuteness of detail, and lucidity of style, make his writings invaluable as record-pictures of the primitive conditions of life on our Western borders a hundred years and more ago.

William Ingles owned a number of slaves at Ingles' Ferry, and gave servants to his children as they were married and settled. These were, in all probability, the *first* slaves ever west of the Alleghanies, and those above mentioned, that had been given to Thomas Ingles, when he went to housekeeping, were probably the *first* to cross New River westward.

Thomas Ingles was now meditating another settlement. He could only be satisfied in the wilderness, but he had had enough of Burke's Garden. As Southwest Virginia was rapidly filling up, he determined to go down into Tennessee, where he made a settlement on the Watauga, a branch of the Holston River. There were then but few settlers in this region, and these few were frequently harassed by the depredations of the Cherokees.

Thomas Ingles managed to live here several years, and had gotten his family pretty comfortably fixed, when the restless spirit of change again seized him. He sold his improvements to immigrants coming in, and moved about fifty miles farther down the river, to another tributary, called "Mossy Creek," then on the frontier; but he found good range there for cattle, and he was very fond of stock-raising. Here he was constantly subject to the same dangers of Indian depredations. Some of his neighbors suffered greatly, but he, fortunately, escaped.

About this time, a military force, under Colonel Knox, was sent still farther down the Holston, to erect a Fort for the protection of the frontier; this was called "Fort Knox."

Thomas Ingles had now remained at "Mossy Creek" about as long as his restless nature would permit him to live at one place, and he again sold out his land and stock, and moved down to the vicinity of Fort Knox.

The security given to settlers by the protection of the Fort induced rapid immigration to this section, and the Fort soon began to grow into the village and town of "Knoxville."

9

Thomas Ingles remained on his farm in this neighborhood for some years longer; he had improved his estate, added to his acres, had large herds of cattle, was prosperous, comfortable, and, apparently, contented. His daughter Rhoda, the infant of Burke's Garden, who had so narrowly escaped massacre at Maxwell's Gap, had grown up to womanhood, was a bright and attractive young lady, and was married to Mr. Patrick Campbell, of Knoxville. One of the earliest recollections of my life, when I could not have been over three or four years old, was a visit from this, then, elderly lady, to my grandfather—her uncle—Colonel John Ingles, of Ingles' Ferry. I remember the earnest and interesting discussions of the family history and adventures, and how they excited my childish imagination. I was too young, of course, to remember details. I only remember the subject, and the interest it excited in me.

CHAPTER XXIV.

THE MOORE FAMILY.

IN another little gem of a valley, not far distant, called "Abb's Valley," from Absalom Looney, its pioneer settler, who came here in 1771, from about Looney's Creek, near Pattonsburg, on James River, another bloody tragedy, similar to that of Burke's Garden, above described, was enacted about four years later.

In July, 1786, a party of Shawanees, from the Ohio towns, led by the same stealthy and blood-thirsty Black Wolf, who had devastated the Ingles-Burke's-Garden settlement, and who had also captured James Moore, Jr., in 1784, came up the Big Sandy, over Tug Ridge and across the heads of Laurel Creek to Abb's Valley, where, on the 14th, they went to the house of Captain James Moore, who, with his brother-in-law, John Pogue, had located here in 1772.

· They found Captain Moore salting his stock, a short distance from the house, and shot him down; then, rushing to the house, they killed two of his children, William and Rebecca, and John Simpson, who, I believe, was a hired man or assistant of Mr. Moore, and sick at the time. There were two other men in a harvest field, who fled and made their escape. These disposed of, the savages proceeded to make prisoners of Mrs. Moore and her four remaining children—John, Jane, Mary and Peggy—and a Miss Martha Evans, of Augusta, who was living with the family.

In their rapid retreat, it soon became evident that the boy, John, who was feeble, was an incumbrance and hindrance in their flight, and he was tomahawked and scalped, in his mother's presence, and left by the wayside. Two days later, little Peggy, the babe, was brained against a tree.

Arriving at one of the Indian towns on the Scioto, they heard of the death of some of their warriors, who had been killed in some engagement with the whites in Kentucky, and they determined, in council, that two of these prisoners should be burned at the stake, in retaliation. This terrible doom fell to the lot of Mrs. Moore and her eldest daughter, Jane—a pretty and interesting girl of sixteen.

They were tied to stakes, in the presence of the remaining daughter and sister, and Miss Evans, and a vast crowd of exulting savages, and slowly and cruelly tortured, after the manner of the fiendish race, with fire-brands and burning splinters of pine, etc., until Death, a now welcome friend, an angel of mercy and messenger of peace, came to release them from their persecutors and their agonizing sufferings.

Can pity lead to inflicting pain? Can kindness kill? Can mercy commit murder? Aye, even so, under some circumstances.

What tender mercy it would have been in Simon Girty to shoot Colonel Crawford, as he piteously begged him to do, to end his fiery tortures! What cruelty it was *not* to kill him!

In this case, an old hag of a squaw, with the feeble spark of humanity that survived in her savage breast kindled to a glow, and being surfeited by the excessive tortures and sufferings of Mrs. Moore, in gentle mercy and the kindness of her heart, gave the final coup de grace to Mrs. Moore, with a hatchet, thus shortening somewhat her already protracted agonies. Mary Moore remained some years a prisoner among the Indians, and, during the latter part of her stay, with a white family, who treated her far more cruelly than the Indians.

In September, 1784, two years prior to the circumstances above related, James Moore, Jr., aged fourteen—eldest son of the above-mentioned Captain James Moore—had been captured near his father's home, in Abb's Valley, by a small party of these Indians, passing through, composed of the same Black Wolf, his son and one other, and taken, first, to the Shawanee towns of Ohio, and, afterwards, to the Maumee settlements in Michigan, and, still later, sold to a white family at or near Detroit. Hearing, through Indian channels, of the terrible fate of his father's family, and that his sister Mary was a captive, not very far from him, he managed to communicate with her, first by message, and, afterwards, in person, and to comfort her.

In October, 1789, James and Mary Moore, and Miss Martha Evans, were all ransomed by their friends, and restored to relatives in the Valley of Virginia, where James Moore, Sr., and wife and Miss Evans had been reared.

James Moore, Jr., not long after, returned to Abb's Valley, where he lived and reared a family, and died,

in 1851, in the eighty-first year of his age, and where
his son, a venerable and honored citizen, now eighty-
four, still owns and occupies, in peace and happiness,
the possessions secured to him and his descendants
by the blood and tears of his ancestors.

Mary Moore married a distinguished Presbyterian
Minister, Rev. John Brown, of Rockbridge County,
and was the mother of a large family, five or six of
whom became Presbyterian ministers; one of whom,
the late Rev. James Brown, D. D., whose memory is
warmly cherished by all the older citizens of this
place (Charleston, W. Va.), was, for a quarter of a
century, pastor of the First Presbyterian Church of
this city.

Dr. James Brown had but two sons who attained
their majority; both were Presbyterian ministers.
The eldest, Rev. Samuel Brown, died at his pastorate
in Greenbriar County, in early life. The younger,
Rev. John Brown, is, and has been for a number of
years, pastor of the Presbyterian Church at Malden,
Kanawha County. Many years ago, Dr. James
Brown, discovering unusual sprightliness in a poor
and friendless Irish boy, took him home with him,
and, in the kindness of his heart, reared and edu-
cated him with his own sons. This (then) poor lad
became the late distinguished Rev. Dr. Stuart Robinson, D. D., LL. D., who achieved a national reputation
as a successful teacher, eloquent preacher and able
author.

The story of the sufferings of James Moore and
family, and especially of the survivor, Mary Moore,
was very touchingly told by the late Rev. James
Brown, her son, in a little volume called " The

Captives of Abb's Valley," published some forty years ago, and which is well remembered by our elderly citizens. From this little volume, chiefly, I have condensed the foregoing sketch.

There is another incident connected with the murder and capture of Captain Moore's family which, I think, is of interest enough to be perpetuated, especially as it illustrates a fact often mentioned by, the early pioneers—that is, that civilized (?) horses have a very strong antipathy to Indians. They scent them at a distance, and show their displeasure and fear by snorting, pawing, etc., and will flee, if they can. After the murders and captures, the Indians proceeded to appropriate the horses, as a matter of course. Captain Moore had a fine black horse, called Yorick—a very powerful and a very vicious horse. He was controllable enough by Captain Moore, and by Simpson, who had attended him, but he would let no one else ride him or handle him. One of the Indians, in attempting to mount him, was knocked down and pawed, and killed or crippled; a second one tried it, and with the same result, when the leader of the party, a very determined and very powerful man, declared that he would ride him or kill him; he mounted him, but was no sooner on than off, and, while down, the horse sprang upon him and, with hoofs and teeth, killed him before he could recover his feet; whereupon the other Indians shot and stabbed the horse to death, after which they buried the large Indian close to the stable and departed.

Dr. Brown does not mention this incident in his narrative, but I have taken the pains to ask of Mr. William Moore, by letter, what he knows or believes

about the tradition. He tells me that he has reason
to believe that it is substantially true, and that when
his father, Mr. James Moore, Jr., the captive, returned to Abb's Valley, he plowed up, in plowing
his fields, near the old stable, a skeleton of unusual
size, which was believed to be that of the large man
killed by the horse.

It is known that the leader of the several parties
who captured Thomas Ingles' family, in Burke's
Garden, in 1782, captured James Moore, Jr., in 1784,
and destroyed the family of James Moore, Sr., in
1786, was named Black Wolf. As he is not afterwards heard of along the borders, I think it strongly
probable that it was the veritable Black Wolf whose
career had been so ingloriously terminated by the horse
Yorick; and this suggests the probable identity of
Black Wolf and Wolf, the son of Cornstalk. It is
said that Cornstalk had a son called Wolf, who went
to Williamsburg with Lord Dunmore, after the
treaty at Camp Charlotte, ostensibly, I believe, as a
hostage, with other Indians, but more likely, really,
to be manipulated in the interest of Dunmore and
the English against the Colonies. When Governor
Dunmore fled, the Indians returned to their wilderness homes. I know of no after history of Wolf,
unless it be as Black Wolf, who had just the huge
physical frame and bold, daring traits of character
that we should expect a son to inherit from such
a father. This, of course, is not history, but simply
conjecture, based upon reasonable probabilities.

CHAPTER XXV

IN 1789, about three years after the destruction of Captain James Moore's family, and about the time of the rcovery, from captivity, of James Moore, Jr., and his sister Mary, the family of one of their former neighbors, Andrew Davidson, were the victims of another raid of the Indians into that region. The family of Mr. Davidson consisted of himself and wife, Rebecca, two little girls and a little boy, and two bound children, a girl and boy.

Andrew Davidson had himself gone on a trip down to the Shenandoah Valley; during his absence, there being no male protector about his house, the Indians suddenly made their appearance, and, in broken English, told Mrs. Davidson she and her family must go with them. This was a terrible fate, under any circumstances, but to Mrs. D., at the time, it was especially painful and trying, as she was about to become a mother; this, however, was no valid excuse in their eyes. Go she must, whatever the suffering to her. She undertook to carry her little boy, less than two years old; seeing that it was too much for her, the Indians took it from her. She expected to see them kill it before her eyes, but was greatly relieved when, instead, they carried it along, good-naturedly, for her.

Somewhere on the route, nature's period being probably somewhat hastened by the unusual physical exertion and mental anxiety, Mrs. Davidson introduced to this world of suffering and sorrow the little expected stranger. Both mother and babe were spared, for the time being; but the circumstance was not allowed to interfere with the progress of the journey. Fortunately for Mrs. Davidson, she enjoyed remarkably fine physical health and strength, unenervated by the inactive life and luxurious habits of the ladies of this day; she was equal to the emergency, and resumed the journey, next morning, with the babe in her arms. After a day or two, the infant became ill and troublesome, when one of the Indians coolly took it from her and pitched it into Tug River and drowned, together, the little life and its sorrows and sufferings, so inauspiciously begun, regardless of the anguish of the sorrowing mother.

When they arrived at the Indian towns, her two little girls, to her great horror, were tied to trees and shot to death, for sport. The little two-year-old boy was given to an old squaw, who started away with him in a canoe, which, by some means, was upset and the little fellow drowned. The two bound children were separated from her, and were never afterwards heard of by her.

Two years after this, Andrew Davidson visited the Indian towns in Ohio, in search of his wife; he found some of those who had participated in her capture; they told him she was alive, but would not tell him where she was. Next year, they sent him word that she was somewhere in Canada; so he started again in search of her. In passing a comfortable farmhouse, in Canada, about noon one day, he stopped to get some dinner, and, while waiting for the meal, a woman passed him, and seemed to examine him very critically; but, as he was deeply absorbed with the thoughts of his wife, and anxious for his dinner, he paid no attention to her. She went on to where the lady of the house (her mistress) was, and said to her, excitedly: "I know who that man is," and, rushing back into his presence, and throwing herself into his arms, cried out: "Andrew Davidson, I am your wife!" And so she was; but, oh, what changes her grief and sorrows had wrought! She was looking thin and haggard, and her once black and glossy hair had turned snowy white, though she was but a young woman.

What happiness! and what sorrow! They were at last restored to each other; but, alas! their little children were all gone.

The gentleman with whom Mrs. Davidson was living proved to be a humane man; he gave her up without ransom or reward, and voluntarily contributed to the expense of her return home, though he had paid the Indians a high price for her.

They returned to their home, where they lived to rear another family.

The Davidsons were related to the Peerys, a prominent family of the Clinch settlement. The Peerys were intermarried with the Crocketts, one of the most numerous families of Southwest Virginia, and the Crocketts and Ingles and Draper families were intermarried.

Mrs. Ingles and Mrs. Davidson knew each other well. With what thrilling interest they must have compared notes and discussed their painful captive experiences!

CHAPTER XXVI.

THE family of Thomas Ingles were hoping that he had gotten well over his wild, roving disposition, and that he would never care to leave his comfortable Knoxville farm and home, but results proved otherwise.

He met with a person just returned from the far-off settlement of Natchez, in the Mississippi Territory. He told Ingles of a man living there who owed him a considerable sum of money. He, also, gave him (Ingles) a glowing description of the new settlement, and the rich lands of that region.

Thomas Ingles at once made up his mind to go to Natchez. He arranged with two traders, who thought they could make a successful trading expedition down the rivers. They procured a boat on joint account, and stocked it with a joint supply of provisions for the trip; the traders got their goods aboard. Thomas Ingles took a pair of saddlebags, with some extra clothing, and the wild adventurers were off on their perilous journey to the far-away, promised land.

They intended to go all the way by water; they proceeded without mishap until they got to the muscle shoals of Tennessee River; these proved to be much rougher and more dangerous than they had anticipated; their boat was violently capsized, and they came near losing their lives, but were assisted by some friendly Indians, who happened to be on the shore, and witnessed their disaster.

They were saved, but were left in a destitute and distressing condition; they were several hundred miles from home, and still farther from their destination, among Indian tribes, remote from any white settlement—their goods lost, their provisions lost, their clothing lost, except only the contents of Thomas Ingles' saddlebags; these he caught with one hand as the boat went over, and he caught and held on to the gunwale of the boat with the other, when it came up again, and until rescued.

They held a consultation on the situation; the unanimous decision was not to turn back, but to go forward.

They got some provisions from the Indians, and on they went, down the Tennessee, down the Ohio, down the Mississippi—meeting many minor troubles and vexations, but no further disasters—and finally reached their objective point, the Natchez settlement.

Thomas Ingles soon found the man he sought; but, of course, he got no money. This he might have known before he went.

He was so charmed with the country, however, and the rich Mississippi lands, that he determined to move his family out. He returned to his home, advised his family of his resolution, then made a last visit to his now aged mother and his brother, John Ingles, at Ingles' Ferry. He spent a week or two with them in pleasant, social and kindred intercourse, talking over and over the terrible scenes and sufferings of their past lives; but the time to part at

last arrived; he bade them a long, last and affecting
farewell, returned to Knoxville, sold his farm, his
furniture, his cattle—whatever he had—for less than
their value, in order to realize promptly, and again,
in 1802, he turned his face towards the setting sun.

How 'long Thomas Ingles lived at Natchez I do
not know, but probably not long, as he was next
heard of at Port Gibson, Mississippi Territory. His
next remove was an involuntary one, and to that far
country whence no traveler returns.

Thomas Ingles left a son, Thomas Ingles, Jr., who
was born in Tennessee in 1791, and removed to
Natchez, with the family, in 1802. He also had a son
John, who, somewhat later, is said to have been
drowned in the Mississippi River.

I remember Thomas, Jr., in 1833, when he returned to Virginia to visit his uncle, Colonel John
Ingles, and to talk over with him the wonderfully
eventful histories of his grandmother and his father
and mother. He urged his uncle to write an outline
sketch of these lives for preservation by the family,
which he did, briefly, and from which I get many of
the facts here related.

The younger Thomas was a worthy and honorable,
though somewhat eccentric, man. He wrote a short
sketch of his father's life (to which I am also indebted for many facts). He also wrote a short auto-
biographical sketch of himself. He seems to have
been "all things by turns, and nothing long." He
says he studied law, medicine, theology and politics,
but did not practice any profession.

He was a book-keeper, deputy sheriff, school
teacher, militia commander, trustee, treasurer, sec-

THOMAS INGLES.

retary, etc., of several corporations—business, religious and literary—a merchant and a planter; but, perhaps, more than anything else, postmaster.

I met him again in 1843, at Augusta, Ky., where, for many years, he was their postmaster, and they never had a better.

Some years later he moved to Cincinnati, where he died in 1863, aged seventy-two. He had been twice married, first to Miss Barnes, the issue being four sons and three daughters; and, second, to Miss Warren, the issue being three sons and two daughters.

CHAPTER XXVII.

WILLIAM INGLES (the elder) died at Ingles' Ferry, in the prime of life, in the fall of 1782, aged fifty-three. Colonel William Christian and Colonel Daniel Trigg were the executors of his will, and received three hundred and forty-six acres of Burke's Garden land for their services. Mrs. Mary Ingles, his widow, lived to a ripe old age, dying at Ingles' Ferry in February, 1815, in her eighty-fourth year.

She retained a large amount of physical vigor and mental clearness to the last. Mrs. Governor John Floyd, who lived near her and knew her well, writing about her in 1843, speaks of meeting her (Mrs. I.) at a religious association, or convention, which she had attended on horseback, thirty miles from home, when past eighty. Her step was then still elastic, her figure erect, and her complexion florid and healthy, though her hair was white as snow.

About this time, some one started a rumor that her brother, John Draper, who was two years older than she, and the second time a widower, was about to marry a young girl. She was very much worried by the report, and, fearing that it might be true, determined to go to her brother's, about twenty miles distant, and learn the facts for herself.

She ordered her favorite saddle-horse, "Bonny," and started, although it was late in the afternoon. When her son, John Ingles, with whom she was living, or, rather, *near* whom, for she kept up her separate establishment as long as he lived, having her own house and garden, servants, horses, cows, etc.—came to the house and learned what had occurred, he was very much disturbed about it, ordered another horse saddled immediately, and started his son, Crockett Ingles, in pursuit, to assure the old lady that it was all a joke, and to bring her back; but Crockett could not overtake her. She got to Draper's Valley after dark, and, satisfying herself that she was the victim of a practical joke, she started back early next morning, and was at home to dinner. Crockett, having failed to overtake his grandmother the night before, stayed all night at a farm-house by the way, and joined her and returned home with her next morning.

Illustrating her wonderful nerve and cool presence of mind, it is related of her that once, when walking in her kitchen garden, among the cabbages and other vegetables, she stepped upon the neck of a large black snake, before seeing it. Instantly the snake, writhing in its pain, coiled itself about her leg. She appreciated the situation at once, but instead of screaming, or fainting, or running away, she stood perfectly still, her weight holding the snake firmly in place, until she called to her cook to fetch her the butcher-knife, with which she soon released herself by cutting the snake in two.

In her youth, Mrs. Ingles had learned to spin on the "little wheel," a most useful and valuable accomplishment in those days, and especially on the frontier, where the pioneers raised their own flax and wool, and where most of their clothes were of home manufacture.

10

Stores were then very remote, and "store clothes" almost unattainable. She kept up her habit of spinning to her latest years. Her temperament was so restless and active that she could not and would not be idle. When she found nothing else to do, instead of sewing or knitting, as most old ladies do, she would get her wheel and put in her time at spinning, often despite the remonstrances of her family, who would have preferred to have her spend her declining years in restful quiet.

Once her wheel got out of order, and she had asked her son, more than once, to send it to a workman and have it repaired. He had neglected to do so, probably intentionally, in order to discourage her spinning efforts; but when he was away from home one day, she ordered her favorite "Bonny" saddled, took the wheel in her lap, rode eight miles to a carpenter, or wheelwright, had it repaired and brought it home; after which the spinning went on as usual, though she was then over eighty years of age.

The old lady delighted, in her latter years, to tell over to her children and grandchildren, the story of her terrible captivity and wonderful escape.

What the theological views or religious professions of these old pioneers of the Ingles and Draper families were I do not know; that they were as honest, moral and kind-hearted people, as true to their own consciences and as charitable to their neighbors as the average church-going people of the present day, I doubt not; but, in the nature of things, it is not probable that actual church-going or other devotional services, public or private, had much part either in their week day or Sunday exercises.

MRS. MALINDA CHARLTON.

As they were mostly of Scotch-Irish descent, it is probable that their denominational proclivities—if they had any—were towards Presbyterianism. Those of their descendants who were or are church members, so far as I know, were or are, with very few exceptions, Presbyterians.

William and Mary Ingles had four children, three daughters and one son, born to them after her return from captivity. They were: Mary, Susan, Rhoda and John.

Mary married Mr. John Grills, of Montgomery County, and had two children.

Susan married General Abram Trigg, of Buchanan's Bottom, New River, and had ten children.

Rhoda married Colonel Byrd Smith, of Dunkard Bottom, and had eight children.

John Ingles, the youngest child, born in 1766, married, first, Margaret Crockett, of Wythe County, and, second, Mary Saunders, of Franklin County; had nine children—all by his first wife.

MRS. CHARLTON.

One of the children of John Ingles and Margaret Crockett, now Mrs. Malinda Charlton, an aged and venerable lady, in her eighty-fifth year, is the last surviving grandchild of William and Mary Ingles. She is still clear in mind, and in a fair state of health and physical preservation. She remembers her grandmother well, having lived in the same house with her from her own infancy until the death of the old lady, in 1815. To her remarkable memory I am indebted for many facts and incidents related in the foregoing sketches of the family.

She is a wonderful connecting link between the past and the present—the old and the new—bringing down the days of her grandmother to those of her own grandchildren, the two lives spanning the great time of one hundred and fifty-four years, or more than a century and a half, from the birth of Mary Draper, at Philadelphia, in 1732, to the present writing, in 1886, and she (Mrs. Charlton) still living. What wonderful changes the world has witnessed in these one hundred and fifty-four years! What a wonderful fact, that a person yet living should have known, and should still remember, the first white woman (at least, of English descent) ever between the Alleghenies and the Pacific; and that woman her own grandmother!

From another branch of this Crockett family sprang the eccentric and renowned Davy Crockett. This Davy Crockett formulated a motto which, for plain matter of fact, concentrated common sense, is one of the wisest ever enunciated. Its authorship alone was enough to immortalize him. Everybody knows Davy Crockett's motto: "Be sure you are right, then go ahead!" as they do, also, that other grand formula, propounded by the great moral teacher, combining the substance and essence of all moral wisdom: "Do unto others as you would have others do unto you." These two companion pictures might be—and, indeed, are—amplified into volumes and libraries, teaching wisdom and purity in all the relations of life—political, social, business, moral and general.

Unfortunately, not every one who is familiar with these wise formulæ governs himself by them, or either of them.

CHAPTER XXVIII.

IN illustration of the customs of half a century and more ago, it may not be without interest to describe here an old-time "family Fall hunt," an institution now obsolete in this part of the world, and even the the recollections of which are fast fading away.

In those days game was very abundant, and the Fall hunt was one of the events of the year. It was looked forward to for months in advance with pleasurable anticipations, by old and young, male and female.

In the days of my youth and earlier, my grandfather, John Ingles, owned large boundaries of wild land on the "Little River," herein above mentioned, and Reed Island Creek, and had a hunting station between them, on "Greasy Creek," a tributary of the latter. There were several log cabins on the premises, for the accommodation of the hunters. A trusted family of old servants lived here to take care of the place, raise poultry and fruit, and keep bees for honey.

About September, invitations would be sent out for twenty or thirty friends, male and female, in several neighboring counties. Out of these, probably a dozen or twenty would attend, of whom about one-third, usually, would be ladies, married and single. Most of the party would rendezvous at Ingles' Ferry,

and go together from there; others would join the
company at the camp.

At the appointed time one or more wagons would
start out with bedding, linen, etc., cooking utensils,
table-ware, table comforts, some medicinal liquors, a
few extra guns and necessary ammunition for those
who might come without their own; a keeper of the
hounds, with a large pack of dogs, necessary cooks,
hostlers, etc., a banjo and a fiddle, a pack of cards and
a few books or magazines for the ladies, and the outfit
was complete.

Arrived upon the ground, and the comfort of the
ladies looked after, the first day's hunt would be
planned by the old campaigners, choosing the ground
over which they should hunt, and allotting each to
his separate duty—some to follow the hounds, some
to still-hunt, and others to be posted at the well
known "stands" where the deer were sure to pass
the gaps or ridges, or cross the streams. This done,
all would retire to an early rest, to dream of the exciting pleasures of the morrow's hunt.

FLINT-LOCKS.

In those days, there was a famous gun-maker in
the neighborhood, named Spangler, who was a born
mechanic, and had acquired great skill and achieved
great reputation in his art. I think he was the second or third of the name, in line, who had followed
the business. No hunter for many counties around
considered his hunting outfit complete, or creditable,
unless he had a rifle with the Spangler brand on it.
They were plain, old-fashioned rifles, with flint-locks,
but wonderfully accurate.

Before day, the keeper of the hounds would sound his horn, which would set all the dogs howling, making longer sleep impossible, and arouse everybody on the place. Breakfast would be ready by daylight, and, by the time that was over, horses were saddled and ready, and "all hands" were off for the stands or the chase.

One half of the dogs would be taken out, and the remainder left in the kennel, and thus alternated day by day, having each day fresh dogs.

It was a disappointment if at least one or more deer or bear were not killed each day, beside turkeys, pheasants, etc. The party would return to the camp about four or five o'clock, depending upon the distance, the luck, etc.

By the time all were in, and washed and ready, a royal game dinner, smoking hot, would be served, probably supplemented by apple dumplings and honey in the comb, all seasoned by that best of all sauces, a sharp appetite.

During and after dinner, the gentlemen would recount the adventures of the day, and plan the hunt for the morrow, after which there might be a game of cards, some music by Sambo, and a little quiet courting among the young folks, if the proper parties happened to be present.

After an early rest and refreshing sleep, all would be ready to renew the pleasures of the chase on the following day; and so on, successively, for a week, or ten days, or two weeks, depending upon the weather, the success of the hunt and the congeniality of the company.

In these everglades and cranberry meadows on the

western slopes of the Blue Ridge, where droves of deer and other game then roved at will, unmolested save by these Fall hunts, once a year, are now settle-tlements, farms and family habitations, and the game and the exciting sport of the chase are gone forever.

In my youth, I attended one of the last, if not, in-deed, the very last, of these formal family Fall hunts, of the order above described. Here I experienced the first touch of the malady termed by the old Nim-rods "buck ague"—not very fatal, usually, at either end of the gun, but violent and exciting while it lasts. There were, as I remember, on the occasion mentioned, about a dozen and a half persons pres-ent, several of them ladies, married and single. I was the youngest person in the party, and I am now, save one other, I believe, the only survivor. All the others have gone over to the happy—or rather, let us hope, the *happier*—hunting ground beyond.

CHAPTER XXIX.

THE INGLES FAMILY CLOCK.

WHILE I write, the grand old family clock is
ticking by my side. As early as I can remember anything, I remember the slow, measured tick,
tick, tick, of this rare old clock, and the sonorous,
silvery notes of its musical bell. And so it has
ticked and struck, and counted off the fleeting hours,
year after year, for generation after generation.

According to the family tradition, the clock was
constructed about 1738, and has been running since
that time, and is now, consequently, nearly a century
and a half old.

Its early history, before the time of William and
Mary Ingles, is not now accurately known, but after
this time it is quite clear, and is identified with the
family history.

It probably ticked for Thomas Ingles (the immigrant) and his children. It certainly ticked for
William and Mary Ingles and their children. It
ticked for John Ingles and his children. It ticked
for his daughter and her children. It is now ticking
for a miserable old bachelor and his—little dog.

William Ingles, when he died, left it to his widow,
Mary Ingles; when she died, she left it to her son,
John; when he died, he left it to his daughter, my
mother; when she died, she left to me; and when
I die, ——?

The clock is a handsome piece of furniture, has a black walnut case, silvered face, brass works, is eight feet high, runs eight days, records the hours, minutes and seconds, the days of the month and changes of the moon, and bids fair to do duty for an indefinite time in the future as an accurate and reliable time-keeper.

From the early date of the Ingles and Draper settlement west of the Alleghenies, I think it safe to assume that this remarkable old clock was the *first* that ever crossed the Alleghenies, and was the first in all that vast territory between the Allegheny Mountains and the Pacific Ocean to tick and tell of the passing moments which, hitherto, through all past time, had glided by unheeded, unmeasured and unrecorded.

This clock suggests some curious and interesting reflections to those inclined to indulge themselves in that way.

If every tick records the departure of a soul from this world, as is claimed, then think of the millions of millions of humans that have played their brief parts on the stage of life and passed on since this clock began its monotonous ticking! Think of how many mighty rulers, Kings and Emperors, have reigned, clothed with brief authority, and gone their way! What Dynasties, great and small, have arisen and gone down! What changes in the maps of the world! What progress in art, science, education, general enlightenment and human comfort!

Look at the changes that have occurred in our own country—then but a scattered British colony along the Atlantic slope, now a grand Republic, the pride of its citizens and the admiration of the world, extending from ocean to ocean, with nearly sixty millions of enlightened people, and with more population now, within a radius of five miles around Trinity steeple, New York, than in the whole country "when this old clock was new."

It is not possible, of course, to tell how long this clock may continue to run, but it is in good and sound condition, and, if it should meet with no disaster or violent end, I see no good reason why it should not last another one hundred and fifty years, or more.

It is a curious thought, and not without sadness, that of all the millions and millions of living beings on earth when this clock ticked its first second, and rang out its first hour, not one is left to bear witness; and, whatever other changes may come in the future, it is safe to say that every soul and every living creature now on earth will have fulfilled its destiny here and gone hence, and their places been filled by countless millions yet unborn, before this old clock ceases to measure, tick by tick, the tiny seconds that go to make up the years and the ages as Time rolls on!

CHAPTER XXX.

CHANGES WITHIN A LIFETIME.

IN writing the foregoing sketches, I have often had occasion to think of the wonderful changes that have occurred in the condition of the world, not only since the Pioneer-Trans-Allegheny-Draper-Meadows-Ingles'-Ferry settlements of nearly a century and a half ago, but of the even more rapid progress that has been made within the much shorter time of my own life and recollections—say within a period of about sixty years.

So much have I been struck and impressed by a review of the rapid advances of this rapidly advancing age, that I am led to believe that a retrospective glance over the period would astonish, interest and, possibly, instruct very many persons who have not had occasion or happened to give the subject special thought.

To aid them in such a retrospect, I will present, from my own recollections, a short sketch of the condition of every-day life existing in a rich, prosperous and representative agricultural and grazing-community, at the time indicated, and will enumerate some of the many items and instances of progress and advance in all the needs, uses and operations of man which scientific invention and discovery have given to them, and to the world at large, within the time named, and let each reader, for himself, compare the past with the present, the old with the new, and each for himself decide whether or not "the good old times" were better than the new.

A large proportion of the families in the region about which I have been writing—now Montgomery and Pulaski Counties, Virginia—were, at the time indicated, wealthy or well-to-do, and largely engaged in cultivating the soil and stock-raising, living upon the fat of the land, very independently and very much within themselves; none the less happy and contented, perhaps, because they lacked the innumerable conveniences and luxuries of this latter day, so many of which now seem to us indispensable.

Each family had among its servants trained and skilled mechanics—a blacksmith to shoe the horses, "upset" the old-fashioned plows, iron the wagons and carts, repair the farm utensils, and other promiscuous work; the carpenter would build and repair the houses, barns, etc., and make or mend the wagons, carts, wheel-barrows, water-pails, butterferkins, etc.; the shoemaker would make and mend the shoes worn by all the family, white and black.

The female servants were all taught to sew, spin and knit, and a certain number of them were taught weaving.

On every large estate, the blacksmith's and carpenter's shop, the shoemaker's shop and the loom house were as invariable as the dwelling house, the barn and the crib.

The servant women spun and wove linen goods for Summer, and woolen flannels and jeans for Winter wear; also, nice bedquilts, counterpanes, etc., and the hosiery was knitted by the older women.

There were fulling mills near, that "fulled" and dyed the woolen goods. They made a beautiful black jeans, then much worn by men and boys.

The mistress of the house was generally expert in cutting the garments, for white and black; and, when so cut out, the females, white and black, would make them up by hand sewing. They raised their geese and made their own feather-beds and pillows.

These farmers raised their own hogs and cured their own bacon for the year. They had beef and mutton, poultry and eggs, butter and cheese, milk and honey, fruit and vegetables, without stint. They never thought of buying any of these things, but sold or bartered their surplus for their sugar, coffee, tea, etc. They never sold, fruit, vegetables, etc., to their neighbors, but divided freely with those who needed.

Most of them distilled their own peach and apple brandies, and enjoyed an apple-jack toddy, or "peach and honey." These were kept on the side-board and offered to all comers. The ladies made a nice domestic wine from currants.

Every Fall, each farmer would send his teams to the Washington County Salt Works for the year's supply of salt, and land plaster for manure.

In season, a stock of wood was provided for Winter fires, the Winter apples were put up, peaches and apples dried, fruits preserved, the cider and apple-butter made, and honey taken for Winter use.

They made their own alkali by leaching wood ashes, and made their own soap from this alkali and the kitchen greases. They made a delicious lie hominy by steeping new corn, in whole grains, in this strong alkali, to remove the outer bran. They also made cracked hominy with home-made hominy mortar and pestle.

They raised their own hemp, spun their own twine and twisted their own ropes, for all domestic uses. Flax was raised, retted, broken, scutched, hackled, spun, woven, cut, made and worn, at home. Wool was raised, carded, spun, woven or knitted, dyed, made and worn, at home.

Servants were allowed private patches, in which they raised their own tobacco, watermelons and some vegetables, and, the more provident, a pig or two and some chickens.

In those days, a few tomatoes, then called "love apples," were raised in gardens, as curiosities, but were not eaten.

The days of canned fruits and vegetables, fish and meats, had not yet arrived. Patent butter, made from tallow or lard, was not then known; the honest cows still held the monopoly of the butter trade.

Horseshoes and horseshoe nails, now made by machinery, were then all made by hand. The modern patent plows and steam plows were not then made. Grain was cut with sickle or cradle, and threshed with the flail or by horses' feet. The patent mowers, reapers, threshers, corn-planters, corn-shellers, and the long list of modern agricultural implements, had not yet taken form in the inventive brains of those who were destined to bless the world with them, and enrich themselves.

The travel of those days was mostly by horseback, or private vehicles, or stage-coaches and canal-boats. There were no railroads then, no telegraphs, tele-

phones, microphones, photophones, autophones, etc.
No bicycles, no roller skates, no patent spring rubber
bottle-stoppers. There were no modern buggies then,
and no eliptical steel springs for wheeled vehicles.
Private carriages, like stages, were hung on leather
belts or bands. There were no lever brakes for
wagons and carriages. Wheels had to be dead-locked
by looped chains. There were no screw-propellers
in steam navigation; no sternwheel boats, and but
few of any sort.

Photography was then unknown. Portraits and
miniatures were painted in oil, or sketched with
crayons.

There were no chromos then, or other cheap pictures; no aniline dyes; no illustrated daily papers.
The number of periodicals then published was but a
beggarly list as compared with to-day.

Percussion caps, needle-guns, fixed ammunition,
modern revolvers, breech-loaders, Gatling and magazine guns, were yet unknown.

The flint-lock rifle was then the standard small
arm, and its accompaniments were the shot-pouch
(generally made of a wild-cat, panther or deer skin),
bullet-molds and a carved powder-horn, and, with
these, a leather belt and a butcher-knife.

There were no rifled nor long-range cannon; no
armor-plated ships; no torpedo boats; no dynamite,
gun-cotton or nitro-glycerine.

No monitors, no submarine armor, no ocean cables,
no suspension bridges, no elevated nor underground
railways, no pneumatic tubes.

The cotton gin was not yet invented. Cotton-seed
oil was not made. Lard oil was not known. Peru-

vian guano and South Carolina phosphates were not
discovered, and chemical manures were not manufactured.

There were no deep-well boring tools, no Diamond
corn-drills, no deep-sea soundings.

The gulf streams and ocean currents were not
then understood. The atmospheric laws and movements were not then known and charted. " Old
Probs," with his weather predictions and records,
had not yet come to the front.

Geology and chemistry were then in their infancy.
Improved telescopes have, since then, made vast
progress in astronomical discovery and knowledge.
The spectroscope, then unknown, has revealed the
secrets of the far distant fixed stars and nebulæ. The
microscope has opened up a new world of wonders
in the opposite direction. The little bacillus " com-
ma," recently discovered by it, may yet be brought
to a "full stop," and the cholera scourge with it. In-
oculation for rabies was not yet tried.

Darwin's evolution theories, now generally accepted by the intelligent, had not then been broached.
The Northwest Arctic passage had not then been
sailed through, and thus demonstrated. Livingstone
and Stanley had not yet opened up the geographical
and race mysteries of Central Africa. The South
African diamond fields were then unknown. The
California and Australia gold mines, Colorado silver
mines, Lake Superior copper mines, and the Missouri
Iron Moutain, were undiscovered.

Sodium, potassium, aluminum, and other metals
and metalloids and their alloys, were unknown.

There were then no "Jetties" to scour out river

11

mouths, and no adjustable dams for river navigation improvement.

There were no steam fire engines, no Holly water system, no steam drills for tunnel boring, no Thames tunnel, no Alpine tunnels for railroads, no railroads for tunnels.

There was then no wood paper pulp, no paper twine, no paper bags, no paper collars, no paper car wheels, no wall-paper, no parchment paper for records, no paper-mache. Probably the first paper mill west of the Alleghenies, and south of Mason's and Dixon's line, was erected in " 'Possum Hollow," between Ingles' Ferry and Draper's Valley.

There were no circular saws, no band saws, nor patent log turners for saw mills. There were no steam-pressure brick machines, no steel wire-lines, no time-locks for bank safes, no elevators nor enunciators for hotels, no aneroid barometers, no anemometers, no self-registering thermometers, no electrical clocks, no water-tube safety boilers, no hard-brick, board-floor street paving, no Nicholson blocks, asphalt or Belgium-block street-paving, no wood or iron planing machines, no gimlet-pointed screws, no coal-digging machines.

There were then no postal stamps, no postal cards, no postal money-orders, no envelopes, no blotting paper. The letter was folded, tucked in and stuck with a wafer, or with sealing-wax. The ink was dried with a dark sand, instead of blotting paper. The writing was done with goose-quill pens; steel and gold pens were yet unknown. There were no type-writers, no manifold writers, no fountain pens, no indelible pencils.

The postage on a letter was 25c., 18¾c., etc., "C. O. D."

Slavery had not then been abolished in America. The Russian serfs had not been emancipated. The African slave trade had not been interdicted by the civilized powers. Universal suffrage and free schools had not been adopted in the United States.

Since then, Uncle Sam has enlarged his domains by a strip of territory extending from the Gulf of Mexico to the Pacific, from Texas to California inclusive, and another Pacific strip from the British line to the frozen oceans. Our population was then but ten millions, and is now nearly sixty millions.

There were then no friction matches, or "Lucifers," as called when first made, and, afterwards, "Locofoco" matches. Gentlemen who smoked carried "sun glasses" in their vest-pockets, and concentrated the sun's rays to light their pipes; and, in the absence of sunshine, resorted to "flint and steel" (usually a jack-knife and a gun flint), and a piece of punk.

The currency, at that day, was reckoned more by pounds, shillings and pence (£ s. d.) than in dollars and cents, but it was based upon the Virginia standard of 16⅔ cents to the shilling. "Uncle Sam" had not then coined the smaller decimal currency. There were no nickels or dimes, but, instead, 6¼ and 12½ cent pieces, called "fourpence-ha'penny" and "ninepence" respectively; 25 cents was "18 pence," 50 cents was "three shillings," 62½ cents was "three and ninepence," 75 cents was "four and sixpence," $1.50 was "nine shillings," $2.50 was "15 shillings," etc. In some places the 12½ cent piece was called a "bit," in others a "levy," and, farther South, the 6¼ cent piece was called a "picayune." Greenbacks were then unknown, and many have but a slight acquaintance with them yet.

Quinine was unknown. Bromine and the bromides were not yet made. Anæsthetics were not yet introduced. If one had to have a tooth pulled, or a leg sawed off, he had to "grin and bear it," taking the pain in the old-fashioned way.

Calomel and jalap, opium and ipecac, bark and the lancet, were the standard remedies of the doctors in those days. The Thompsonian remedies, Nos. 1 to 6, were much in vogue with the quacks. The modern great patent medicine trade was not then developed. The pedagogues of that day prescribed and administered "oil of birch" with great freedom. Parties differed as to the "happy effects" according to the stand-point from which the subject was considered. The preachers prescribed caloric and sulphur with a reckless disregard to economy.

Sanitary measures were then less perfectly understood and practiced, and the average duration of human life was considerably less than at present.

For lights at night, the common dependence was upon the home-made tallow-dips, with accompanying candlestick and snuffers; and, for a better light, the wax or the spermaceti candle. Star candles were not yet known, and petroleum and coal-oil lamps were far in the future.

There were no gas lights (I believe New York was first lighted with gas in 1827), no gas engines, no electric lights, no electric motors. There were no street railroads, no horse-cars.

Modern cook stoves and ice machines were alike

unknown. There were no baking-powders, nor patent yeast-cakes. Gas-well fuel was unknown.

There were no India-rubber nor gutta-percha goods. Jute fiber was not yet utilized. The long lists of patent churns and washing machines were not yet invented.

There were no steam tanneries, no steam pumps, no steam hammers, no drawn or lap-welded tubes, no turning lathes for shoe-lasts, axe-handles and other irregular forms, no electro-plated goods, no sand-blast carving or glass-cutting, no four-pronged silver table-forks, nor silver-plated knives. There were no cotton compresses, no grain elevators, no coal elevators. No beet root sugar, sorghum molasses, nor glucose; no rolling mills, no iron, steel nor paper hulls for boats, no iron or steel bridges, no iron house-fronts, iron roofs, iron mantels, iron bank safes, iron power plate-punches and shears, no metallic coffins, no machine-made barrels, no steam-cut nor cylinder-sawed barrel staves, no roller-process flour.

Wood was the domestic fuel of the country. Iron was melted with charcoal. Anthracite was but just discovered. Coke was not yet manufactured.

World's Fairs and National Expositions, those great public educators, had not yet been inaugurated. Sewing machines had not yet come in response to the "Song of the Shirt" and the wail of the women. "Home, Sweet Home" and "Dixie" had not then been composed and sung; "The Star-Spangled Banner" was but newly written and sung, and even "Hail Columbia" was not old.

Knitting machines, spinning jennies and power-looms had not yet appeared. Lager beer had not then tickled the throats of the thirsty. Spring-bed mattresses were unknown luxuries. Mosquito bars were equally unknown. Modern extension dining-tables and adjustable reclining chairs were not known. Wooden shoe-pegs were not yet made, nor pegged shoes, nor metal-tipped shoes. There were no "incline" tracks and passenger cars in use for elevated sites, like those up the Cincinnati hills. There were no steam whistles to torture human tympanums; no steam calliopic music; no steam radiators for warming buildings.

In the matter of dress, there have been striking changes, as in other things. Ladies' dresses, and the styles and fashions thereof, come and go, changing often; as the new becomes old, the old becomes new again. I am not learned in the mysteries of ladies' wear and fashions. I only know that the ladies are all pretty, and they lend beauty and charm to the fashions.

Gentlemen's styles change more slowly. Many elderly gentlemen, at the time I write of, still wore queues, ruffled shirts, knee-breeches and long stockings, knee and shoe buckles, etc. Pantaloons were then made with a square flap in front, instead of the up and down seam, as now. Gentlemen's every-day wear was home-made jeans; the formal dress goods was "broadcloth."

There were then no button gaiters, nor patent-leather boots and shoes. Spotted calico shirts, and celluloid cuffs and collars, and even detached linen cuffs and collars were not then worn, or known, by the young bloods.

Pins and needles were still made by hand; cloth-covered button$ were unknown; hooks and eyes were largely used by the ladies, instead of buttons.

This seems a formidable list, though it is far from exhaustive, and could easily be very greatly extended; but this is enough to show what tremendously progressive strides the world has taken within a lifetime, and to excite the wonder of the present generation as to how former generations got along without the comforts, conveniences and luxuries which we now take "as a matter of course," and enjoy unthoughtedly and unthankfully.

Will the world continue to advance as it has done? is a question often asked. That continued and rapid progress will still be made seems certain; but that the next or any future sixty years will witness as wonderful a forward bound as the last sixty—which has grown largely out of the unparalleled development of steam and electricity—may well be doubted; although, in view of the infinite mysteries and resources of Nature to be discovered, explored and developed, and the, as yet, unknown limit of the power and scope of the human mind to grapple them, it becomes us to be very modest and conservative in limiting our predictions as to future progress.

"He is a very bold man," said the wise Frenchman, "who dares to pronounce the word *impossible.*"

CHAPTER XXXI.

DANIEL BOONE.

THE fact that so remarkable a man as Daniel Boone was, for about twelve years, a resident of the Kanawha Valley deserves, I think, more than a mere passing notice, especially as the fact is not well known to the public, and not now very generally known, even here. A year or two ago I published, in pamphlet form, a short history of his residence in this valley, and will here give a condensed sketch from facts therein contained.

His biographers, of whom there are half a dozen or more, devote themselves to his wonderful Kentucky experiences, from 1769 to about 1785, after which they seem to know but little about him, although he lived for thirty odd years after leaving Kentucky. His Kanawha experiences are disposed of in a paragraph or two, to the effect that, about 1792, he settled for a time in Western Virginia, and about 1797 went to Missouri, etc. Instead of in 1792, he probably settled at the mouth of the Kanawha as early as 1786, as there is a deed for land in Kentucky, signed and acknowledged by himself and wife, at Point Pleasant, April 28, 1786, and on record in Fayette County, Ky. While at Point Pleasant, tradition says, he lived on the bank of Crooked Creek, made famous by the battle of the Point. Elderly persons at the Point still remember the log cabin, now long gone, in which he is said to have lived.

It is supposed that he moved up to this neighborhood about 1788 or '89, and, while here, lived on the south side of the river, nearly opposite the original salt spring.

Dr. L. C. Draper, LL. D., who has in preparation and, it is hoped, will shortly publish, an exhaustive biography of Boone, is inclined to think that his residence opposite the salt spring was not a settled family residence, but only a hunting camp, of which he had many. The local traditions here indicate that it was his regular family residence, and his son, Jesse Boone, lived at the same place until about 1816.

When I came to the county, in 1840, there were still living old men who had hunted and trapped with him; one of them, Mr. Paddy Huddlestone, interested me greatly by relating the incidents of their joint hunting, trapping and camping experiences. Mr. Jared Huddlestone, son of Paddy, still living, remembers well to have heard his father tell of his first acquaintance with Boone. A stranger, with rifle and pack, came to his father's (Paddy's) house one evening, about dusk, and asked to stay all night; he seemed tired, did not tell who he was, had but little to say, and soon retired to rest. Next morning, when the family got up for the usual early breakfast, the stranger, with his rifle, was out and gone, but his pack remained, indicating that he had not gone far. It was not long until he came in and got his breakfast, remarking that, as he was an early riser, he had been looking around a little to see if there were any signs of game about, and told them he had discovered fresh beaver signs near the house. He asked if they had any traps; they told him they had no beaver traps, but had a steel trap for catching foxes. " Well," said he to Paddy, "come, young man, get your trap and go with me, and I will show you how to catch beaver." The first day they caught five, and, within a few days, exterminated the colony—about a dozen in all.

The sign which Boone had found was two sap-plings cut down from a triangle of them, and the beavers had commenced on the third. Catching the beavers saved the third sappling, which, to-day, is a red oak tree, about two feet in diameter, standing at the upper end of Long Shoal, a few miles below the Kanawha Falls.

On the 6th of October, 1789, Kanawha County was organized. Of the military organization, Colonel Samuel Lewis, brother of General Andrew, was Colonel, and Daniel Boone, Lieutenant Colonel. The county was entitled to two Representatives in the Legislature. The first year, George Clendenin, the founder of Charleston, and Andrew Donnelly, the defender of Donnelly's Fort, in Greenbriar, in 1778, were elected. The next year Daniel Boone and George Clendenin were elected. Boone went to Richmond and returned, on foot.

Boone spent much of his time in surveying while here. Mr. T. A. Mathews, surveyor, tells me that in rerunning the lines of two surveys, of one hundred thousand acres each, running from the site of Boone C. H. to the Kentucky line, he finds the lines plainly marked, and the names of the party cut in the bark of the trees still legible; they were: "Daniel Boone, George Arnold, Edmund Price, Thomas Upton and Andrew Hatfield. 1795."

I have a report of survey made out by him, in his own handwriting, still clear and well preserved. The following is a fac-simile copy:

June The 14th 1791

Survede of for William Allin ten acres of Land Situate on the South Este Side of Conocks Crick in the County of Cockanorway as followeth viz Begining at a Red oke and Sticking thence North 56 West 23 poles to a Stake thence North 34 Este 58 poles to a Stake thence South 56 Este 23 poles to a Stake thence South 34 West 58 poles to the Begining — —

Daniel Boone

58/1600(2
116
440
464
24

59
27
1683
1593

26   57   58
60   27   28
1560   514   464
270   60   3   464
1620   165   3   31624

The last survey made by Boone, before leaving the valley, was on September 8th, 1798; Daniel Boone, marker; Daniel Boone, Jr., and Mathias Van Bibber, chainmen, as shown by the surveyor's books.

In one of Boone's hunting and trapping expeditions, up Gauley River, he brought back the top of a sprout of yew pine, an unusual growth, and hitherto unknown to him. He left the brush of pine needles to the end to show to his friends; when it had served this purpose, the end with the needles was cut off, leaving a nice walking-stick. When he left Kanawha, he gave this to his friend, " Tice" Van Bibber, and he left it to his son, David Van Bibber, still living, at about ninety. The cane was presented to me a few years ago, and is now in my possession.

" In an early day," exact date not known, the family of John Flinn, the earliest settlers on Cabin Creek, this county, were attacked by Indians, and Flinn and wife killed. One daughter made her escape alone to Donnelly's Fort, Greenbriar, and one daughter and son, Cloe and John, were captured by the Indians.

This daughter, Cloe, was afterwards rescued by Boone, and, being an orphan, was reared by Boone in his own family, so states Mr. St. Clair Ballard, her grandson, who was a member of the Legislature from Logan County, in 1847. When it was proposed to form a new county from Kanawha and Logan, Mr. Ballard related the circumstances of this capture and recovery, and the generous action of Mr. Boone, and proposed, in personal gratitude, and by way of public acknowledgment to Boone, that the new county be called Boone, and his motion was carried by a unanimous vote.

The son, John Flinn, who had escaped, or been

rescued, was afterwards recaptured by the Indians, going down the Ohio, with Skyles, May and Johnson, and burned at the stake.

Jesse Boone, son of Daniel, was the first State Salt Inspector here, when salt was the dominant interest of this valley. His son, Colonel Albert Galletin Boone, himself a famous early explorer, true to the Boone instinct, in the Far West, was born here. He was the first white man to camp on the present site of the city of Denver, in 1825.

I have examined the old assessors' books to see what property Daniel Boone had, when here. I find he was not blessed, or cursed, with a large share of this world's goods. He was assessed for taxation with two horses, one negro and five hundred acres of land; the land remained on the books in his name until 1803.

Boone left here for Missouri in 1799. His starting was the occasion of the gathering of his friends and admirers, from all the region round about, to bid him a friendly adieu and God-speed. They came by land and water—on boats, by horseback and in canoes—and, at the final leave-taking, it is said there was many a dimmed eye and moistened cheek among those hardy, weather-beaten warriors, hunters and pioneers. Boone started from here by water, in canoes, embarking at the junction of Elk and Kanawha Rivers. His friend and companion, Tice Van Bibber, went with him to Missouri, but returned to Kanawha.

Boone was never again in Kanawha, but twice returned to Kentucky, once to identify the beginning corner of an important survey, made some twenty or twenty-five years before, and again to liquidate some long-standing, scattering indebtedness, which he had been unable to pay, owing to the loss of all his lands by the gross wrong done him, or permitted, by the State of Kentucky and the General Government.

The final payments of these debts, which had so long borne upon and disturbed his peace of mind, was, by his own account, one of the happiest incidents and reliefs of his life. While he had but little, it was, he said, a consolation to know that he did not owe a dollar, and that no man could say he had ever wronged him out of a cent.

Boone died at the house of his youngest son, Colonel Nathan Boone, on the Feme-Osage River, Missouri, September 26th, 1820. Colonel Albert Galletin Boone, his grandson, still living, told me, some years ago, that he was with him at the time, and says he passed off gently, after a short illness, almost without pain or suffering.

Thus ended the mortal career of one of the most remarkable men the country has ever produced, leaving an imperishable name and fame to after ages. He stands out in history as the great type, model and exemplar of the pioneer, frontiersman, hunter, explorer, Indian fighter and pilot of civilization.

His fame is secure forever, without the fear of a rival. The world does not now, and can never again, present an opportunity to duplicate or parallel his life and history.

His praises have been sung in the glowing lines of Lord Byron (in " Don Juan "), and by the eloquent tongues and pens of Tom Marshall, Bryan, Flint, Bogart, Filson, Abbott, and others, and the history of his wonderful adventures is read with thrilling interest in the mansions of the rich, and the humblest log cabins of the remotest Far West.

CHAPTER XXXII.

THE battle of Point Pleasant, considered merely in relation to the numbers engaged, or the numbers slain, on either side, or both sides, was but an insignificant affair, compared with many of the conflicts of the Revolution, which immediately followed, or the mighty shocks of arms of the late Civil War; but, up to the time of its occurrence, it was the most evenly balanced, longest continued and desperately contested battle that had occurred in our Western country, and its results were freighted with greater, more lasting and far-reaching effects than any other that had occurred.

It was a pivotal turning-point, upon which hinged, in great measure, the future destinies of the country. The result of this battle was probably the determining weight in the scale of Fortune, so evenly balanced, that decided the fate of the colonies in their struggle for independence.

It is, indeed, generally considered, in view of the relations then existing between the colonies and the mother country, and the course pursued by the Governor, as the initiatory battle of the Revolution; and, by demoralizing the Indian tribes, checking for a time their aggressions on the Western frontiers, and their co-operation with the English, it gave the

colonies, who were correspondingly encouraged by
their success, time and better opportunities to con-
centrate their powers and efforts for the mighty
struggle about to be, or already, inaugurated.

Instead of relating simply the isolated story of the
fight at the Point, with which persons in this region
are already more or less familiar, I have thought that
it might add to the general understanding of the
battle and its relations, and a fuller appreciation of
its extraordinary importance, to pass in review, briefly
and unincumbered by voluminous details, the long
series of preceding steps that led up to, and prepared
the way for, this event and the following revolutionary struggle.

Beginning this outline review, I shall go back to
1748, the date of the Ingles-Draper pioneer-trans-
allegheny settlement, the first on western-flowing
waters.

At this time, the French occupied Canada and
Louisiana, and, by virtue of the earlier discoveries of
La Salle, Marquette, and others, they were claiming
the entire Mississippi and Ohio Valleys, while Virginia claimed that her boundaries extended from
ocean to ocean. The French, to make their claim to
the Ohio Valley more formal, sent a company of
engineers down the Ohio, in 1749, with engraved
leaden plates, which they planted at the mouths of
prominent tributaries of the Ohio, claiming for the
French crown all the lands drained by the respective
streams.

About the same time, the " Ohio Land Company,"
recently organized, was making a move to acquire
and colonize five hundred thousand acres of lands

lying along the Ohio, and the "Loyal Land Company" was organized, based upon a grant of eight hundred thousand acres, lying north of the North Carolina line and west of the mountains and New River.

In 1750–51, Christopher Gist was dispatched by the "Ohio Company" to examine and select desirable lands along the Ohio.

The French, meanwhile, were establishing fortified trading posts, intending to have a chain of them from the Lakes to the Gulf.

In 1753, when serious trouble seemed to be brewing between the French and English, the conflicting claimants of this vast Western region, Governor Dinwiddie, of Virginia, dispatched George Washington, a then promising young man, who had been private surveyor of Lord Fairfax, official surveyor of Culpepper County, etc., on a tour of observation, with letters of inquiry and protest, addressed to the French commander on the Upper Allegheny. Washington took with him John Davidson, Indian interpreter; Jacob Van Brahm, French interpreter; Christopher Gist as guide, and four attendants. He was courteously received at head-quarters by the French commander, M. De St. Piere, as a matter of course, but as positively as politely informed that they should maintain their claims to the country.

Washington returned at once to Williamsburg, the then seat of government, and in his report, which was printed, and copies of which were sent to England, he laid stress, among other things, upon the very eligible site for a fortification at the forks of the Ohio, which would command both streams.

In 1754, the "Ohio Company" sent a force there, accompanied by a force of forty Virginia militia, under Lieutenant Trent, sent by the State. Before their work was completed, the French commander, Captain Contrecour, sent down a largely superior force, drove them off, took possession of their Fort, built it stronger, and called it Fort Du Quesne, after the Governor of Canada. This was the overt act that launched the long and bloody French and English war which raged with violence on both continents for several years.

Virginia immediately organized a large force, under Colonel Joshua Fry and Lieutenant-Colonel Washington, to recapture the position; Colonel Fry dying, en route, the command devolved upon Colonel Washington. The expedition resulted in the surprise of a party of French, under Captain Joumondville, near the Great Meadows, in which the leader, Captain Joumondville, was killed, and all his party either killed or captured. Later, Washington was attacked at Fort Necessity, which he had hastily fortified, by a largely superior French force, and was obliged to capitulate.

In the following year (1755), the English Government sent over General Braddock, with two regiments of English regulars, to co-operate with the Virginia troops. This expedition ended in the disastrous defeat of Braddock's army, almost in sight of Fort Du Quesne, by the French and their Indian allies.

In 1758, another and more formidable army was organized, under command of General Forbes, who finally succeeded in capturing and holding Fort Du

12

Quesne, and, the following year, a formidable strong-
hold was built and called Fort Pitt, after the then
English Premier.

The subsequent engagements between the English
and French along the Lakes and the St. Lawrence
need not be followed here (being beyond the geographical limits treated of), except to state that, upon
the capture of Quebec, the French finally surrendered,
to the English, Canada and all their possessions and
claims east of the Mississippi, thus terminating the
long and bloody war—the final treaty of peace being
ratified at Paris in 1763.

The French were now out of the way of settlements, but their savage allies, whom they had instigated and encouraged to resist the encroachments of
the whites upon their territory, were still there to
dispute every advance upon their hunting grounds;
and, although the march of settlement continued
steadily westward, every pioneer trail was a trail of
blood, and every pioneer family numbered among its
members victims of the tomahawk and scalping
knife.

The expedition sent out from Fort Pitt in 1764,
under Colonel Boquet, into the Indian country, resulted in checking their atrocities for a time, in the
recovery of over three hundred white prisoners,
mostly from the Virginia borders, and a treaty of
peace, concluded with Sir William Johnson, the following year.

This peace gave an impetus to Western emigration,
and by 1772–73 settlements had reached the Ohio at
several points, and the main tributary streams and
their smaller branches.

Another serious and general colonial trouble was now brewing, growing out of the levying of taxes on the colonies by the mother country, for the expenses of the French and Indian wars, and for a standing army to protect them from the Indians.

These and other measures the colonies considered unjust and onerous, and they protested against them with great earnestness and strong feeling.

In this state of the case, it was charged that the English instigated the Indians to harass the Western borders, so as to occupy the attention of the colonial forces in their protection, and thus prevent resistance to the oppressive measures contemplated by the English in the East.

Early in the Spring of 1774, it was evident that the Indians were combining for aggressive action. About this time, several murders were committed by both parties, on the Upper Ohio. A white man in a trading boat was killed by Indians, some distance above Wheeling Creek; within a few days, early in April, Captain Michael Cresap and party killed two Indians, near Wheeling, in a canoe, and followed a larger party down the river, to about the mouth of Captina, where they were surprised in camp and nearly all killed. Within a few days, still in April, Daniel Greathouse and a party of whites attacked an encampment of Indians, about the mouth of Yellow Creek, near Baker's house, opposite; after plying them with whisky, they were nearly all murdered. In these two Indian parties—at Captina and Yellow Creek—some in each, were all of Logan's family, and they were all killed. Logan charged Captain Cresap with the murder of his kin at Yellow Creek, but this is probably a mistake.   He was undoubtedly responsible for the killing at Captina (whether justifiable or not, it is impossible to decide now), but it has been pretty conclusively shown that he was not present at the Yellow Creek massacre.

About this time, Bald Eagle, an old and friendly Delaware Chief, was wantonly murdered by some straggling whites, set up in his canoe, with a pipe in his mouth, and sent floating down the Monongahela, not the Kanawha, as stated by some.

The Indians were terribly exasperated by these murders, and it was soon unmistakably evident that they meant to be avenged.   Dr. Connally and Captain Cresap sent messengers to Williamsburg to apprise the Governor of the state of affairs.   He dispatched Colonel Angus McDonald, with four hundred Virginia militia, in June, to make an incursion into Indian territory, to occupy them at home and prevent their raids on the border settlements.

Later, when the Indians seemed determined on a general border war, Connally and Cresap again communicated with the Governor, who sent for General Andrew Lewis, then a member of the House of Burgesses for Bottetourt County, to consult about a plan of campaign.   It was decided that an army of two divisions should be organized as speedily as practicable—one to be commanded by General Lewis, and the other by Lord Dunmore, in person.

General Andrew and his brother, Colonel Charles, then a member from Augusta County, started at once to the Valley of Virginia to get together their army from Augusta, Bottetourt and Fincastle Counties, while the forces of Governor Dunmore were to be raised in Frederick, Dunmore (now Shenandoah) and adjacent counties.

The Governor dispatched Daniel Boone and Michael Stoner to Kentucky, to notify the several surveying parties and the few land hunters and explorers then there; while from the Greenbriar region, Captain John Stewart dispatched two runners (tradition says Philip Hammond and John Pryor) to warn the few settlers on Kanawha, from Kelly's Creek to Campbell's Creek, of the approaching danger.

General Lewis' army rendezvoused at Camp Union (Lewisburg), about September 1st, and was to march from there to the mouth of Kanawha; while Governor Dunmore was to go the Northwest route, over the Braddock trail, by way of Fort Pitt, and thence down the Ohio River, and form a junction with General Lewis at the mouth of 'Kanawha. The army of General Lewis was made up as follows:

1. Regiment of Augusta troops, under Colonel Charles Lewis, the Captains being George Mathews (in whose company not a man was under six feet in height, and most of them over six feet two inches), Alexander McClannahan, John Dickinson, John Lewis (son of William), Benjamin Harrison, William Paul, Joseph Haynes and Samuel Wilson.

2. Bottetourt Regiment, under Colonel William Fleming. The Captains were Matthew Arbuckle, John Murray, John Lewis (son of Andrew), James Robertson, Robert McClannahan; James Ward and John Stewart (author of memoir, etc.).

3. An independent company of seventy men, under Colonel John Field, raised by him in Culpepper County.

4. The force under Colonel William Christian consisted of three independent companies, under Captains Evan Shelby, William Russell and —— Herbert, from the Holston, Clinch and New River settlements, then Fincastle County; a company of scouts under Captain John Draper, of Draper's Valley, and an independent company under Captain Thomas Buford, of Bedford County.

The aggregate strength of this Southern division of the army was about eleven hundred; the strength of the Northern division, under Lord Dunmore, was about fifteen hundred.

On the 11th of September, General Lewis broke camp, and, with Captain Matthew Arbuckle, an intelligent and experienced frontiersman, as pilot, marched through a pathless wilderness, making, as they went, such road as was necessary to get the pack-horses, bearing ammunition and provisions, and their beef cattle over.

Their route was by Muddy Creek, Keeny's Knobs, Rich Creek, Gauley, Twenty Mile, Bell Creek and Kelly's Creek, to Kanawha, and down Kanawha to the mouth, following the Indian trail at the base of the hills, instead of along the river bank, for the obvious reason that it was thus easier to cross or avoid the creeks and ravines. They reached the Point on the 30th day of September, after a fatiguing march of nineteen days.

When Lewis' army started its march from Camp Union for the mouth of Kanawha, Colonel Field, who, in previous service with Lewis in the Northwest, had been the senior in command, now manifested some unwillingness to take position under

General Lewis, and, as his company was an independent one, raised by himself ouside of the State order for troops, and as he had recently twice passed through the wilderness, from Camp Union to Kelly's Creek and back, and knew something of its topography, he started out with his command by a route of his own; on the next or following day, however, two of his men, named Clay and Coward, strayed from the main body to hunt; they were attacked by two Indians, probably spies watching the movements of the army. Clay was shot and killed by one of them, while the other was killed by Coward.

After this, Colonel Field, acting with judicious discretion, joined the main body of the army, and they marched together harmoniously the remainder of the way.

At the mouth of Elk (the present site of Charleston) the army halted long enough to construct some canoes, or "dug-outs," into which the commissary stores, ammunition, etc., were transferred from the backs of pack-horses, and taken the remainder of the way by river.

In most or all the accounts of the battle, it is stated that Colonel Christian and his regiment were delayed in getting together, and did not arrive in time for the battle. This is, in part at least, an error. Colonel Christian did not arrive until late in the afternoon, when the fighting was nearly over, bringing with him the portions of his companies that had been too late in reaching the rendezvous; but Captains Russell, Shelby and Buford, and parts of their companies, were certainly on the ground at the beginning of the fight.

The four men who had made a daylight hunting
excursion up the Ohio River bank, on the morning
of the 10th, who were the first to see the Indians,
and one of whom (Hickman) was killed—the first
blood drawn—were members of Captains Russell's
and Shelby's companies; and Captain Buford was
present, and himself wounded during the day.

The army had been gotten together hastily, as were,
also, the supplies, which were not overly abundant.
The army was neither well clad nor well fed; they
were, perforce, " teetotalers." They had no spirit
rations, and neither tea nor coffee, yet they were in
good health and spirits, though tired and worn by
the hard march through the wilderness.

General Lewis waited several days, anxiously expecting the arrival of Lord Dunmore, who, by appointment, was to have joined him here on the 2d of
October. Having no intelligence from him, Lewis
dispatched messengers up the Ohio River to meet
him, or learn what had become of him. Before his
messengers returned, however, three messengers
(probably McCulloch, Kenton and Girty) arrived at
his camp on Sunday, the 9th of October, with orders
from Lord Dunmore to cross the river and meet him
before the Indian towns in Ohio.

This is, substantially, the current version of mat-
ters; but authorities differ. Some say the messengers arrived on the night of the 10th, after the battle
was fought; others say they did not arrive until the
11th, the day after the battle, and Colonel Andrew
Lewis, son of General Andrew, says his father received no communication whatever from Lord Dunmore after he (Lewis) left Camp Union, until after

the battle had been fought, and Lewis, of his own
motion, had gone on into Ohio, expecting to join
Dunmore and to punish the Indians, when he received
an order to stop and return to the point. This order
(by messenger) Lewis disregarded, when Lord Dunmore came in person, and, after a conference and as-
surances from Dunmore that he was about negotiating a peace, Lewis reluctantly retraced his steps.

In the very excited state of feeling then existing
between the colonies and the mother country, it was
but natural that the sympathies of Lord Dunmore, a
titled English nobleman, and holding his commission
as Governor of Virginia at the pleasure of the crown,
should be with his own country; but it was not only
strongly suspected, but generally charged, that, while
he was yet acting as Governor of Virginia, and before he had declared himself against the colonies, he
was unfairly using his position and influence to the
prejudice of his subjects.

These suspicions, and the supposed grounds for
them, will be more fully discussed in a subsequent
chapter on Lord Dunmore.

According to the account of Colonel Stewart, when
the interview was over between General Lewis and
the messengers of Lord Dunmore, on the 9th, Lewis
gave orders to break camp at an early hour next
morning, cross the river, and take up their march
towards the Indian towns; but the Fates had decreed
otherwise. At the hour for starting, they found
themselves confronted by an army of Indian braves,
eight hundred to one thousand strong, in their war
paint, and commanded by their able and trusted
leaders, Cornstalk, Logan, Red Hawk, Blue Jacket

and Elinipsico, and some authors mention two or three others.

Instead of a hard day's marching, Lewis' army had a harder day's fighting—the important, desperately contested, finally victorious, and ever-memorable battle of Point Pleasant.

No "official report" of this battle has been preserved, or was ever written, so far as I can learn. There are several good reasons, apparently, for this omission. In the first place, the time, place and circumstances were not favorable for preparing a formal official report. In the second place, Lord Dunmore, the superior officer, to whom General Lewis should, ordinarily, have reported, was himself in the field, but a few miles distant, and General Lewis was expecting that the two divisions of the army would be united within a few days; and, in the third place, the "strained relations" between the colonies and the mother country were such, and the recent action of Governor Dunmore so ambiguous, that General Lewis was probably not inclined to report to him at all.

In the absence of an official report, I give below an account of the battle which, I think, comes nearer to it than anything else extant.

Being in Belfast, Ireland, in 1874, a short time before the centennial celebration of the battle at Point Pleasant, and knowing that Belfast, Ulster district, and the North of Ireland generally, had sent a large early emigration to the Valley of Virginia, many of whose descendants were, no doubt, in General Lewis' army, and in this battle, I went to the City Library to see if I could find anything there relating to the battle. In examining the files of the "Belfast News

Letter," a city paper, which I found preserved in annual bound volumes from its commencement, in 1737 (and now nearly one hundred and fifty years old), I turned to 1774, and my search was soon rewarded by finding the following very interesting letter, a copy of which I sent to the "Charleston Courier" in time for publication and circulation at the Point Pleasant celebration :

BELFAST.

Yesterday arrived a mail from New York, brought to Falmouth by the Harriot packet boat. Captain Lee.

WILLIAMSBURG, VA., November 10th.

The following letter is just received here from the camp on Point Pleasant, at the mouth of the Great Kenhawa [as then spelled], dated October 17, 1774:

"The following is a true statement of a battle fought at this place on the 10th instant: On Monday morning, about half an hour before sunrise, two of Captain Russell's company discovered a large party of Indians about a mile from the camp, one of which men was shot down by the Indians; the other made his escape, and brought in the intelligence. In two or three minutes after, two of Captain Shelby's company came in and confirmed the account.

"Colonel Andrew Lewis, being informed thereof, immediately ordered out Colonel Charles Lewis, to take command of one hundred and fifty of the Augusta troops, and with him went Captain Dickinson, Captain Harrison, Captain Wilson, Captain John Lewis, of Augusta, and Captain Lockridge, which made the first division. Colonel Fleming was also ordered to take command of one hundred and fifty more of the Bottetourt, Bedford and Fincastle troops, viz.: Captain Thomas Buford, from Bedford; Captain Love, of Bottetourt; Captain Shelby and Captain Russell, of Fincastle, which made the second division.

"Colonel Charles Lewis' division marched to the right, some distance from the Ohio, and Colonel Fleming, with his division, on the bank of the Ohio, to the left.

"Colonel Charles Lewis' division had not marched quite half a mile from the camp when, about sunrise, an attack was made

on the front of his division, in a most vigorous manner, by the
united tribes of Indians—Shawnees, Delawares, Mingoes, Tawas,
and of several other nations—in number not less than eight hundred, and by many thought to be one thousand.

"In this heavy attack, Colonel Charles Lewis received a
wound which, in a few hours, caused his death, and several of
his men fell on the spot; in fact, the Augusta division was
obliged to give way to the heavy fire of the enemy. In about a
second of a minute after the attack on Colonel Lewis's division,
the enemy engaged the front of Colonel Fleming's division on the
Ohio, and in a short time the Colonel received two balls through
his left arm, and one through his breast, and, after animating
the officers and soldiers in a most calm manner to the pursuit of
victory, retired to the camp.

"The loss in the field was sensibly felt by the officers in particular; but the Augusta troops, being shortly after reinforced
from the camp by Colonel Field, with his company, together
with Captain McDowell, Captain Mathews and Captain Stewart,
from Augusta; Captain Paulin, Captain Arbuckle and Captain
McClannahan, from Bottetourt, the enemy, no longer able to
maintain their ground, was forced to give way till they were in a
line with the troops, Colonel Fleming being left in action on the
bank of the Ohio.

"In this precipitate retreat Colonel Field was killed. During
this time, which was till after twelve, the action in a small degree
abated, but continued, except at short intervals, sharp enough
till after one o'clock. Their long retreat gave them a most advan-
tageous spot of ground, from whence it appeared to the officers
so difficult to dislodge them that it was thought most advisable to
stand as the line was then formed, which was about a mile und
a quarter in length, and had sustained till then a constant and
equal weight of the action, from wing to wing.

"It was till about half an hour of sunset they continued firing
on us scattering shots, which we returned to their disadvantage.
At length, the night coming on, they found a safe retreat.

"They had not the satisfaction of carrying off any of our
men's scalps, save one or two stragglers whom they killed before
the engagement. Many of their dead they scalped, rather than
we should have them, but our troops scalped upwards of twenty
of their men that were first killed.

"It is beyond doubt their loss, in number, far exceeded ours,
which is considerable.

"The return of the killed aftd wounded in the above battle, same as our last, as follows:

"Killed—Colonels Charles Lewis and John Field, Captains John Murray, R. McClannahan, Samuel Wilson, James Ward, Lieutenant Hugh Allen, Ensigns Cantiff and Bracken, and forty-four privates. Total killed, fifty-three.

"Wounded—Colonel William Fleming, Captains John Dickinson, Thomas Buford and I. Skidman, Lieutenants Goldman, Robinson, Lard and Vance, and seventy-nine privates. Total wounded, eighty-seven; killed and wounded, one hundred and forty."

Looking further through the "Belfast News Letter" to see if I could find any additional particulars, I found the following Williamsburg letter in relation to the movements of Governor Dunmore:

"AMERICA.

"WILLIAMSBURG, IN VIRGINIA, December 1, 1774,

"We have it from good authority that His Excellency, the Governor, is on his way to this capital, having concluded a peace with the several tribes of Indians that have been at war with us, and taken hostages of them for their faithful complying with the terms of it, the principal of which are that they shall totally abandon the lands on this side of the Ohio River, which river is to be the boundary between them and the white people, and never more take up the hatchet against the English.

"Thus, in a little more than the space of five months, an end is put to a war which portended much trouble and mischief to the inhabitants on the frontier, owing to the zeal and good conduct of the officers and commanders who went out in their country's defense, and the bravery and perseverance of all the troops."—Copied from the "Belfast News Letter" of February 10, 1775."

It will be observed that the foregoing Point Pleasant letter has no signature to it. The letter was, doubtles, signed when written, but why the name was omitted at Williamsburg or Belfast is not known.

While there is no name to the letter as printed, it is circumstantially conclusive, I think, that it was written by Captain Matthew Arbuckle, whom General Lewis had left in command of the garrison, and charged with the care of the wounded at the Point.

There were no enterprising newspaper correspondents at the front in those days; no literary camp-followers or hangers-on; no amateur aids-de-camp, or other fancy gentlemen, to write sensational battle reports; there was no Point Pleasant town there then; no citizens nor neighbors to write army letters or battle reports. Outside of Captain Arbuckle's camp, there was absolutely not a white man within one hundred miles of Point Pleasant, or nearer than the armies then out on Pickaway Plains. I assume, therefore, that the letter was written by Captain Arbuckle, possibly by order of General Lewis, to be forwarded to the State capital. It was, probably, sent by runners to Camp Union, forwarded thence to Williamsburg, and published in the little weekly "Virginia Gazette," published by Purdie & Dixon, and the only newpaper then published in the State.

This report of the battle is quite meager, it is true, and it is to be regretted that it had not given more of detail; but, as far as it goes, it is evidently a true and accurate account of what transpired, as seen by the writer, himself an active participant throughout. The style of the letter is plain, simple and clear, with no effort at fine writing; no thought of making or glorifying pet heroes, and no wish to be sensational. It was written on the ground, just one week after the battle, with all the facts fresh and clear upon his own mind, and the memories of his garrison and wounded, with whom, doubtless, he had discussed the exciting events over and over, and compared notes, day by day, during the week past.

Though short, the simple and unpretentious style of the report is probably calculated to give the average general reader as clear a comprehension of the prominent facts and features of the battle as a half-dozen-column article from a modern army correspondent, largely made up of fulsome flattery of incipient heroes, and of sensational incidents of doubtful authenticity.

About ten years after the battle, Colonel John Stewart, who had been one of the first permanent settlers of Greenbriar, and who had taken a most active and efficient part in the prominent Indian wars and raids of the period, in this region, wrote a not very full, but exceedingly interesting, memoir of these early times and troubles, including the battle of the Point; and to this memoir, probably more than to any other one document, we are indebted for what has been preserved of the eventful history of this valley at that period, and it is the basis of much of the history of the region since written.

Many years later, Dr. S. L. Campbell, of Rockbridge, wrote a somewhat similar sketch, the material being gathered from the recollections of those who had taken part in the events described, chiefly from Mr. Alexander Reed and Mr. William Moore, of Rockbridge.

Later, Colonel Andrew Lewis, of the Bent Mountain, Va., son of General Andrew, gave, briefly, his recollections of the long ago; and many other longer or shorter sketches relating to the battle of the Point, and other events of this region, have been written mostly from traditions, more or less imperfectly and inaccurately transmitted from those who were personal actors or witnesses.

Each of these sketches contains some fact, item or incident unknown to or omitted by the others, but as each item fills a gap and helps to make up the general picture, it is only possible now to get a tolerably full and clear idea and understanding of the conditions then existing by gleaning from all the accounts, each of which, alone, gives so little of circumstantial detail.

That there are some discrepancies, and conflicts of statement is but natural and to be expected under the circumstances; they are generally unimportant, however, and must be reconciled by comparisons and weight of probabilities.

Colonel Stewart, one of the first to write about the battle, after Arbuckle's short account, was himself present, was well known to General Lewis (and a relative by marriage), says General Lewis received a message from Governor Dunmore, on the 9th, telling him to cross the Ohio and join him, and he (Stewart) mentions McCulloch as one of the messengers.

Burk, and others, say the messengers came after the battle, and mention Simon Kenton and Simon Girty among the messengers.

Colonel Andrew Lewis says his father received no communication of any sort from Governor Dunmore, until ordered to return from Ohio.

Dr. Campbell says there was considerable dissatisfaction in Lewis' camp, for some days before the battle, growing out of the manner of serving the rations, and especially the beef rations; the men claimed that the good and bad beef were not dealt out impartially. On the 9th, General Lewis ordered that the poorest beeves be killed first, and distributed to all alike. The beef was so poor that the men were unwilling to eat it, and, although it was positively against orders to leave camp without permission, about one hundred men started out before day, next morning (the 10th), in different directions, to hunt and provide their own meat. Many of these did not get back, nor know of the battle, until night, when it was all over.

This was a serious reduction of the army at such a time. This circumstance has not been mentioned, so far as I know, by any other of the early writers.

Of the several men belonging to Captains Russell's and Shelby's companies who went immediately up the bank of the Ohio, the two (Hickman and Robinson) who first encountered the Indians belonged, as Arbuckle tells us, to Captain Russell's company. Of these, Hickman was killed, as above stated, and Robinson escaped to the camp with all speed, and reported an army of Indians that would cover four acres or more.

When the approach of the Indians was reported, it is said that General Lewis first quietly lighted his pipe, and then coolly gave his orders for the disposition of the forces as described by Captain Arbuckle, and generally confirmed by others.

Nearly all the accounts of the battle state that Colonel Charles Lewis was shot down on the first round, and soon expired at the root of a tree. Dr. Doddridge

13

says he was carried to his tent by Captain Morrow and Mr. Blair, from Captain Paul's company, while Colonel Andrew Lewis says he received his wound early in the action, but did not let it be known until he had gotten the line of battle extended from the Ohio to Crooked Creek; he then asked Captain Murray, his brother-in-law, to let him lean on his shoulder and walk with him to his tent, where he expired about twelve o'clock. This does not conflict with the statement of Captain Arbuckle, who says: " He received a wound which, in a few hours, caused his death."

The terrific grandeur of a battle scene can not well be described in cold, common-place language. I shall not attempt the elevated strain necessary to do the subject justice, but will quote, briefly, from two authors who have written on this battle. De Hass says:

"The battle scene was now terribly grand. There stood the combatants—terror, rage, disappointment and despair riveted upon the painted faces of one, while calm resolution and the unbending will to do or die were marked upon the other. Neither party would retreat, neither could advance. The noise of the firing was tremendous. No single gun could be distinguished— was one common roar.

"The rifle and the tomahawk now did their work with dreadful certainty. The confusion and perturbation of the camp had now arrived at its greatest height. The confused sounds and wild uproar of the battle added greatly to the terror of the scene. The shouting of the whites, the continued roar of firearms, the war-whoop and dismal yelling of the Indians, were discordant and terrific."

Colonel J. L. Peyton, in his valuable history of Augusta County, says:

" It was, throughout, a terrible scene—the ring of rifles and the roar of muskets, the clubbed guns, the flashing knives—the fight, hand to hand—the ·scream for mercy, smothered in the death-groan—the crushing through the brush—the advance—the retreat—the pursuit, every man for himself, with his enemy in view—the scattering on every side—the sounds of battle, dying away into a pistol-shot here and there through the wood, and a shriek—the collecting again of the whites, covered with gore and sweat, bearing trophies of the slain, their dripping knives in one hand, and rifle-barrel, bent and smeared with brains and hair, in the other. No language can adequately describe it."

After these eloquent and thrilling descriptions of the desperate conflict, one can hardly fail to be surprised, when he comes to foot up results, to find that the casualties are so few.

Different accounts of the battle state the losses on the part of the whites, in killed and wounded, at one hundred and forty to two hundred and fifteen; but I assume that Captain Arbuckle's account, above given, is correct; that is, nine officers and forty-four privates (53) killed, and eight officers and seventy-nine privates (87) wounded; total, killed and wounded, one hundred and forty.

All the early writers claim that the losses of the Indians were greater than those of the whites, but this, I think, admits of much doubt. The historians all claim that the Indians were seen throwing their dead into the river all day, but it seems only a vague "they say" sort of statement, not given upon the positive authority of any reliable person who saw it. While, per contra, Colonel James Smith, who was several years a prisoner among the Indians, spoke their language, knew many of them well, and communicated with them after this battle, says they only admitted the loss of twenty-eight killed outright,

and eight who died from their wounds—total, thirty-
six; but as they had no muster-rolls, and the tribes
scattered, they had probably overlooked at least five,
as twenty-one were found lying as they fell, and
twelve where their friends had partially buried or
secreted them, making thirty-three, and the eight
who afterwards died from their wounds would increase their loss to forty-one—one of whom Cornstalk himself had killed.

This Colonel Smith was one of the most intelligent and observant of the many early pioneers who
had the hard fate to serve a captivity of several years
among the Indians; but to his misfortune we are indebted for his published narrative, after his release,
of his personal adventures and results of his observations, which is probably the best record extant, of
the manners and customs, and every-day life of the
Indians at that period of their history.

Among the eighty-seven wounded whites, it would
seem probable that some died of their wounds in the
hospital; but, if so, I have seen no list or mention
of them.

To Colonel Christian, who, as generally stated, arrived about four o'clock, when the battle was nearly
over, was assigned the duty of gathering up and
burying the dead whites; most of them were buried
in a common grave or trench, with only their blankets
for coffins and shrouds. A few, whose friends wished
to remove them, were buried in separate graves.

The Indians were not given burial at all, but left
to pollute the air until the birds, the animals and the
elements had disposed of them.

The Indians, during the battle, had some of their

warriors stationed on both sides of the river, below the Point, to prevent the possible escape of the whites by swimming the river from the extreme point, in the event of defeat.

Colonel Fleming was early wounded by two balls through his left wrist, but he contined to give his orders with coolness and presence of mind, calling loudly to his men: "Don't lose an inch of ground! Try to outflank the enemy! Get between them and the river!" but he was about to be outflanked himself, and was only saved by the timely coming up of Colonel Field, with reinforcements, when he was again shot, through the lungs, and carried off the field. Several times the Indians retreated, to draw out the whites from cover—a favorite ruse of theirs—and then advanced again. During one of these moves, Colonel Field was leading on his men in pursuit, when he was fatally shot.

General Lewis, warned by the loss of so many brave officers and men, of the danger of possible disaster, put a large force of his reserves to cutting and felling trees in a line across the angle between the rivers, making a breastwork for his men, and protection for the camp, if he should be driven back to it.

It is rather remarkable that not one of the Indian leaders was killed or wounded. They certainly fought bravely.

During the battle, it is said that the stentorian voice of Cornstalk was often heard, commanding and encouraging his men.

Captain Stewart at one time asked some one near him, who understood something of the Indian language, what it was that Cornstalk was saying; in reply he said, the English equivalent of the expression was: "Be strong! Be strong!"

To punish an individual act of cowardice, during the battle, and to serve as a warning to others, and, possibly, prevent demoralization in his army, it was said that Cornstalk cleft the skull of one of his own men with his tomahawk. This, I believe, is given on the authority of Cornstalk himself, subsequently obtained; he also stated that he had opposed the battle, and advised a conference with General Lewis, on the eve of the fight, to treat for peace, but he was overruled, when he said to them: "Then if you will fight, you shall fight, and I will see that you do fight!"

It was about four o'clock in the afternoon when General Lewis detailed Captains Shelby, Matthews and Stewart to make a detour and flank movement up Crooked Creek. This was entirely successful, and was the decisive move of the day. As soon as the Indians discovered it, thinking it was Colonel Christian arriving with fresh reinforcements, they began their final retreat. They kept up a show of fighting by desultory firing, to keep the whites in check while getting away with their wounded, which they accomplished with entire success.

Some historians of the battle claim that the Indians were pursued, on their retreat, by the whites, from one to three miles, but the evidence is not satisfactory. General Lewis' army had fought from sunrise to sunset, without food or rest, and were, consequently, fatigued, hungry and exhausted, and in no condition to pursue. To have attempted it in the darkness of night would have been to risk being ambushed and exterminated. In the exhausted condition of the armies, I assume that one side was as glad to be let alone as the other, and that there was no pursuit.

Probably the first man killed when the battle opened, and after the hunter, Hickman, had been killed a mile above the camp, was Captain Frogg. He was not commanding a company, but was a sutler. When the order was given to advance, he took his gun and volunteered to fight with the rest. He was a nervous, excitable man, and kept not only even with the front rank, but generally several steps in advance, as there were yet no Indians in sight. He was gaudily dressed in bright colors, and had his hat rigged with ribbons or feathers; suddenly the Indians arose from an ambush in a pawpaw thicket, and fired a volley into the advance. Captain Frogg, from his advanced position and gaudy dress, had probably been mistaken for an officer of rank, and was riddled with bullets. He had, unfortunately for himself, drawn the fire of the enemy, and, possibly, saved the lives of several others.

A few days after the battle, there was a sale, at auction, of sundry articles captured from, or lost by, the Indians during the day. They brought, in the aggregate, £74. 4s. 6d.

These two last items I give on the authority of Colonel B. H. Smith's centennial address at Point Pleasant in 1874, and he got them from the traditions of his ancestors, who were in the battle.

It is said that three Indians were successively shot down over one body in the, at last, unsuccessful effort to secure a much-coveted scalp.

The wonderful powers of endurance of the Indians may be estimated from the facts that they occupied the night of the 9th in crossing the river, marched three miles by sunrise on the morning of the 10th, fought from sunrise till dark, remarched three miles, and recrossed the river on the night of the 10th, with little or no opportunity for food or rest.

Collins, in his admirable history of Kentucky, says that Captain James Harrod, who had a company of forty-two colonists in Kentucky, taking up lands and building improvers' cabins, in 1774, left the country with the surveyors and others, when warned out by Boone, took most of them with him up to the Point, and "lent a helping hand" in the bloody fight.

The weather on the 10th of October, the day of the memorable battle, was clear and pleasant, and the rivers were low. On Tuesday, the 11th, General Lewis strengthened the Fort, provided for the wounded and prepared for the march, and on Wednesday, the 12th, crossed the Ohio and started to join Lord Dunmore. It is believed that he crossed not far below the mouth of "Old Town Creek," and about where the Indians had crossed and recrossed.

The original camp and Fort at the Point stood in the angle of the rivers, a little nearer the Ohio, and a little below the present Virginia street; and here the brave Virginians, who had lost their lives in defense of her borders and their own homes, were laid to rest. Since that day the Ohio has cut away its banks very much, encroaching upon the site.

One of the last official acts of Governor Dunmore,

before fleeing from the wrath of his unloving subjects, was to order the disbanding of the garrison at the Point, in 1775, hoping thus to encourage and facilitate Indian raids upon the Western settlements. The Governor was then fully committed to the English side in the Revolutionary struggle.

It was not long, however, till a larger Fort was constructed, changing the location to the site of the large brick storehouse of the late James Capeheart, and it was called Fort Randolph.

How long this Fort stood, I do not know, but Colonel Andrew Lewis says he was at the Point in 1784, when there was little or no sign of it left.

CHAPTER XXXIII.

LORD DUNMORE.

IT has been stated that there were not only suspicions, but grave charges, that Governor Dunmore acted a double part, and that he was untrue and treacherous to the interests of the colony he governed.

As he is inseparably connected with this campaign (often called the Dunmore war), and its accompanying history, and the inauguration of the Revolution, it may be well to briefly allude to his official course just before, during and after the campaign, that his true relations to it, and to the colony, may be understood; and, also, to show that the "Revolution" was really in progress; that this campaign was one of the important early moves on the historical chess-board, and that the battle of Point Pleasant was, as generally claimed, the initiatory battle of the great drama.

In the Summer of 1773, Governor Dunmore made, ostensibly, a pleasure trip to Fort Pitt; here he established close relations with Dr. Connally, making him Indian Agent, Land Agent, etc. Connally was an able, active and efficient man, who thereafter adhered to Dunmore and the English cause.

It is charged that Connally at once began fomenting trouble and ill-feeling between the colonies of

Virginia and Pennsylvania in regard to the Western frontier of Pennsylvania, then claimed by both colonies, but held by Virginia, hoping by such course to prevent the friendly co-operation of these colonies against English designs; and, also, to incite the Indian tribes to resistance of Western white encroachments upon their hunting grounds, and prepare the way for getting their co-operation with England against the colonies, when the rupture should come.

In December, 1773, the famous "cold-water tea" was made in Boston harbor. In retaliation, the English Government blockaded the port of Boston, and moved the capital of the colony to Salem. When this news came, in 1774, the Virginia Assembly, being in session, passed resolutions of sympathy with Massachusetts, and strong disapproval of the course of England; whereupon Governor Dunmore peremptorily dissolved the Assembly. They met privately, opened correspondence with the other colonies, and proposed co-operation and a Colonial Congress.

On the 4th of September, 1774, met, in Philadelphia, the first Continental Congress—Peyton Randolph, of Virginia, President; George Washington, R. H. Lee, Richard Bland, Patrick Henry, Benjamin Harrison and Edmund Pendleton members from Virginia.

They passed strong resolutions; among others, to resist taxation and other obnoxious measures; to raise minute men to forcibly resist coercion; and, finally, resolved to cease all official intercourse with the English Government.

In the meantime, Dr. Connally had been carrying out the programme of the Northwest. He had taken possession of the Fort at Fort Pitt, and renamed it Fort Dunmore; was claiming lands under patents from Governor Dunmore, and making settlements on them; had been, himself, arrested and imprisoned for a time by Pennsylvania; had the Indian tribes highly excited, united in a strong confederacy and threatening war; then came the massacre of Indians above Wheeling, at Captina and at Yellow Creek, said to have grown out of Connally's orders.

While the Continental Congress was passing the resolutions above mentioned, and which created a breach between the colonies and the mother country past healing, Governor Dunmore and General Lewis were organizing and marching their armies to the West. Instead of uniting the forces into one army, and marching straight to the Indian towns and conquering or dictating a lasting peace, Lord Dunmore took the larger portion of the army by a long detour by Fort Pitt, and thence down the Ohio, picking up, on the way, Dr. Connally and Simon Girty, whom he made useful.

At Fort Pitt, it is said, he had held a conference with some of the Indian Chiefs, and came to some understanding with them, the particulars of which are not known.

Instead of uniting with Lewis at the mouth of Kanawha, as had been arranged, but which was probably not intended, he struck off from the Ohio River at the mouth of the Hockhocking and marched for the Indian towns on the Pickaway plains, without the support of Lewis' army, delaying long enough for the Indians to have annihilated Lewis' division, if events had turned out as Cornstalk had planned. He

(Cornstalk) said it was first their intention to attack. the "Long Knives" and destroy them, as they crossed the river, and this plan would have been carried out, or attempted, but for the long delay of Lewis, awaiting the arrival of Lord Dunmore. They afterwards, upon consultation, changed their plans, and determined to let Lewis cross the river, and then ambush him somewhere nearer their own homes, and farther from his (Lewis') base; but the Indians have no organized commissary or transportation arrangements, and can only transport such amount of food as each brave can carry for his own sustenance; this is, necessarily, a limited amount, and Lewis' delay in crossing had run their rations so short that they were obliged to cross, themselves, and force a fight, or break camp and go to hunting food. They crossed in the night, about three miles above the Point, on rafts previously constructed, and expected to take Lewis' army by surprise; and it has been seen how near they came to accomplishing it. It was prevented by the accident of the early hunters, who were out before daylight, in violation of orders.

Colonel Andrew Lewis (son of General Andrew), in his account of the Point Pleasant campaign, says: "It is known that Blue Jacket, a Shawanee Chief, visited Lord Dunmore's camp, on the 9th, the day before the battle, and went straight from there to the Point, and some of them went to confer with Lord Dunmore immediately after the battle."

It is also said that Lord Dunmore, in conversation with Dr. Connally, and others, on the 10th, the day of the battle, remarked that "Lewis is probably having hot work about this time."

When Lewis had crossed the river, after the battle, and was marching to join Dunmore, a messenger was dispatched to him twice in one day, ordering him to stop and retrace his steps—the messenger, in both instances, being the afterwards notorious Simon Girty. General Lewis had, very naturally, become very much incensed at the conduct of Lord Dunmore, and took the high-handed responsibility—advised and sanctioned by his officers and men—of disobeying the order of his superior in command, and boldly marching on towards his camp.

When within about two and a half miles of Lord Dunmore's head-quarters, which he called Camp Charlotte, after Queen Charlotte, wife of his master, George III., he came out to meet Lewis in person, bringing with him Cornstalk, White Eyes (another noted Shawanee Chief), and others, and insisted on Lewis' returning, as he (Dunmore) was negotiating a treaty of peace with the Indians. He sought an introduction to Lewis' officers, and paid them some flattering compliments, etc.

Evidently, it did not comport with Lord Dunmore's plans to have General Lewis present at the treaty, to help the negotiation by his suggestions, or to have the moral support of his army to support them.

So much did Lewis' army feel the disappointment and this indignity, that Colonel Andrew, his son, says it was with difficulty General Lewis could restrain his men (not under very rigid discipline, at best) from killing Lord Dunmore and his Indian escort. But the result of the personal conference was that General Lewis, with the utmost reluctance of himself and army, consented to return, and to disband his army upon his arrival at Camp Union, as ordered.

Suppose Lewis had attempted to cross the river, and been destroyed, or had crossed and been ambushed and demolished in the forest thickets of Ohio, or that Cornstalk had succeeded, as he came so near doing, in surprising him in his own camp, on the morning of the 10th, or after that; suppose the Indians had succeeded in turning the so evenly balanced scale in their favor, during the fight, as they came so near doing, and had annihilated Lewis' army, as they might then have done, having them penned up in the angle of two rivers, who can doubt, in view of all the facts above noted, that Lord Dunmore would have been responsible for the disaster? Who can doubt, as it was, that he was responsible for the unnecessary sacrifice of life, at the Point, on the 10th? Who can doubt that, with the two divisions of the army united, as per agreement, and Lord Dunmore and Lewis acting in unison and good faith, they could have marched, unopposed, to the Indian towns, and utterly destroyed them, or dictated a favorable and lasting peace, and maintained it as long as they pleased, by holding important hostages? But, clearly, the policy of the Governor was dictated by ulterior and sinister motives; his actions were not single-minded.

Colonel Andrew Lewis says: "It was evidently the intention of the old Scotch villain to cut off General Lewis' army." Burk, the historian, says: "The division under Lewis was devoted to destruction, for the purpose of breaking the spirit of the Virginians." Withers, Doddridge, and others, ex-press the same views.　General Lewis and his army were convinced of the fact; Colonel Stewart had no doubt of it, and nearly every one who has written on the subject has taken the same view of it.　A few only are willing to give him the benefit of a doubt.

If this design to destroy Lewis' army had succeeded, it is almost certain that the English, through Lord Dunmore, would have perfected an alliance, offensive and defensive, with the victorious Indians, against the colonies, and every white settlement west of the Alleghenies would probably have been cut off.　It would have been difficult or impossible, for a time, to raise another army for the defense of the Western border; the Tory element would have been encouraged and strengthened, the Revolutionary element correspondingly discouraged, the Rebellion (?) crushed, and Lord Dunmore would have been the hero of the age.

Upon what slender and uncertain tenures hang the destinies of Nations, and the fate of individuals! The closely-won success of Lewis was not only an immediate victory over the Indians, but a defeat of the machinations of the double-dealing Governor, and the projected Anglo-Indian alliance.

In this view of it is established the claim of the battle of Point Pleasant as being the initiatory battle of the Revolution; and, although small in itself, when its after results and influences are considered, it stands out in bold relief as one of the important and decisive victories of history.

A few words more and we shall be done with Lord Dunmore.

Upon his return to Williamsburg, the Assembly,

upon his own ex parte statement of the results of the campaign, passed a vote of thanks for his "valuable services," etc., which, it is said, they very much regretted when they learned more of the facts.

Just after the battle of Lexington (April 18, 1775), he had all the powder that was stored in the colonial magazine at Williamsburg secretly conveyed on board an armed English vessel lying off Yorktown, and threatened to lay Williamsburg in ashes at the first sign of insurrection.

Patrick Henry raised a volunteer force to go down and compel him (Dunmore) to restore the powder; but as this was impracticable, he agreed to pay, and did pay, for it, and then issued a proclamation declaring " One Patrick Henry and his followers rebels." He had previously threatened Thomas Jefferson with prosecution for treason, and had commenced proceedings.

About this time, having previously sent his family on an English naval vessel, he made his own escape, by night, to the English fleet, and commenced a system of depredations along the coast, burning houses, destroying crops, etc.

He tried to bring his scheme of Indian co-operation to bear, and sent a message to his old friend, Connelly, with a commission as Colonel, and instructed him to secure the co-operation of as many of the Western militia commanders as possible, by large rewards; to form an alliance with the Indians, collect his forces at Fort Pitt, and march through Virginia and meet him. Fortunately, Colonel Connelly was captured and imprisoned, and the scheme exposed and thwarted.

He (Dunmore) issued a proclamation granting

14

freedom to all the slaves who would flock to his standard, and protection to the Tories.

Among other acts of violence, he burned Norfolk, the then largest and most important town in Virginia.

Upon his flight, the Assembly met and declared his office vacant, and proceeded to fill it; and, for the first time, Virginia had entire "home rule."

Upon the petition of citizens of Dunmore County, which had been named in his honor, the name was abolished, and the county called Shenandoah.

In 1776, Lord Dunmore and his fleet and hangers-on were at Guynne's Island, in the Chesapeake Bay, where, as an interesting example of poetic or retributive justice, General Lewis, in command of the Virginia troops, attacked, defeated and drove them off, with heavy loss, General Lewis, himself, firing the first gun, soon after which the ex-Governor, a sadder and wiser man, "left the country for the country's good."

>|-|-|<

CHAPTER XXXIV.

POINT PLEASANT was a sort of developing high
school, which prepared a class of military heroes
and statesmen from the apt pupils who had been
learning and practicing the preliminary lessons of
border warfare in the isolated settlements, and occasional Indian raids that had been made upon their
families, all along the Western frontiers, and sent
them out to serve their country usefully, and make
honorable records for themselves, in after years, all
along the borders and newly developing Western
States, and elsewhere.

A brief sketch of, or allusion to, the more prominent
persons known to have been present on this memorable occasion, or otherwise connected with it, may
be of interest.

General Andrew Lewis, one of the high professors
and proficients in this military school, had had eventful experiences. He commenced his military career
with Washington at Great Meadows and Fort Necessity, in 1754, where he was twice wounded. In the
following year, with three brothers, he was with
Braddock and Washington, in Braddock's disaster,
where three of the four brothers were wounded.

In the following year (1756), he commanded the

"Big Sandy expedition" against the Shawanees; in 1758 he was with General Forbes and Washington at the capture of Fort Du Quesne, where he was again wounded. Subsequently, he was in the service of his colony in defending her Western borders, acting as commissioner in negotiating treaties, or as member of the House of Burgesses. It was at the treaty of Fort Stanwix that the Governor of New York, in commenting on his majestic figure and commanding appearance, said of him: "He looks like the genius of the forest, and the very ground seems to tremble under him as he walks along." Colonel Stewart, in his memoir, says of him: "He was upwards of six feet high, of uncommon strength and agility, and his form of the most exact symmetry. He had a stern countenance, and was of a reserved and distant deportment, which rendered his presence more awful than engaging." Mr. Alexander Reed, of Rockbridge, who was in the battle of the Point, says of him: "He was a man of reserved manners, and great dignity of character—somewhat of the order of General Washington."

It is known that Washington considered him one of the foremost military men of the country, and recommended him as Commander-in-Chief of the armies. General Lewis had, beside his brother Charles, three sons in the battle of Point Pleasant; John, a Captain, and Samuel and Thomas, privates. Samuel was wounded. There were a number of others here, his relatives by blood or marriage, and a large part of his army was composed of the sons of his friends and neighbors. It was a class of material not accustomed to restraint, and not amenable to very rigid discipline. This may account for the statement sometimes made that the discipline of his camp was somewhat lax. He knew their metal, and knew that when fighting was to be done he could depend upon them, and contented himself with this knowledge. Up to this time, General Lewis had fought under British colors, against the French and against the Indians, but this battle was the pivotal point; henceforth his guns were turned against the British flag (and, strangely enough, in conjunction with the French), until it was driven from our shores. Like Moses of old, he was not permitted to enter into the rewards of his long and arduous labors. He was taken ill with fever, not long before the surrender at Yorktown, and started for his home on the Roanoke, in then Bottetourt, now Roanoke, County, but died on the way, at the house of his friend, Colonel Buford, at the Eastern base of the Blue Ridge. He was brought home and buried on his own magnificent estate, called "Dropmore," lying just outside of the limits of the town of Salem, where he rests, solitary and alone, under the spreading branches of the forest trees, on an eminence overlooking, for many miles, up and down, the river and valley of the beautiful Roanoke.

But there is yet more to be told, though it is painful to report the sad condition of this lonely grave; there is no marble shaft, nor granite column, nor slab of stone, nor mound of earth, to mark the spot where the hero sleeps. It is enclosed by no wall of stone, or brick, no railing of brass, or iron, or wood, and loose stock roam over it at will.

Shall the grave of the old patriot, who fought his

country's battles for twenty-seven years—from 1754
to 1781—from "Great Meadows" almost to Yorktown; who mingled his own blood with the first
French blood shed in the first engagement of the
great Anglo-French war; who saw his brother slain
and his son wounded at the battle of the Point, the
first blood shed in the great Revolution that gave us
our liberties, and who drove the last foreign Governor from our colonial shores; the friend and companion of the immortal Washington, longer suffer
this cold neglect?

Will not some appreciative and patriotic American—I need not say Virginian—in our halls of Congress, do himself the honor to bring this matter to
the attention of our justice-loving and merit-reward-
ing Government, that is spending millions in pen-
sions to the brave men who fought her more recent
battles, and hundreds of thousands to honor the
memories of the brave officers who led them, or served
their country in other fields, and give them the opportunity to honor themselves by doing the tardy
justice to embalm in marble, or granite, or brass,
either on the site of his grave or at the capital of
the Nation, the memory of the "Hero of Point
Pleasant?"

Colonel Charles Lewis, a younger brother of General Andrew, and the youngest of five brothers, was,
by many, considered "the flower of the flock." He
was a man of magnificent physique, as were all the
family. He was credited with a more amiable temperament and genial disposition than General Andrew,
and was more beloved by his neighbors and his
soldiers, while both, alike, were honored and esteemed

for their acknowledged bravery, high character and spotless integrity.

Colonel Charles was said to be the idol of the army. He had had large, active and honorable military experience, from Braddock's war down to date, and it is believed that he would have achieved greater honors and distinction in the Revolutionáry struggle if his life had been spared; but his brilliant career was ended in glory on this field.

The remains of Colonel Charles were afterwards removed from the Point to the mouth of Old Town Creek, on the Ohio, four miles above, where they are well cared for in the family burying-ground of his descendants.

Colonel William Fleming was a Scotchman of high lineage by birth, a doctor by profession, a resident of Bottetourt County, a man of learning and culture. He was thrice severely wounded in this battle, but recovered, and was afterwards, for a time, Acting Governor of Virginia, but not an elected Governor, as sometimes stated.

Colonel John Field was a native of Culpepper County, Va., had seen active service in Braddock's war and after, had been on the Kanawha a few months before, entering and surveying lands at Field's Creek (named after him), and Kelly's Creek, where Walter Kelly was shot down by his side, and he narrowly escaped by running eighty miles through the wilderness, to the Greenbriar settlements.

Colonel Field raised a force of volunteers in his own county for this campaign, and united it with General Lewis' army. It was his timely and vigorous advance on the field that checked the retreat both of Lewis' and Fleming's forces, when both leaders had been wounded. He received his fatal wound at the front, after he had succeeded in turning the tide of battle, and was bravely leading on his command in active pursuit of the then retreating foe. Colonel Field's remains were never removed from the Point, but still lie there, surrounded by the other brave men who fell around him.

Colonel Christian was descended from an ancient Scotch family of high degree, who lived on the Isle of Man. The immediate ancestors of Colonel William were among the earliest to settle in the Valley of Virginia, on Christian's Creek, near the site of Staunton. Colonel William was a man of education and refinement. He married a sister of Patrick Henry. He was not, himself, present in the early part of the battle of the Point, though a portion of his regiment was, and he arrived, with the remainder, about four o'clock in the afternoon, when the fighting was nearly over. He removed to Kentucky a few years after this date, and was finally killed, near the Falls of the Ohio, while in pursuit of a raiding party of Indians, who had committed some depredations upon his neighbors.

Colonel William Preston, of Smithfield, intended to accompany General Lewis and participate in the events of this campaign, but as his young wife was on the eve of becoming a mother, he remained at home to await the interesting event, which occurred about the date of the battle, and too late for him to join the army. The child born afterwards became Governor James Preston, of Virginia, the father-in-law of Governor John Floyd, and the grandfather of Governor John B. Floyd.

Captain Evan Shelby, originally from Maryland, settled on the Holston, in Southwest Virginia, about 1771. He raised a volunteer company for Lewis' army, and joined Colonel Christian's regiment. He was present when the fight began. After Colonels Lewis, Fleming and Field had been killed or disabled, he was the ranking officer, until Colonel Christian arrived. He it was who led the three companies (his own, Matthews' and Stewart's) on the flank movement up Crooked Creek, which was so successful in finally putting the Indians to flight, and deciding the fortunes of the day. Captain Shelby afterwards became Colonel Evan Shelby, and had a distinguished career in Kentucky and Tennessee.

Captain George Matthews, of Augusta County, with his splendid company, nearly every man of whom, as heretofore stated, was over six feet two inches in height, was one of the three Captains who made the successful Crooked Creek detour. He afterwards became the distinguished General George Matthews of the Revolution, hero of Brandywine, Germantown and Guilford, Governor of Georgia, United States Senator, etc.

Captain John Stewart, one of the first permanent settlers and defenders of Greenbriar, and one of the three Captains who executed the Crooked Creek flank movement, afterwards became Colonel John Stewart, took an active part in several subsequent Indian engagements, built on his estate a private fort, called "Fort Spring," was first Clerk of Greenbriar County, author of the fullest account of this battle, and ancestor of a large and honorable family of descendants.

Captain William Russell raised a volunteer company in the Clinch and New River settlements, and joined Colonel Christian's regiment. He was in the battle at its commencement; the first blood shed was that of Hickman, one of his men, who had started out for an early hunt up the Ohio River. Captain Russell afterwards became Colonel William Russell, and father of Colonel William Russell, both distinguished citizens of Kentucky.

Captain Moore became General Andrew Moore, of Rockbridge County, United States Senator, etc.

Captain McKee became Colonel William McKee, of Kentucky.

Lieutenant Shelby became General Isaac Shelby, a prominent factor at King's Mountain, Long Island (Holston), battle of the Thames, and other engagements, first Governor of Kentucky, and afterwards Secretary of War, under Monroe.

Lieutenant Thomas Ingles, who had been the first white child born west of the Alleghenies, and had been thirteen years prisoner among the Indians, became Colonel Thomas Ingles, and had a very eventful career, as herein elsewhere related.

William and John Campbell became General William and Colonel John Campbell, the heroes of King's Mountain.

Charles Cameron became Colonel Charles Cameron, of Bath County, Va.

Bazaleel Wells became General Bazaleel Wells, a distinguished citizen of Ohio.

John Steele, who was shot through the lungs here, survived and became Colonel John Steele, of the Revolution, a large land owner and salt dealer in this valley, and Governor of Mississippi.

John Lewis became Major John Lewis, a prominent citizen of Monroe County, Va.

Lieutenant Tate became General Tate, a distinguished citizen of Washington County, Va.

Lieutenant John Draper, who had been one of the founders of the "Draper's Meadows" settlement, was the ancestor of the prominent and honorable family of Draper's Valley, Va.

Captain Ben Harrison, according to the family tradition, was engaged in the successful flank movement up Crooked Creek, with Shelby and others. The Harrisons were a prominent and influential family in the Valley of Virginia, and founders of Harrisonburg; related to Benjamin Harrison, signer of the Declaration of Independence, President W. H. Harrison, etc.

Captain Daniel Smith was with Colonel Charles Lewis at the front, when Lewis received his fatal wound. Captain Smith was afterwards a prominent man in the Valley of Virginia, was long the presiding justice in his county, was the ancestor of Judge Daniel Smith, of that district, and of Colonel B. H. Smith, of this city.

Captain John Dickinson, a few years later, "entered" and surveyed the five hundred and two acres of land at and about the mouth of Campbell's Creek, containing the original salt spring, or Buffalo Licks.

George Clendenin afterwards became the founder of Charleston, the capital of West Virginia; was first member of the Legislature from Kanawha County, and, next year, fellow-member with Daniel Boone. He was father-in-law of Governor Return Jonathan Meigs, of Ohio.

William Clendenin (brother of George) became Colonel William Clendenin, a prominent citizen and long-time representative, first of Kanawha, and afterwards of Mason County, in the Legislature.

James Trimble was afterwards the founder of the distinguished family of that name in Kentucky and Ohio, father of Governor Allen Trimble, United States Senator Trimble, etc.

Anne Trotter, made a widow by the death of her husband in this battle, remarried and became the eccentric and renowned " Mad Anne Bailey," the useful border scout, reliable messenger and valuable conveyor of ammunition, etc., between the Forts at Point Pleasant, Charleston, Lewisburg and Jackson's River. She is still remembered by some of our older citizens, and is said to have been nearly one hundred and twenty years old when she died.

Captain Matthew Arbuckle, who is said to have been the first white man to pass down through this valley to the Ohio and return (in 1764), and was guide and pilot of General Lewis' army to the Point, was the commander of the garrison left at the Point after the battle, and was probably the author of the first written account of the battle, above given.

James Welch was afterwards appointed, by Governor Patrick Henry, first surveyor of Greenbriar County. After the death of Captain Arbuckle, Mr. Welch married his widow, and, upon his death, his brother, Mr. Alexander Welch, succeeded to the surveyorship.

John and Peter Van Bibber, brothers, came with the army from the Greenbriar, and afterwards settled in this valley, and became the ancestors of a large and prominent family. One of them, Matthias, called "Tice," was the companion of Boone in his hunting and trapping excursions, and chain carrier on his surveys. He became the father-in-law of Jesse Boone, Colonel Andrew Donnally, Colonel John Reynolds and Mr. Goodrich Slaughter, all prominent citizens of the valley, and, still later, through the daughters of Jesse Boone, he became the grandfather-in-law of Governor Boggs, of Missouri, and Mr. Warner, a member of Congress from Missouri.

Captain James Harrod, who brought up his colonists from Kentucky and took part in the battle, as elsewhere related, next year founded Harrodsburg, Ky., became Colonel James Harrod, and one of the most prominent citizens of the State.

Philip Hammond and John Pryor, who had come down from Camp Union to warn the few settlers on the Kanawha, remained in the garrison at the Point, and, in 1778, volunteered as runners to Greenbriar, to warn the citizens of the approach of the Indians, and then helped to fight them at Donnally's Fort, having passed the Indians on the way.

Mr. Robertson, one of the two soldiers who met the Indians above the Point, on the morning of the battle, and who made his escape, his companion (Hickman) having been killed, became Brigadier-General Robertson, of Tennessee.

Colonel Daniel Boone was not in the battle, but was the commander of three frontier garrisons (believed to have been the three Greenbriar Forts), to protect the citizens while the fighting men were absent with the army. He, next year, founded Boones-

borough, Ky.   He will be treated of briefly in a separate chapter.

Simon Kenton was not in the fight, but was pilot,
scout and messenger for Lord Dunmore, in connection with Simon Girty, and, on account of the friendship then formed, Girty afterwards saved his life,
when a prisoner, and after Girty had gone over to
the Indians.   Kenton was the first white man ever
to camp in, this valley (1771), and he was the first to
raise corn in Northern Kentucky.   He became
Colonel Simon Kenton, and had a most eventful
career as frontiersman, Indian fighter, etc.

Samuel McCulloch was one of Lord Dunmore's
scouts and messengers.   He was one of the bearers
of orders from Dunmore to Lewis, on the day before
the battle.   He lived to become one of the most renowned and successful Indian fighters on the Western borders.

Captain Logan, afterwards General Benjamin Logan, was with Dunmore.   He became, next year, the
founder of St. Azaph, or Logan's Fort, one of the
first permanent centers of settlement in Kentucky,
and a distinguished commander in the early Kentucky Indian troubles.

George Rogers Clark was with Dunmore; had,
probably, joined him at Wheeling, where, it is said,
he planned and laid out the Wheeling Fort, called
Fort Henry.   He went to Kentucky the following
year, where he, Boone, Harrod, Logan and Kenton,
became the founders, developers and defenders of a
great commonwealth.   A little later, General George
Rogers Clarke became the hero of Vincennes and Kas-
kaskia, among the most brilliant achievements in

history, winning for himself the proud appellation of "The Hannibal of the West."

Major (afterwards Colonel) Crawford, the unfortunate, was also with Dunmore.

William Eastham was the father of Mr. A. G. Eastham, a prominent citizen of Mason County, some time member of the West Virginia Legislature, and now, as he believes, the last surviving immediate descendant of any of the participants in the Point Pleasant battle.

The admittedly last survivor of those who personally participated in this memorable fight was Mr. Ellis Hughes, one of the remarkable family of border settlers and Indian fighters of that name. After Wayne's treaty, he and a neighbor, Radcliff, removed to Ohio, and were the first to settle in (now) Licking County. Hughes died in 1845, near Utica, aged in the nineties.

There were, probably, others connected with this memorable Point Pleasant campaign, who afterwards attained to positions of prominence or eminence in the stirring times that followed; as most of them, when disbanded, re-enlisted in the Revolutionary armies, but of whose connection with this event no record has been preserved.

While the names of those above mentioned will long be remembered and cherished with pride and pleasure by their descendants, there is one other whose "bad eminence" will ever be remembered with execration and horror.

Simon Girty had joined Dunmore at Fort Pitt and was acting as scout and pilot. He had not then turned Judas, forsworn his race and betrayed his color, kith and kin; he was an active and useful scout, and probably, up to that time, loyal to the whites.

There is a tradition that, while at the Point, with the other scouts and messengers (McCulloch and Kenton), the day before the battle, Girty made some demand of General Lewis in regard to pay for his services. General Lewis, very properly, replied that it was not his business to settle such accounts, and referred him to the proper authority; at this Girty became quite insolent to General Lewis, who rapped him severely, with his cane, over the head, and put him out of his tent. Girty left, bleeding profusely from his scalp wounds, threatening vengeance, and swearing that the camp should " run with blood " for the insult.

This incident was, doubtless, considered trifling at the time, and, in view of the tragical events of the following day, was probably very nearly lost sight of and forgotten; but, it seems highly probable, if the account of this incident be true, that Girty's defection and renegadeism dated from this time, and was probably occasioned by this unfortunate circumstance, as he very soon, if not immediately after, joined his fortunes with the Indians and the English, and became the bitter, relentless and dangerously efficient enemy of his former friends, probably causing them, directly and indirectly, more bloodshed and suffering, for the next twenty years, than any half dozen of the most bloodthirsty Indian warriors. Girty had not far to go when he "went over to the enemy;" he did but little violence to his feelings. He, with his brothers, George and James, had been captured near Fort Pitt, in their infancy or very early youth, and retained as captives eight or nine years, trained up in all the habits and imbibing the feelings and prejudices of the Indians, learning their language thoroughly, while nearly forgetting their own, acquiring a strong taste and lasting fondness for the roving, unrestrained and exciting Indian life, and thus these wild Irish lads were converted into wilder savage Indians. It has frequently been said that it is impossible to make a white man of an Indian, but very easy to make an Indian of a white man; the history of the Girtys fully illustrates the latter.

Of the Indians who participated in this memorable battle of the Point, two—Cornstalk and Logan— stand out in bold relief above all the rest. In physical development, manly beauty and intellectual capacity, they were magnificent specimens of their race. For bravery they could not be excelled, and for self-composed dignity of bearing, ease of manner and fervid eloquence they will, from the accounts we have of them, compare favorably with the best orators of any age. Mr. Jefferson, who has immortalized Logan and his touchingly eloquent speech, thought him the equal of any of the ancient Greek or Roman orators. It has been doubted by many whether Logan was the author of the speech, but it has also been doubted whether Mr. Jefferson was the author of the Declaration of Independence; whether Shakespeare or Lord Bacon wrote Hamlet; William Tell has been pronounced a myth, and Barbara Fritche is said never to have had visible, tangible existence.

15

There are always believers—always doubters. I give the speech of Logan as it was reported by Colonel John Gibson, who was with Lord Dunmore at Camp Charlotte, who claimed to have heard it direct from Logan, and vouched for its authenticity. Let those believe who can, those doubt who must. Voltaire said: "History does not *always* lie."

When Lord Dunmore was holding his peace conference with the Chiefs, at his camp, it was observed that Logan was not present. Feeling the importance of securing his assent to the terms of the treaty, Lord Dunmore sent Colonel Gibson to his tent, where he found him brooding over his wrongs. In reply to the request to attend the council, he said: "I am a warrior, not a councilor, and I will not go," but instead he sent the following speech by Colonel Gibson:

LOGAN'S SPEECH.

"I appeal to any white man to say if he ever entered Logan's cabin hungry, and he gave him not meat; if ever he came cold and naked, and he clothed him not. During the course of the last long and bloody war, Logan remained idle in his cabin, an advocate of peace. Such was my love for the whites that my countrymen pointed as they passed, and said: 'Logan is the friend of the white man.' I had even thought to live with you, but for the injuries of one man. Colonel Cresap, the last Spring, in cold blood and unprovoked, murdered all the relations of Logan, not even sparing my women and children. There runs not a drop of my blood in the veins of any living creature. This called on me for revenge. I have sought it. I have killed many ; I have glutted my vengeance. For my country, I rejoice at the beams of peace; but do not harbor a thought that mine is the joy of fear. Logan never felt fear. He will not turn on his heel to save his life. Who is there to mourn for Logan? Not one."

Logan, weighed down by his sorrows, gave himself up to intemperance, becoming a sot, and was finally murdered by a brother-in-law, on his return from a trip to Detroit.

The dominant character, not only in this Indian army, but probably throughout the Ohio tribes, at this period, was the great Shawanee chief, and king of the confederacy, Cornstalk. He was born in this valley, within the present limits of Greenbriar County, says Colonel Peyton in his "History of Augusta County."

Colonel Benjamin Wilson, who was with Lord Dunmore at Camp Charlotte, heard Cornstalk at this peace conference, and says of him:

" When he arose, he was in no wise confused or daunted, but spoke in a distinct and audible voice, without stammering or repetition, and with peculiar emphasis. His looks, while addressing Dunmore, were truly grand and majestic, yet graceful and attractive. I have heard the first orators in Virginia—Patrick Henry and Richard Henry Lee—but never have I heard one whose powers of delivery surpassed those of Cornstalk on this occasion."

Some one else present says:

" His clear, bugle voice could be distinctly heard all through the camp."

Colonel Andrew Lewis (son of General Andrew) says:

" I have often heard my father speak of his being the most dignified looking man, particularly in council, he ever saw."

That greatness and great misfortunes are apt to go together there are many examples among the illustrious names of the white race, and the histories of Cornstalk, Logan, Pontiac, Tecumseh, and others, illustrate the same rule in their race.

CHAPTER XXXV.

DEATH OF CORNSTALK.

THREE years after the battle of the Point, the brave Cornstalk, who had here led his army almost to victory, who had himself withstood the flying bullets of a thousand murderous rifles, from sunrise to sunset, and escaped; who was now here as a messenger of peace, unarmed, and trusting his life to the protection of the garrison, was foully and and shamefully murdered. The most reliable, indeed, the only reliable, account of it is that by Colonel John Stewart, who happened to be present on the occasion, and was an eye-witness of the unfortunate occurrence. I quote, entire, Colonel Stewart's account, as it also gives valuable collateral history:

"In the year 1777, the Indians, being urged by British agents, became very troublesome to frontier settlements, manifesting much appearance of hostilities, when the Cornstalk warrior, with the Red Hawk, paid a visit to the garrison at Point Pleasant. He made no secret of the disposition of the Indians, declaring that, on his own part, he was opposed to joining in the war on the side of the British, but that all the nation, except himself and his own tribe, were determined to engage in it; and that, of course, he and his tribe would have to run with the stream (as he expressed it). On this, Captain Arbuckle thought proper to detain him, the Red Hawk, and another fellow, as hostages, to prevent the nation from joining the British.

"In the course of that Summer, our Government had ordered an army to be raised, of volunteers, to serve under the command of General Hand, who was to have collected a number of troops at Fort Pitt, and, with them, to descend the river to Point Pleasant, there to meet a reinforcement of volunteers expected to be raised in Augusta and Bottetourt Counties, and then proceed to the Shawanee towns and chastise them so as to compel them to a neutrality. Hand did not succeed in the collection of troops at Fort Pitt, and but three or four companies were raised in Augusta and Bottetourt, which were under the command of Colonel George Skillern, who ordered me to use my endeavors to raise all the volunteers I could get, in Greenbriar, for the service.

"The people had begun to see the difficulties attendant on a state of war, and long campaigns carried on through wildernesses, and but a few were willing to engage in such service. But as the settlements which we covered, though less exposed to the depredations of the Indians, had showed their willingness to aid in the proposed plan to chastise the Indians, and had raised three companies, I was very desirous of doing all I could to promote the business and aid the service. I used the utmost endeavors, and proposed to the militia officers to volunteer ourselves, which would be an encouragement to others, and by such means to raise all the men who could be got.

"The chief of the officers in Greenbriar agreed to the proposal, and we cast lots who should command the company. The lot fell on Andrew Hamilton for Captain, and William Renick, Lieutenant. We collected, in all, about forty, and joined Colonel Skillern's party on their way to Point Pleasant.

"When we arrived, there was no account of General Hand or his army, and little or no provision made to support our troops, other than what we had taken with us down the Kanawha. We found, too, that the garrison was unable to spare us any supplies, having nearly exhausted, when we got there, what had been provided for themselves. But we concluded to wait there as long as we could for the arrival of General Hand, or some account from him.

"During the time of our stay, two young men, of the names of Hamilton and Gilmore, went over the Kanawha one day to hunt for deer; on their return to camp, some Indians had concealed themselves on the bank, among the weeds, to view our encampment, and as Gilmore came along past them, they fired on him and killed him on the bank.

"Captain Arbuckle and myself were standing on the opposite

bank when the gun fired, and while we were wondering who it could be shooting, contrary to orders, or what they could be doing over the river, we saw Hamilton run down the bank, who called out that Gilmore was killed.

"Gilmore was one of the company of Captain John Hall, of that part of the country now Rockbridge County. The Captain was a relative of Gilmore's, whose family and friends were chiefly cut off by the Indians in the year 1763, when Greenbriar was cut off. Hall's men instantly jumped into a canoe and went to the relief of Hamilton, who was standing in momentary expectation of being put to death. They brought the corpse of Gilmore down the bank, covered with blood and scalped, and put him into the canoe.

"As they were passing the river, I observed to Captain Arbuckle that the people would be for killing the hostages as soon as the canoe would land. He supposed that they would not offer to commit so great a violence upon the innocent, who were in no wise accessory to the murder of Gilmore; but the canoe had scarcely touched the shore until the cry was raised, 'Let us kill the Indians in the Fort,' and every man, with his gun in his hand, came up the bank, pale with rage. Captain Hall was at their head, and leader. Captain Arbuckle and I met them, and endeavored to dissuade them from so unjustifiable an action, but they cocked their guns, threatened us with instant death if we did not desist, rushed by us into the Fort, and put the Indians to death.

"On the preceding day, the Cornstalk's son, Elinipsico, had come from the nation to see his father, and to know if he was well or alive. When he came to the river, opposite the Fort, he hallooed. His father was, at that instant, in the act of delineating a map of the country and the waters between the Shawanee towns and the Mississippi, at our request, with chalk upon the floor. He immediately recognized the voice of his son, got up, went out, and answered him.

"The young fellow crossed over, and they embraced each other in the most tender and affectionate manner. The interpretor's wife, who had been a prisoner among the Indians, and had recently left them, on hearing the uproar the next day, and hearing the men threaten that they would kill the Indians, for whom she retained much affection, ran to their cabin and informed them that the people were just coming to kill them, and that because the Indians who had killed Gilmore had come with Elinipsico the day before. He utterly denied it; declared that he knew nothing of them, and trembled exceedingly.

"His father encouraged him not to be afraid, for the Great Man above had sent him there to be killed and die with him. As the men advanced to the door, the Cornstalk rose up and met them. They fired upon him, and seven or eight bullets went through him.

"So fell the great Cornstalk warrior, whose name was bestowed upon him by the consent of the nation, as their great strength and support. His son was shot dead as he sat upon a stool.

"The Red Hawk made an attempt to go up the chimney, but was shot down. The other Indian was shamefully mangled, and I grieved to see him so long in the agonies of death.

"The Cornstalk, from personal appearance and many brave acts, was undoubtedly a hero. Had he been spared to live, I believe he would have been friendly to the American cause, for nothing could induce him to make the visit to the garrison at the critical time he did but to communicate to them the temper and the disposition of the Indians, and their design of taking part with the British.

"On the day he was killed we held a council, at which he was present. His countenance was dejected, and he made a speech, all of which seemed to indicate an honest and manly disposition. He acknowledged that he and his party would have to run with the stream, for that all the Indians on the Lakes and northwardly were joining the British. He said that when he returned to the Shawanee towns, after the battle at the Point, he called a council of the nation, to consult what was to be done, and upbraided them for their folly in not suffering him to make peace on the evening before the battle. 'What,' said he, 'will you do now? The Big Knife is coming on us, and we shall all be killed. Now you must fight, or we are undone.' But no one made an answer. He said: 'Then let us kill all our women and children, and go and fight till we die.' But none would answer. At length he rose and struck his tomahawk in the post in the center of the town-house. 'I'll go,' said he, 'and make peace,' and then the warriors all grunted out, 'ough! ough! ough!' and runners were instantly dispatched to the Governor's army to solicit a peace, and the interposition of the Governor on their behalf.

"When he made his speech in council with us, he seemed to be impressed with an awful premonition of his approaching fate, for he repeatedly said: 'When I was a young man and went to war, I thought that might be the last time, and I would return no more. Now I am here among you; you may kill me if you please. I can die but once, and it is all one to me, now or another time.' This declaration concluded every sentence of his speech. He was killed about one hour after our council."

Thus fell this rude child of Nature, and denizen of the forest, who, with the lights before him, and true to the nature within him, had lived and acted well his part. His creed required an eye for an eye, blood for blood, life for life, and he had lived up to it bravely and fearlessly. He had fought for his country and his race when duty, as he saw his duty, required it; but he was a lover of peace, and a councilor of peace, when peace was practicable. He was here now, this rude savage, in the interest of peace, when he and his son, the pride of his heart, and his companion in arms, Red Hawk, were cruelly murdered by those who had been reared in the light of the eighteenth century civilization, and under the teaching and preaching of peace gospels. Which were the savages?

RED HAWK.

Kercheval, in his "History of the Valley," says, on the authority of Major Lawrence Washington, that Dr. Daniel Craig, of Winchester, met this Indian brave, Red Hawk, soon after Braddock's defeat, when Red Hawk told him that he had fired eleven well aimed shots at Washington during that memorable day, and had then desisted, believing Washington to to be under the protection of the Great Spirit, as his gun never missed its mark before.

It is related by one of the biographers of Washington that, in 1770, when at the mouth of the Kanawha, looking after his lands, he met an Indian, who gave him the same story. This was probably Red Hawk himself, though no name is given.

Cornstalk was first buried not far from the camp where he fell, near the intersection of the present Virginia and Kanawha streets, but in after years (1841) his remains were removed to the court house enclosure, where they yet remain; but, like the grave of his illustrious adversary of 1774, there is neither stone nor mound—*nothing*—to indicate the spot. I am informed by Mr. V. A. Lewis, however, a citizen of the county, and well informed in her history, that the spot is where a westward extension of the southern jail wall bisects a southern extension of the western old court house wall. Prior to the late civil war, Mr. Charles Dawson, son of the then jailor, at his own expense and pains, put a rail fence around the grave, and his sister, Miss Susan Dawson, in the kindness of her heart, planted rose bushes upon it, but during an occupation of the town by Federal troops, about 1863, they burned the rails and fences, and stock destroyed the rose bushes, since when the grave has had no care.

When General Lewis' monument shall be erected, as I predict it will be, shall not Cornstalk also be remembered, in acknowledgement of the good that was in him, and in atonement of wrong that was done him?

The directing brain and executing right arm of the great Cornstalk were stilled forever, but his blood cried aloud to his tribe and his race for revenge, and revenge they took in large measure. Who can estimate the amount of blood-shed, the number of innocent lives sacrificed, and the consequent heart-aches, all along the Virginia border, in retaliation for the wicked murder of Logan's kindred, and Cornstalk and his party? It is said that Logan, in retaliation for his wrongs, himself brought in nineteen scalps and one prisoner, and yet he was kind to that prisoner, a Mr. Robinson, and he afterwards helped Girty to save Simon Kenton's life, when Girty was about to fail. Would the slayers of his family, and of Cornstalk, have been as humane under like circumstances?

Many of the individual murders, interior raids, and attacks in force on the Forts, all along the frontier, from the Kanawha to the Monongahela, within the next year or two, were largely due to the determination, on the part of the Indians, to avenge the death of their honored chief.

When the news of Cornstalk's death, and the attendant circumstances, reached the capital, the Governor of Virginia, Patrick Henry, offered a reward for the apprehension and conviction of the guilty parties. As a result, Captain Hall and some of his men were arrested in their county (Rockbridge), and went through the forms of a pretended trial, but there was scarcely a family in that region that had not, at some time, suffered from Indian raids and murders, or had not lost friends or relatives in the battle of the Point, or other Indian wars, and their prejudices were so strong against Indians generally, that, although the facts were generally known, there was no one to prosecute, no one to testify; the trial

was a farce, and the case was dismissed by default.
Public sentiment went so far as to condemn the act,
but was not willing to punish the guilty parties.

In the Fall of 1777, not long after the death of
Cornstalk, a small party of Indians made their appearance near the Fort at Point Pleasant, and Lieutenant Moore was dispatched from the garrison, with
some men, to drive them off. Upon his advance,
they commenced retreating, and the Lieutenant,
fearing they would escape, ordered a quick pursuit.
He did not proceed far before he fell into an ambuscade. He and three of his men were killed at the
first fire; the rest of the party saved themselves by
a precipitate flight to the Fort.

In the following May (1778), a few Indians again
came in view of the Fort, but as the garrison had
been reduced by the removal of Captain Arbuckle's
company, and the experience of the last season had
taught them prudence, Captain McKee, the then
commander, forebore to detach any of his men in
pursuit of them. Disappointed in their expectations
of enticing others to destruction, as they had Lieutenant Moore in the Winter, the Indians suddenly
rose from their cover, and presented an unbroken
line, extending from the Ohio to the Kanawha River,
and in front of the Fort. A demand was then made
for the surrender of the Fort, and Captain McKee
asked till next morning to consider it. In the course
of the night the men were busily employed bringing
water from the river, expecting that the Indians
would continue before the Fort for some time.

In the morning, Captain McKee sent his answer
by the Grenadier squaw (sister to Cornstalk, and who,

notwithstanding the murder of her brother and nephew, was still attached to the whites, and was remaining at the Fort in the capacity of interpretor), that he could not comply with their demand.

The Indians immediately began the attack, and for one week kept the garrison closely besieged. Finding, however, that they made no impression on the Fort, they collected the cattle about it, and, instead of returning towards their own country with the plunder, proceeded up the Kanawha River towards the Greenbriar settlements.

Some accounts state that Captain McKee and three or four others met as many of the Indians, under a flag of truce, and had a conference. Captain McKee disclaiming for himself and garrison all part in the murder of Cornstalk, explained that it was a sudden act of lawless violence, done under excitement, deprecated and deplored by all conservative people, etc. Some of the Indians seemed satisfied and returned home, but the larger number were bent on revenge, and moved off up the Kanawha.

Satisfied that so large a force would be able to destroy these settlements, if unadvised of their approach, Captain McKee started two men to Colonel Andrew Donnally's (the then frontier house), with intelligence. These men soon came in view of the Indians, but finding that they were advancing in detached groups, and dispersed in hunting parties through the woods, they despaired of being able to pass them, and returned to the Fort.

Captain McKee then made an appeal to the chivalry of the garrison, and asked: "Who would risk his life to save the people of Greenbriar?" John

Pryor and Philip Hammond at once stepped forward and replied: "We will." They were then habited after the Indian manner, and painted in Indian style by the Grenadier squaw, and departed on their hazardous, but noble and generous, undertaking.

Traveling night and day, with great rapidity, they passed the Indians at Meadow River, where they were killing and eating some of Mr. McClung's hogs for their breakfast, and arrived, about sunset that day, at Donnally Fort, twenty miles farther on. Colonel Donnally at once had all the neighbors advised, and during the night they collected at his house. He also dispatched a messenger to Captain John Stewart, at Fort Union, to acquaint him with the facts, and made every preparation practicable to resist the attack. Pryor and Hammond explained how the precaution of Captain McKee in providing a plentiful supply of water had saved the garrison at the Point from suffering, and advised similar precaution here. Accordingly, a hogshead was filled and rolled behind the door of the kitchen, which adjoined the house.

Early next morning, John Pritchet (a servant of Colonel Donnally's) went out for some firewood, and was fired at and killed. The Indians then ran into the yard, and endeavored to force open the kitchen door, but Hammond and Dick Pointer (a negro belonging to Colonel Donnally), who were the only persons within, aided by the hogshead of water, prevented their accomplishing it. They next proceeded to cut the door in pieces with their tomahawks.

Hammond, seeing that they would soon succeed in this way, with the assistance of Dick, rolled the hogshead to one side, and, letting the door suddenly fly open, killed the Indian at the threshold, and the others who were near gave way. Dick then fired among them with a musket heavily charged with swan shot, and no doubt with effect, as the yard was crowded with the enemy. A war club with swan shot in it was afterwards picked up near the door.

The men in the house, who were asleep at the commencement of the attack, being awakened at the firing of Hammond and Dick, now opened a galling fire upon the Indians. Being chiefly upstairs, they were enabled to do greater execution, and fired with such effect that, about one o'clock, the enemy retired a short distance from the house. Before they retired, however, some of them succeeded in getting under the floor, when they were aided by the whites below, in raising some of the puncheons of which it was made. They (the whites) did this for a purpose, and profited by it. Several Indians were killed in this attempt to gain admittance, while but one white man received a wound, which but slightly injured his hand.

When intelligence was conveyed to Captain Stewart of the approach of so large a body of savages, Colonel Samuel Lewis was with him, and they both exerted themselves to save the settlement from destruction, by collecting the inhabitants at Fort Union (now Lewisburg). Having succeeded in this, they sent two men to Donnally's, to learn whether the Indians had advanced that far. As they approached, the firing became distinctly audible, and they returned with the tidings.

Captain Stewart and Colonel Lewis proposed marching to the relief Donnally's Fort with as many men as were willing to accompany them, and in a short time commenced their march with sixty-six men. Pursuing the most direct route, without regard to road, they approached the house from the rear, and thus escaped an ambuscade of Indians placed near the road to intercept and cut off any assistance which might be sent from the upper settlements.

Adjoining the yard was a field of well grown rye, into which the relief from Fort Union entered about two o'clock, but as the Indians had withdrawn to a distance from the house, there was no firing heard. They soon discovered the savages, however, in the field, looking intently towards Donnally's, and it was resolved to pass them. Captain Stewart and Charles Gatliff fired at them, and the whole party rushed into the yard, amid a heavy discharge of balls from the savage forces.

The people in the Fort, hearing the firing in the rear of the house, soon presented themselves at the port-holes to resist what they supposed was a fresh attack on them; but quickly discovering the real cause, they opened the gates, and all the party, led by Stewart and Lewis, entered safely.

The Indians then resumed the attack, and maintained a constant fire at the house until near dark, when one of them approached, and, in broken English, called out: "Me want peace." He was told to come in and he should have it; but he declined the invitation to enter, and they all retreated, dragging off those of their slain who lay not too near the Fort.

Of the whites, only four were killed by the enemy—

Pritchet before the attack commenced, James Burns
and Alexander Ochiltree as they were coming to the
house, early in the 'morning, and James Graham,
through a port-hole, while in the Fort. It was impossible to ascertain the entire loss of the Indians.
Seventeen lay dead in the yard, and they were known
to have carried off others of their slain.

There were twenty-one men at Donnally's before
the arrival of the reinforcements under Stewart and
Lewis, and the brunt of the battle was over before
they came. The Indian force exceeded two hundred men.

It was believed that the invasion of the Greenbriar
country had been projected some time before it was
actually made. During the preceding season an Indian, calling himself John Hollis, had been very
much through the settlements, and was observed to
take particular notice of the different Forts, which
he entered under the garb of friendship. He was
with the Indians in the attack on Donnally's Fort,
and was recognized as one of those who were left
dead in the yard.

On the morning after the Indians departed, Captain Hamilton went in pursuit of them with seventy
men, but following two days, without perceiving that
he gained on them, he abandoned the chase and returned.

After this unsuccessful attack on Donnally's Fort,
the Greenbriar settlements were not again molested
until sometime in 1780, when a party of twenty-two
warriors made a raid into that country. The first
act of atrocity committed was at the house of Lawrence Drennon, above the Little Levels. Here they

shot Henry Baker and Richard Hill. Baker was killed, but Hill escaped into the house.

Mr. Drennon dispatched a messenger to the Little Levels for assistance. He soon returned with twenty men, who remained all night, but next morning, seeing nothing of the Indians, and supposing they had departed, they buried Baker, and, with Drennon and family, started to the Levels. Two brothers, named Bridges, to save distance, took a narrow pathway, which the Indians had waylaid, supposing the whites would go that way. They were both killed.

The Indians next proceeded to the house of Hugh McIver, whom they killed, and made his wife prisoner.

In going from here, they met John Pryor and his wife and child, on their way to the south side of the Kanawha. Pryor was shot through the breast, but, anxious for the fate of his wife and child, stood still, till one of the Indians came up and laid hold of him. Notwithstanding the severe wound he had received, Pryor proved too strong for his opponent, and disengaged himself from him. Pryor then, seeing that no violence was offered his wife or child, walked off without any attempt being made to stop or otherwise molest him. The Indians, it was supposed, suffered him to depart, expecting that he would obtain assistance and endeavor to regain his wife and child, and that an opportunity would be given them of waylaying any party coming with this view. Pryor returned to the settlement, related the facts above mentioned, and died that night. His wife and child were never again heard of. It was supposed that they were murdered by the Indians on the way,

16

being unable to travel as rapidly as the Indians wished.

Thus, at last, perished the brave John Pryor and his family. He was a noble fellow and deserved a better fate. I can not learn what became of Philip Hammond, his partner in danger, and equal in daring and endurance. They deserve to be remembered by their country.

This party of Indians next went to a house occupied by Thomas Drennon and a Mr. Smith, and captured Mrs. Drennon, Mrs. Smith and a child. Thence, going towards their homes, they wounded Captain Samuel McClung, and killed an old man named Monday.

Withers, to whom, chiefly, I am indebted for this account, says this was the last murder committed by them in the Greenbriar settlements, but there was at least one other instance of murder. During the same season, Mr. William Griffith, his wife and daughter, were killed, and a son, a lad, taken prisoner. In passing through the Kanawha Valley, some hunters got on their trail. Mr. Atkinson says that John Young, Ben Morris, Bob Aaron, William Arbuckle, and two others, followed them across to Elk, up Little Sandy and branches, towards Poca, and discovered their camp. There were but two men and a boy. They fired and killed one man, the second man took to his heels, and the boy was unhurt. The man killed proved to be a white man painted as an Indian, the man who escaped was an Indian, and the boy was the captive Griffith lad.

The stream on which this incident occurred is, to this day, called White Man's Fork of Aaron's Fork of Little Sandy.

HANNAH DENNIS AND GREENBRIAR SETTLEMENTS.

In 1760, a party of Shawanees made a raid by way of the Kanawha and Greenbriar Rivers, then unsettled, over to the then frontier settlement in that direction, on Jackson's River. They killed several persons, among them Robert Renix and Thomas Dennis, and took a number of prisoners, among them Mrs. Hannah Dennis, and Mrs. Renix and her five children. They were pursued by a party of whites, under Captain Matthews; they were overtaken, and in the engagement that followed nine Indians and three whites were killed, but the remainder of the Indians made good their escape, with their prisoners. In accordance with the stipulations of Colonel Boquet's treaty, Mrs. Renix and her sons, William and Robert, were returned to their friends in 1765. William and Robert became prominent citizens of Greenbriar; another son, Thomas, came in, in 1783, but returned and settled on the Scioto. Joshua never returned; he married an Indian wife, became a Miami Chief, and rich and influential among the tribe. The daughter, Betsy, died in captivity.

Mrs. Hannah Dennis was separated from the other captives and allotted to live at the Chillicothe towns. She learned their language, she dressed and painted herself as they did, and conformed to their manners and customs. Finding them very superstitious, she professed witchcraft, and claimed to be a prophetess. She was attentive to the sick and wounded, and soon became a great favorite with them, and acquired great influence over them. She was all the while meditating an escape, and awaiting a favorable opportunity.

At last, in June, 1763, she made a start; she was pursued, but, after many hair-breadth escapes, she reached the mouth of Kanawha, where she crossed the Ohio on a drift log, and then made her way up Kanawha and Greenbriar Rivers. She traveled chiefly by night to avoid discovery, and lived upon river muscles, green grapes, herbs, etc. She finally sat down by Greenbriar River utterly exhausted with fatigue and hunger, and gave up, thinking it impossible to proceed any farther. Here she was found by Thomas Athol and three others, who took her to Archibald Clendenin's house, where she was kindly cared for, and, when sufficiently recuperated to travel, was sent on horseback to Young's Fort, on Jackson's River, and to her relations.

At this time there were but two settlements in the Greenbriar country; these were on Muddy Creek and the Big Levels, and the two contained about twenty families, or, say, one hundred souls of all ages. Within a few days after Hannah Dennis had left Clendenin's, in the Muddy Creek settlement, about sixty Indian warriors made their appearance, led by the afterwards distinguished Cornstalk. They came professing friendship, and, as the French and English war had but recently been terminated by treaty of peace, the settlers did not doubt their sincerity, and treated them with hospitable kindness; when, suddenly, they fell upon the unsuspecting whites and killed every man, and killed or made every woman and child prisoners. They then hurried on to the Big Levels, fifteen miles distant, where the same treacherous and murderous scenes were re-enacted. Mr. Archibald Clendenin had just returned from a successful hunt, bringing in three fine elk, upon which they had a glorious feast, and after which, at a concerted signal, the massacre was executed upon their helpless victims. Thus, within a few hours, two prosperous and happy settlements were exterminated.

Only Conrad Yolkum, out of the one hundred persons in both settlements, escaped death or capture by timely flight. The brave Mrs. Clendenin, as below related, made her escape from captivity, but with the sacrifice of her infant child.

At Clendenin's, a negro woman, who was endeavoring to escape, was followed by her crying child. To facilitate her own escape, and to prevent the child falling into Indian hands, she stopped and murdered it herself.

Mrs. Clendenin, who seems to have been a woman of fearless nerve and strong force of character, boldly denounced the Indians for their perfidy and treachery, alleging that cowards only could act with such duplicity. To silence her, they slapped her face with the bloody scalp of her husband, and raised a tomahawk in a threatening attitude over her head; but she was not to be silenced nor intimidated. She would not hold her peace, nor her tongue.

In passing over Keeny's Knobs, on the retreat, the Indians being in the front and rear, and the prisoners in the center, Mrs. Clendenin handed her infant to another woman to hold, and she slipped aside in the brush, and succeeded in making her escape. The crying of the child soon led to the discovery of her absence, when one of the Indians, observing that he could "bring the cow to her calf," took it by its heels and beat its brains out against a tree.

Mrs. Clendenin returned to her home, about ten miles distant, that night. She covered the remains of her husband with brush, and weeds, and fence-rails, to protect it from the wild beasts, and after an effort to get some rest and sleep in an adjoining corn-field, tortured by visions of murderers and murders, she resumed her flight and finally reached, in safety, the settlements on Jackson's River.

These melancholy events, occurring so immediately after the escape of Mrs. Hannah Dennis, whom they were so unwilling to lose, induced the supposition that the raid was made in pursuit of her. If such were the fact, dearly were others made to pay the penalty of her fortunate deliverance.

CHAPTER XXXVI.

BELIEVING that dates, systematically arranged, very much aid the general reader in understanding the relation of facts to each other and help the memory to retain them, I herewith give a table of dates, chronologically arranged, of the more important and interesting events that have occurred all along the Western Virginia border, but more especially along the New-River-Kanawha and tributaries.

To get early historical dates with accuracy is no easy task, as those who have tried it know. This trouble arises from the fact—heretofore stated—that those who made the history did not themselves record it, at the time. This was generally done years after, either by themselves, or by their friends from their dictation, after the dates—never much regarded by them—had become somewhat dim and uncertain.

"IN AN EARLY DAY."

Those who have enjoyed the pleasure of listening to the interesting traditions of old, as related by the lingering members of the rear guard of a generation now past and gone, those whose experiences dated back to the primitive days of border life, can not fail

to remember how often they used this almost stereo-
typed phrase in recounting the incidents of "the
long, long ago," away back in the dim distant past.
"The good old times," which they remembered with
so much interest and pleasure, forgetting, or but
dimly remembering, the dangers and hardships
which accompanied their daring but successful, and
therefore pleasurable, adventures.

Their goings and comings and their doings were
not guided by fixed rules nor programmes, nor
cramped and fettered by cold records. They had a
contempt for calenders and a negligent disregard of
dates.

Facts they remembered, and could relate with
minutest detail; but they neither knew nor cared
whether the events related occurred five, or ten, or
twenty years earlier or later; all that they knew or
cared to remember was, that they occurred "in an
early day"—in the dim, indefinite and distance-
enchanted past.

I have taken great pains, however, to examine and
compare dates, as given by all the authorities,
records, traditions and other sources available to me,
and believe that the accuracy of those given below
may be relied on with reasonable certainty.

1654. Colonel Abraham Wood was the first to
cross the Blue Ridge, and the first to discover New
River, and to name it "Wood's River."

1666. Captain Henry Batte was the next to cross
the Blue Ridge. It is possible that he was in the
Kanawha Valley, as he says he followed a westerly
flowing river for several days to near where a tribe
of Indians made salt.

1716. Governor Spottswood crossed the Blue Ridge with his Knights of the Golden Horse Shoe; and, seeming to be ignorant of the two preceding expeditions mentioned, claimed the honor of being the first to cross it, and was knighted for the feat. He crossed at Swift Run Gap, and not at Rock Fish Gap as generally stated.

1726. Morgan Morgan, a Welshman, is said to have been the first white man to settle and build a house west of the Blué Ridge and south of the Potomac.

1727. Cornstalk was born in this valley. Colonel J. L. Peyton, in his valuable history of Augusta County, says he was born 1747, within the present limits of Greenbriar County, but the date is wrong by twenty years. His son, Elinipsico, was a commanding officer under him at the battle of Point Pleasant.

1730. John Salling, captured on James River, crossed New River on his way to the Cherokee towns. He was probably the first white man to cross it.

1732. Joist Hite, John Lewis and others first settled the valley of Virginia.

1734. Orange County was formed, and embraced all Virginia territory west of the Blue Ridge.

1735–6. Christian, Beverly, Patton, Preston, Borden and others, made settlements in this valley of Virginia.

1736. John Salling, above mentioned, who had escaped after six years captivity, made a settlement at the forks of the James River, below the Natural Bridge, the first settlement on James River, west of the Blue Ridge.

1738.   Augusta County was formed, but was not organized until 1745.

Staunton was laid out and commenced building, and Winchester had but two houses.

1744.   Rapin DeThoyer's map issued, giving wild guesses at the geography of the Great West.

1748.   Dr. Thomas Walker and party crossed New River westward and were the first, from this direction, to penetrate into Kentucky.

Draper's Meadows settlement made by Ingles and Draper.

1749.   The Loyal Land Company, organized by Walker, Patton and others, based on a grant of 800,000 acres of land, lying north of the North Carolina line and west of the mountains.

In April, first Indian depredation west of the Alleghenies, upon Adam Harmon, one of the Draper's Meadows settlers.

A lunatic from about Winchester wandered across the mountains westwards.   He was much surprised to find the waters flowing westward and reported the fact on his return.

1749.   Captain De Celeron, a French engineer, planted an inscribed leaden plate at the mouth of Kanawha, claiming all the country drained by the River for the French crown.

1750.   William Ingles and Mary Draper were married, at Draper's Meadows, the first white wedding west of the Alleghenies.

Jacob Marlin and Stephen Sewell, influenced by the account of the lunatic above mentioned, came out and settled on the waters of Greenbriar, in what is now Pocahontas County.   They occupied the same camp for a time in peace and harmony; but, one being a Catholic and the other a Protestant, they quarreled on religious subjects and separated; the seceder taking up his abode in a hollow tree, within speaking distance of his late associate. Every morning, when they got up, they exchanged salutations across the way, and that was the last communication of the day. They were thus found by Colonel John Lewis, who came to survey lands on the Greenbriar, in 1751. Soon after this, Marlin returned to the settlements; Sewell came, alone, down to New River, about Sewell Mountain and Creek, which bear his name, and was there killed by the Indians.

Dr. Thomas Walker made his second trip with a second party, crossing New River and going up Peak Creek, Cripple Creek, Reed Creek, over to Holston, to Clinch, to Cumberland Gap, etc. Returning, he came along the Flat Top Mountain, by the present site of Pocahontas, down Blue Stone to New River, down New River to Greenbriar, up Greenbriar and Anthony's Creek, over the mountains, and by the Hot and Warm Springs, home.

1751. Thomas Ingles born at Draper's Meadows; the first white child born west of the Alleghenies.

Colonel John Lewis and son, Andrew, surveying lands on Greenbriar River, which they so name from the green briars which greatly annoyed them in their surveying; and the county was named from the river.

1752. Peter Fontaine, a surveyor, by order of the Governor of Virginia, made a map, giving what was then known of the Western part of the State. See map.

"The Ohio Land Company" established a station

at the mouth of Red-stone Creek, on the Monongahela, the extreme Northwestern post at that date.
It was built of stone.

1753. Colonel James Patton and William Ingles
taking up lands, under the " Loyal Land Company,"
on Peak Creek and in Burke's Garden.

Frazier, an Indian trader, erects a little cabin on
the Monongahela, ten miles from the mouth.

1753–54. George Washington, accompanied by
Christopher Gist and others, was the bearer of a
communication from the Governor of Virginia to the
commander of the French forts in the Northwest.
He says that Frazier's cabin, above mentioned, was
then "the ultima thule of Western settlement."

1754. The Ohio Land Company, and a force of
Virginia militia, commence fortifying the forks of
the Ohio (Duendaga), as advised by Washington, but
were driven off by a superior force of French.

Washington surprises a party of French, under
Captain Joumonville, near Great Meadows. The
commander was killed and the entire party killed or
captured. This was the first blood shed that
launched the long French and English war of both
continents, that resulted in the loss of Canada to the
French, and her other American claims east of the
Mississippi.

Washington was compelled to capitulate to a
superior French force, at Fort Necessity, which he
had hastily fortified.

Ingles' Ferry located and settlements about it
begun.

James Burke settles in Burke's Garden and is murdered by Indians.

Two families settle on Back Creek, opposite Draper's Meadows.

James Reed settles and names the first "Dublin," of this neighborhood. (See history of Dublin, Pulaski County.)

A McCorkle family (Dunkards) settle at Dunkard Bottom, near Ingles' Ferry.

Two families settle on Cripple Creek, a few miles above.

One family settles at or near the head of Reed Creek.

All these being on the west side of New River.

Christopher Gist made a settlement at the foot of Laurel Hill, not far from where Uniontown, Pa., now stands.

David Tygart and a Mr. Files settled near each other, on an eastern branch of the Monongahela, since known as Tygart's Valley River. Files settled at the mouth of a creek, where Beverly, the county seat of Randolph, now stands, and Tygart a few miles higher up the river. They had not been here a great while when they concluded that it was not safe, and determined to go back to nearer the border settlements; but before they had found it convenient to do so, the family of Files was attacked by Indians, and every member killed, except a son, who was absent from the house, but within hearing and sight of the terrible massacre. He fled to the house of Tygart, and the timely warning given by him enabled the Tygart family to escape and leave the country.

1755. Simon Girty and his brothers, George and James, were captured at Girty's Run, not far from Fort Du Quesne.

Draper's Meadows settlement attacked, and all present massacred or captured.

Braddock's disastrous defeat near Fort Du Quesne.

Mary Ingles and Bettie Draper, the first white persons ever in Kanawha Valley.

Mrs. Ingles and Mrs. Draper help make the first salt ever made by white persons in Kanawha, or elsewhere west of the Alleghenies.

1756. Settlements again made west of New River.

Vass' Fort built under direction of Captain Hogg, and advice of Colonel George Washington.

A Stockade Fort built at Draper's Meadows, under direction of Captain Stalnaker.

Vass' Fort captured by a party of French and Indians, and the inmates murdered or taken prisoners.

The Big Sandy expedition, under Major Andrew Lewis, was made.

1757. Another Big Sandy expedition was projected, but afterwards abandoned.

The New River Lead Mines were discovered by Colonel Chiswell, and operations begun.

Daniel Boone married on the Yadkin, North Carolina, and settled on the head of the Holston, Virginia.

1758. Fort Du Quesne captured by General Forbes, and called Fort Pitt; two hundred of Washington's command left to garrison the place.

Fort Chiswell, in (now) Wythe County, Va., built under direction of Colonel William Byrd.

Dr. Thomas Eckerly and two brothers, from Pennsylvania, settle on the Monongahela, eight or ten miles below the present site of Morgantown. The Eckerlys were Dunkards, and the creek at the mouth of which they settled was named Dunkard's Creek. From this point the Eckerlys explored the surrounding country, and ultimately selected and settled on a fine bottom on Cheat River, which they called Dunkard Bottom. Here they built a cabin, planted and raised corn, vegetables, etc., got their supplies of meat by their guns, and their clothes from skins and furs; they had lived here in this way, for some years, in peace and quiet, when it became necessary to visit the settlements to procure a supply of ammunition and other necessaries. Dr. Eckerly took a pack of furs and skins and went to a trading post on the Shenandoah. On his return, upon getting in sight of where his cabin had stood, he saw but a pile of ashes. On approaching nearer, he found the mutilated and decaying remains of his brothers in the yard, and the hoops upon which their scalps had been dried lying near. After burying the remains of his unfortunate brothers, the doctor returned to the settlements on the south bank of the Potomac.

Thomas Decker, and others, settled on the Monongahela, at the mouth of a creek, now called Decker's Creek.

1759. This Decker settlement was broken up, and nearly every one killed. One of the party, who escaped, made his way to Fort Red-stone and reported the disaster. Captain Paul, the commander, dispatched a runner, with information, to Captain John Gibson, at Fort Pitt. He left the Fort under command of Lieutenant Williamson, and, taking thirty men, attempted to intercept the raiding party on their return to their towns. He did not find the party he was seeking, but came on a party of Min-

goes on Cross Creek, near where Steubenville now
stands. In an engagement which followed, Kiskepila,
or Little Eagle, a prominent Mingo Chief, and Captain Gibson came into close quarters. Captain Gibson, being a very powerful man, entirely severed the
head of Little Eagle from his body with one stroke
of his sword. This was a novel experience to the
Indians, and they fled precipitately, two others being
shot down. Upon reaching their towns, they reported that the white Captain had cut off the head
of Little Eagle with a "long knife." This gave to
the Virginia militia generally the name of the "Long
Knives," or the "Big Knife Nation."

A more substantial and defensible Fort was built
at Fort Pitt.

A Fort was built at Red-stone, under direction of
Colonel Byrd; also, a number of smaller Forts for
local defense. Among them were Westfall's and
Cassino's, on Tygart's Valley River; Prickett's, on
Prickett's Creek; Jackson's, on Ten Mile Creek;
Shepherd's, on Wheeling Creek; Nutter's, near
Clarksburg, and several others.

1760. An Indian raiding party surprised by William Ingles, and others, near Ingles' Ferry; six or
seven Indians killed, and a few escaped. One white
man killed. This was the *last* Indian raid or trouble
that occurred in that region.

Selim, the Algerine, of remarkable history, passed
up the Kanawha Valley in search of the white settlements to the East. Selim was a wealthy and edu-
cated young Algerine; he was captured in the Med-
iterranean by Spanish pirates; was sold to a Louisiana planter, escaped, made his way up the Missis-

sippi, and up the Ohio. Somewhere below the
Kanawha he met with some white prisoners; and a
woman among them told him, as best she could in
sign language, to go towards the rising sun, and he
would find white settlements. As it was just about
this time that an Indian raid had been made through
this valley over to the Jackson's River settlements,
and captured the Renix family and Mrs. Hannah
Dennis, I think it is possible, and even probable, that
they were the prisoners he met, and who told him of
the Eastern settlements. At any rate, he turned up
Kanawha, then Greenbriar, etc., and was finally discovered, nearly entirely naked, and on the point of
starvation, not far from Warm Springs, and kindly
taken care of. Through a Greek Testament in possession of some minister who saw him, it was discovered that he was a good Greek scholar; and thus
communication was opened up between him and the
minister, who understood Greek. Selim studied
English, became a Christian, returned to his home in
Algiers, was repudiated by his parents because he
had given up the Moslem for the Christian religion.
He returned to America, heart-broken, and finally
died in an insane hospital.

1761. The Cherokee war was terminated.

John and Samuel Pringle, William Childers and
Joseph Linsey deserted from the garrison at Fort
Pitt; they went up the Monongahela to the mouth
of George's Creek, where Albert Gallatin afterwards
founded New Geneva; after remaining here a while,
they crossed over to the Glades of the Youghiogheny,
where they remained a year or so. Making a trip to
the settlements on South Branch, Childers and Linsey

17

were captured as deserters, but the Pringles escaped and returned to the Glades.

1762. Archibald Clendenin, and others, settled on Muddy Creek and the Big Levels, now Greenbriar County.

Ingles' Ferry established by law—the first on New or Kanawha Rivers.

1763. Mrs. Hannah Dennis, having escaped from Indian captivity, made her way up through this Valley, and, after great suffering, reached the Muddy Creek settlement.

Soon after this, a large Indian raiding party, under Cornstalk, passed up the valley to Greenbriar, and exterminated the Muddy Creek and Big Levels settlements.

Final treaty of peace between the French and English, at Paris.

1764. John and Samuel Pringle explored the Valley River and the Buchanan Branch; finally settled at the mouth of Turkey Creek, taking up their abode in a hollow sycamore tree, where the town of Buchanan, Upshur County, now stands, while Hacker, and others, settled a little higher up the river.

John Simpson, who had hunted and trapped all over this region, discovered and named Simpson's Creek. Going thence, westwardly, he got over on to a stream he called Elk, at the mouth of which he camped and where he remained till permanent settlements were made in the vicinity and Clarksburg started.

Captain Paul, pursuing a returning raiding party of Indians with prisoners, surprised them in camp at the mouth of Indian Creek, on New River, killed several and recovered the prisoners.

Matthew Arbuckle, a hunter and trapper from the Greenbriar region, passed down the Kanawha Valley with peltries, to a trading post at the mouth, and returned, being the first white man to do so.

Colonel Boquet's expedition into Ohio, against the Indians, recovered about three hundred prisoners, mostly from the Virginia frontiers.

1765. Sir William Johnson's treaty of peace with the Indians, the result of the Boquet campaign.

Settlements were rapidly made in the Northwest, especially about Redstone, upon the conclusion of this treaty of peace. Michael Cresap owned three hundred acres, and built the first house.

1766. Butler and Carr hunted and trapped about the heads of Bluestone and Clinch.

Colonel James Smith, Joshua Horton, Uriah Stone and William Baker passed by New River and Holston settlements, and explored the country between the Cumberland and Tennessee Rivers.

1767. Butler, Carr, and others, settled families about the heads of Clinch and Bluestone.

Adam Ice, and others, had a settlement at Ice's Ferry, on Cheat River; Adam Ice, Jr., was born there.

1768. The Pringle brothers brought out, as settlers, John, Edward and George Jackson, Hacker, Hughes, Radcliffe, and others, and they located on Buchanan River, Turkey Run, Hacker's Creek, Bushy Fork, etc.

Jacob Van Meter, John Swan, Thomas Hughes, and others, settled on Muddy Creek, of Monongahela, the site of the present Carmichaelstown.

David and Zackwell Morgan settled at the mouth

of Decker's Creek, where the Deckers had been killed, in 1759, remained a while and left, to return later.

Tennessee first began to be settled.

1768–69.   George Washington, R. H. Lee, F. L. Lee and Arthur Lee petition King George for two and a half million acres of Western lands, for "The Mississippi Company."

1769.   Ebenezer, Silas and Jonathan Zane were out locating lands about the mouth of Wheeling Creek.

A man named Tygart had then a solitary cabin on the river, below Wheeling Creek.   His history and fate are unknown.   Could he have been the same Tygart who settled in Tygart's Valley, in 1754?

John Stewart, Robert McClennahan, Thomas Rennix and William Hamilton settled in the Greenbriar country, about where Frankfort now is.

Daniel Boone, John Finley, and others, go to Kentucky.

Richard and Hancock Taylor, and others, were the first to go by water from Fort Pitt to the mouth of the Mississippi River.

The Pringles brought in other settlers from the North Branch of the Potomac and located them in the now Beverly region.

1770.   The Pringle colony brought out their families, and their settlements were permanently established.   These Pringles, starting out into the wilderness, originally, as deserters and fugitives, had been the most active and useful men in the Northwest, in exploring the wilderness, locating settlements, and bringing in colonies.

Joseph Tomlinson and brother, and Mrs. Rebecca Williamson, their sister, made the first actual settlement on the Ohio River, below Fort Pitt, at the mouth of Grave Creek, the present site of Moundsville.

David Morgan, who had been at Decker's Creek (Morgantown), in 1768, with Prickett, Hall, Ice, and others, settled at Prickett's Creek, now Monongalia County, five miles below Fairmount.

Captain James Boothe and John Thomas settled on Boothe's Creek, a branch of the West Fork, and site of Boothesville, above Fairmount.

George Washington, says Collins (History of Kentucky), surveyed for John Fry 2,084 acres of land at the forks of Big Sandy, the present site of Louisa. Washington was also at the mouth of Kanawha the same year, looking after his own lands, and his agent, Colonel Crawford, is said to have been with him.

Camp Union, or Fort Savannah (now Lewisburg), was built.

Captain (afterwards Colonel) Knox's party of "long hunters" hunted in Southwest Virginia and Kentucky.

1771. Kenton, Yeager and Strader, the first white men to camp in Kanawha Valley, settled about the mouth of Two-Mile Creek of Elk River.

Absalom Looney, from Looney's Creek, on James River, settled in Abb's Valley, on the Bluestone.

1771–72. Colonel Andrew Donnally built "Donnally's Fort;" Colonel John Stewart, "Fort Spring;" and Captain Jarrett, the " Wolf Creek " or " Jarrett's Fort," all in the Greenbriar country.

1772.   Daniel Davidson settled the *first family* on the present site of Clarksburg; Nutter, Cottrail, Beard, Hickman, and others in the vicinity.

The medicinal virtues of the Greenbriar white sulphur waters first tested by the whites.   It had long been a famous elk and deer lick, among the Indians.

John Powers, James Anderson and Jonas Webb settled along Simpson's Creek, a branch of the West Fork of the Monongahela, now Harrison County.

Settlements were made in Tygart's Valley by Hadden, Riffle, Connelly, Whiteman, Westfall, and others, and there were large accessions, this year, to the Buchanan and Hacker's Creek settlements.

Captain James Parsons settled at the "Horse Shoe," on Cheat River, and near him Robert Cunningham, Henry Fink, John Goff and John Minear; and Robert Butler, William Morgan, and others, at "Dunkard Bottom."

A German, named Stroud, settled in the Glades of Gauley River, where his family were murdered by the Indians.

Indian Captain Bull and five families, living at Bull-town, Little Kanawha, were murdered by William White and William Hacker, in retaliation for the Stroud massacre.

Zackwell Morgan returned with his family, and made a permanent settlement at the mouth of Decker's Creek, the present site of Morgantown.

1772–73.   The Tomlinsons bring out their families to Grave Creek, and, soon after, the Zanes, McCullochs, Wetzels and Shephard bring their families to Wheeling Creek.

1773.   John Doddridge, George Lefler, Benjamin

Briggs, Daniel Greathouse, Joshua Baker and Andrew Swearengen settled above Wheeling Creek, on Short Creek, Buffalo Creek, and vicinity.

Tradition (from Ballinger, the recluse,) of the highest water ever known in New River or Kanawha.

Boone, with several families, started to Kentucky; were attacked by Indians, near Cumberland Mountains, several killed, and the trip delayed till 1775. Boone took his family to the Clinch settlement.

Walter Kelly, a refugee from South Carolina, settled at the mouth of a creek nineteen miles above Charleston, now Kelly's Creek.

Colonel Thomas Bullitt, Thomas Alsbury, Joshua Morris, John Campbell, and, perhaps, others, were in this valley, looking up lands.

Kenton, Yeager and Strader were attacked at their Two-mile camp by Indians, Yeager being killed, and the other two wounded.

The McAfee brothers, McCown, Adams, and others, from the New River settlements, joined by Colonel Bullitt, Hancock Taylor, and others, on Kanawha, go to Kentucky to locate and survey lands. Bullitt surveyed Big Bone Lick, July 5th; McAfee brothers and Hancock Taylor, the site of Frankfort, July 15th; and Bullitt, the site of Louisville, August 5th.

John and Peter Van Bibber, Rev. Joseph Alderson, and another (probably Matthew Arbuckle), came down through the Kanawha Valley from the Wolf Creek Fort.

The Kanawha Burning Spring was first discovered by these parties, on this trip.

Fort Pitt was abandoned by the English Government, and was taken possession of by Dr. Connelly, in the name of Virginia, and called "Fort Dunmore."

Captains Thomas Hedges and Thomas Young surveyed a tract of land, and built an "improvers' cabin," on the Ohio River, five miles below where Augusta, Kentucky, now stands. They had to abandon it, but Captain Hedges returned to it in 1775. This, says Collins, was the *first* cabin built within the limits of Kentucky.

1774. Captain Cresap sold his house and land at Redstone to the Brown brothers, who founded Brownsville, and he (Cresap) settled on the Ohio, near the mouth of Little Kanawha.

Captain James Harrod, Abram Hite, James and Jacob Sandusky, and about forty others, came by boat from Redstone to Kentucky, to secure land and build "improvers' cabins."

William Morris settled at the mouth of Kelly's Creek, on Kanawha, Leonard Morris at the mouth of Slaughter's Creek, John Flinn on Cabin Creek, and Thomas Alsbury, and perhaps others, at points lower down.

The family of John Lybrook, on Sinking Creek, now Giles County, was attacked by Indians; five of the children were murdered, and Lybrook narrowly escaped by secreting himself in a cave.

In the same neighborhood, Jacob and John Snidow, and a smaller brother, were captured and taken to the Indian country. Jacob and John made their escape and returned, not long after; but the boy remained among them until he was completely Indianized; and, although he afterwards came home on a visit, he returned to the Indians and spent his life with them.

A Miss Margaret McKinsie was, also, captured; she remained a prisoner eighteen years, when she was recovered and returned to New River; she married a Mr. Benjamin Hall, and lived to a very old age.

In April of this year, several unfortunate murders occurred on the Upper Ohio, by the Indians, by Cresap, and by Greathouse, which, it is believed, were largely instrumental in precipitating the war which culminated, the following Fall, in the battle of Point Pleasant, and treaty of Camp Charlotte.

When a general outbreak seemed inevitable, the Governor of Virginia, in June, dispatched Colonel Angus McDonald, with four hundred Virginia militia, to penetrate the country north of the Ohio, to hold the Indians in check, while he (Governor Dunmore) and General Lewis were arranging and preparing a more formidable campaign, to follow, later.

The Wheeling Fort—first called "Fort Fincastle," and, afterwards, "Fort Henry"—was built. It is said to have been planned by George Rogers Clarke.

Governor Dunmore dispatched Daniel Boone and Michael Storer to Kentucky, to warn the surveying parties, land hunters and settlers, of the impending danger.

Captain Stewart, of Greenbriar, was notified, and he dispatched runners (tradition says Hammond and Pryor) to notify the few settlers on Kanawha.

Walter Kelly was killed at the mouth of Kelly's Creek (Kanawha), Colonel Field narrowly escaping.

General Lewis' army, about eleven hundred strong, left Camp Union (now Lewisburg), September 11th, piloted by Captain Matthew Arbuckle.

Daniel Boone left in command of three frontier garrisons (probably Camp Union, Donnally's Fort, and Wolf Creek or Jarrett's Fort).

The first Continental Congress met at Philadelphia, September 5th, and passed strong resolutions of resistance to, and non-intercourse with, the English Government.

General Lewis' army arrived at Point Pleasant, September 30th.

October 9th, three messengers arrive in camp, with dispatches from Lord Dunmore, changing the plans of the campaign. No one authority mentions the names of all the messengers, but McCulloch, Kenton and Girty, one by one, are mentioned by several authors, and I have seen no other names mentioned by any.

There is a tradition that, for some insolence on the part of Girty, on this occasion, General Lewis caned him over the head and drove him out of his tent.

October 10th, the ever-memorable battle of Point Pleasant was fought.

October 12th, General Lewis crossed his army over the Ohio, and started to join Lord Dunmore before the Indian towns.

Captain Matthew Arbuckle was left in care and command of the wounded and the garrison at the Point.

1774–75. Augusta County, Va., held courts alternately at Staunton and Fort Pitt. The latter was still considered to be part of Virginia territory, and, as such, a part of Augusta County.

1775. Boone cut the Boone trail, or wilderness road, from Long Island, in Holston, into Kentucky.

Boone, Harrod, Kenton and Logan founded permanent settlements in Kentucky.

Generals Washington and Lewis "took up" two hundred and fifty acres of land at and embracing the famous Kanawha Burning Spring.

Rev. Joseph Alderson cut out the first wagon road across the mountains as far west as the Greenbriar.

Thomas Ingles settled on Wolf Creek.

1776. Virginia defined the boundaries of "West Augusta," and then divided it into three counties— Ohio, Monongalia and Youghiogheny. When the disputed Pennsylvania and Virginia State boundaries were settled, Youghiogheny County was abolished, and the lines of the other two conformed to the new State line.

Colonel Christian, in an expedition against the Cherokees, burned their towns, and compelled them to sue for peace.

Robert Hughes, the first settler at the mouth of Hughes Creek, Kanawha, was captured by Indians, and remained two years a prisoner.

General Andrew Lewis, in command of the Virginia troops, drove Lord Dunmore, and his fleet and rabble, from Gwyne's Island, with heavy loss, soon after which Dunmore left the country.

1777. At Black's Cabin, on Short Creek, Ohio County, January 6th, was organized the first civil court in the Mississippi Valley.

John Finley, the long-time frontiersman and wilderness pilot, being old, and poor, and wounded, asks Washington County, Va., for aid.

Cornstalk, Elinipsico, Red Hawk, and another Indian, murdered at Point Pleasant.

Desperate attack on Fort Henry (Wheeling) by three hundred Indians. All earlier historians say they were led by Simon Girty, but McKnight, and later athorities, think Girty was not present at this siege.

Authorities, also, differ as to whether the heroic and famous gunpowder feat occurred at the first or second siege of Fort Henry, with the probabilities in favor of the second. Authorities, also, differ as to whether Bettie Zane or Mollie Scott was the true heroine.

The brave, but unfortunate, Captain Foreman, and his party, were destroyed at Grave Creek Narrows.

Augusta, Bottetourt and Greenbriar volunteers, under Colonel Skillern, march to Point Pleasant, to join forces under General Hand, from Fort Pitt, but Hand's forces did not arrive.

Lieutenant Moore, and three men, killed by a small party of Indians, near the Fort, at Point Pleasant—Fort Randolph.

1778. Virginia declared Colonel Henderson's land purchases and Transylvania operations in Kentucky, null and void.

Fort Randolph (Point Pleasant) was besieged by a large force of Indians. Having failed to take the Fort, they started up Kanawha towards the interior settlements. Captain McKee, then in command, called for volunteer "runners," to go to the Greenbriar settlements and warn the settlers of the approach of the Indians. Hammond and Pryor at once volunteered, and, being rigged out in Indian disguise, by the "Grenadier squaw," then at the Fort, acting as interpreter; they reached the settlements safely, and their timely notice, no doubt, saved a terrible massacre.

Donnally's Fort was attacked, in May, by the Indian party above mentioned; but, having been forewarned by Hammond and Pryor, and reinforced by volunteers from Camp Union, under Stewart and Lewis, they successfully resisted the attack; the Indians retired with considerable loss.

Thomas Ingles settled in Abb's Valley.

1780. Dr. Thomas Walker and Colonel Daniel Smythe, Commissioners of Virginia, ran the boundary line between Virginia and North Carolina, now Kentucky and Tennessee.

Thomas Ingles resettled Burke's Garden.

An Indian raid into Greenbriar resulted in the killing of John Pryor, one of the brave messengers, and Hugh McIver, and the capture of their wives; also, Henry Baker and two Bridger brothers, and an old man, named Monday, and his wife, were killed, and the wives and children of Thomas Drennon and Mr. Smith made prisoners.

A little later, William Griffith, his wife and daughter, were murdered, and a son, a lad, taken prisoner. This was the last Indian raid made, or murder committed, in the Greenbriar country.

The trail of this last raiding party, only two in number, was discovered and followed by John Young, Benjamin Morris, William Arbuckle and Robert Aaron, as they passed down Kanawha, crossed Elk and went up Little Sandy; their camp was discovered on a fork of a fork of Sandy; they were fired on, one killed and one escaped; the lad, young Griffith, was recovered. The one killed proved to be a white man, disguised as an Indian. The fork on which he was killed was, from this circumstance, called White Man's Fork of Aaron's Fork (from Bob Aaron) of Little Sandy.

A Mr. Carr and two children murdered near the mouth of Bluestone, and a woman at Culversom's Bottom.

1782. Thomas Ingles' family captured, and part murdered, in Burke's Garden.

Lewisburg established as a town, with Samuel Lewis, James Reid, Samuel Brown, Andrew Donnally, John Stewart, Arthur Matthews, William Ward and Thomas Edgar, trustees.

Thomas Teays, captured below the mouth of Coal River, taken to Ohio and condemned to be burned, with Colonel Crawfard. He was recognized and saved by an Indian, with whom he had hospitably divided his salt, when surveying in Teay's Valley, the year before.

Second desperate attack on Fort Henry, this time certainly led by Girty, if not before. The heroic powder feat, probably occurred at this time.

Rice's Fort, on Buffalo Creek, was bravely and successfully defended by six men, against one hundred Indians, losing but one man of the six.

1783. Captain James Neal surveyed, for Alexander Parker, who had bought the Tomahawk title of Robert Thornton, the land at the mouth of Little Kanawha, upon which Parkersburg now stands.

1784. Virginia and Pennsylvania accept and adopt the report of Engineers Mason and Dixon, establishing the inter-State line, since known as "Mason and Dixon's line, and which had been in dispute since 1752.

James Moore, Jr., captured in Abb's Valley.

1785. Captain James Neal, and others, make a settlement on Little Kanawha, about a mile from the mouth, called Neal Station, or Monroe.

Captain John Dickinson located five hundred and two acres of land at and about Campbell's Creek, including the " Big Buffalo Lick," or Salt Spring.

Judge Joseph Wood, and others, mostly Scotch families, settled at and built Belleville, on the Ohio, a few miles below the mouth of Little Kanawha.

West Liberty, Ohio County, first town organized in the Mississippi Valley, November 29th.

1786. The first wagon road, called "Koontz's new road," was opened from Lewisburg to the Kanawha River. Its route was by Muddy Creek, Keeney's Knobbs, Rich Creek, Gauley, Twenty-Mile, Bell Creek and Campbell's Creek, with side trails down Kelly's Creek and Hughes' Creek to the "Boat Yards."

James Moore, Sr., of Abb's Valley, and two of his children killed, and the balance of the family made prisoners.

1787. Maysville, lately Limestone, on land of John May and Simon Kenton, was organized as a town, December 11th.

The State of Virginia ordered the construction of a wagon road from Kanawha Falls to Lexington, Ky.

1788. George Clendenin built the first house and Fort where Charleston now stands. (See chapter on Charleston.)

James Rumsey, the truly original inventor of the steamboat, exhibited his working model to General Washington, and others, on the waters of the Potomac, near Berkeley Springs.

Lewis Tackett was captured by Indians, and, on the way down the Kanawha River, was tied to a pine tree at Knob Shoals, while his captors went off hunting; a rain storm coming on, loosened his buckskin thongs, and allowed him to make a remarkable escape. The "Tackett pine" stood until within the last few years, a prominent landmark.

Tackett, after this, built a Fort at the mouth of Coal River, lower side.

Later, this Fort was captured, and several persons murdered. There are two versons of the story of the capture of Fort Tackett. I adopt that given by Mr. Atkinson, in his history of Kanawha, derived from Mr. George Harmon. It is the less sensational, but probably the most reliable. John and Lewis Tackett, and their mother, were captured near the Fort, while gathering turnips. Chris. Tackett and John McElhany were the only men in the Fort when captured. Chris. Tackett was killed in the action, McElhany and wife, Betsy Tackett, Sam Tackett, and a small boy, were taken prisoners; McElhany was tomahawked near the Fort. John Tackett succeeded in making his escape, but Lewis Tackett and his mother were taken to the Indian towns on the Scioto, where they remained, as prisoners, two years, when they were ransomed and returned. In the Young family, of this valley, is preserved an interesting tradition in relation to the capture of Tackett's Fort. When the attack commenced, John Young, with a young wife and a one-day-old babe, was in the Fort, but upon the final surrender, and under the friendly cover of the approaching shades of night, Young picked up his wife and babe, and the pallet on which they lay, made his way, unobserved, to a canoe at the bank, laid them in, and, through a drenching rain, poled his canoe, with its precious freight, up the river, during the night, to Clendenin's Fort, and they were saved. Neither father, mother nor babe suffered any harm from the effort, fright or exposure. That babe, Jacob Young, died but recently, aged about ninety years, leaving a large family of worthy descendants in this valley.

Ben. Eulin was out in the hills below Point Pleasant, hunting; he was pursued by Indians, and, to escape them, jumped over a cliff, just below and in sight of the Point, which proved to be fifty-three feet high. He fell in a clump of pawpaw bushes and grape vines, which broke his fall and saved breaking his neck; he then jumped over another cliff, twelve feet high, and finally escaped, but little worse for the wear and tear.

About this time, the family of Captain John Van Bibber was attacked, near the Point; his daughter, Miss Rhoda, was killed and scalped, and Joseph, a younger brother, taken prisoner to Detroit; he escaped and returned home, in 1794, soon after Wayne's victory. Captain Van Bibber, aided by his faithful negro servant, Dave, killed two or three Indians during the attack above mentioned.

1788–89. Daniel Boone and Paddy Huddlestone caught the first beavers in Kanawha Valley, at Long Shoal.

1789. Mad Ann Bailey made her famous solitary ride, through the wilderness, to Camp Union, for ammunition for the Clendenin Fort.

The first settlement on Big Sandy River was by

18

Charles Van Couver, about the forks, on the Virginia side, but not far from the present site of Louisa. It was on the survey made by George Washington for John Fry, in 1770, the first ever made on the river.

Kanawha, or "Kenhawa," County was formed. (For organization, etc., see chapter on Charleston.)

William Wyatt, who lived at the mouth of Paint Creek, dreamed that he was bitten by a snake, and interpreted it to mean that he would be shot by an Indian. To quiet his fears, his young wife went with him to the field, where he was working, and kept watch over him; but, sure enough, he was shot and killed by an Indian.

A party left the Clendenin settlement by boat, bound for the new settlements of Maysville and Lexington, Kentucky. They consisted of John May, after whom Maysville was named; Jacob Skyles, a large land operator, and the father-in-law of James Rumsey, the original inventor of the steamboat; Charles Johnson, from Bottetourt County, the agent and clerk of Skyles; and John Flynn, Jr., once an Indian captive, and son of the murdered John Flynn, of Cabin Creek. At Point Pleasant, they picked up the Misses Fleming, two sisters, recently from Pittsburgh. The expedition had a most thrilling and tragical ending. Descending the Ohio River, they were attacked by Indians; John May and one of the Misses Fleming were killed, Skyles badly wounded, and Johnson, Skyles, Flynn and the remaining Miss Fleming taken prisoners. Skyles and Johnson, after enduring great privations and tortures, succeeded in making their escape, by separate routes, and returned to the settlements; John Flynn was burned at the stake, and Miss Fleming was rescued, after being sentenced to be burned, tied to the stake and wood piled up around her. Charles Johnson, after his escape, published in book form a history of the personal experiences of each of the members of this unfortuate expedition; and it is one of the most thrilling narratives of early border dangers, sufferings and hairbredth escapes that has ever been published.

Matthias (Tice) Van Bibber and his little brother, Jacob, were fired on by Indians, near Point Pleasant. Tice was struck in the forehead and slightly wounded, but succeeded in escaping. Jacob, the lad, was caught and made prisoner; he made his escape and got home, some two years later.

William Carroll and family, of Carroll's Branch, Kanawha, narrowly escaped being murdered; they escaped, but the Indians burned their house.

1790. Leonard Cooper and William Porter made the first settlements on Elk River, about Cooper's Creek and Porter's Island.

'Squire Staten was killed, on his way home from court in Charleston, at the mouth of a branch which still bears the name of "Staten's Run."

James Hale was killed in the branch opposite the Clendenin Fort, which still bears the name of "Hale's Branch."

Fleming Cobb poled a canoe, with ammunition for the Clendenin Fort, sixty miles, up stream, from Point Pleasant, in fourteen hours.

The Indians killed some cows on a creek in the upper end of Kanawha County, and hung the bells on swinging limbs, so they would ring as the wind blew. When the citizens went out to bring their cows home they were shot down. The creek was named, from this circumstance, " Bell Creek."

1791. Jerry and Ben Carpenter, and some others, from Bath County, settled on the Upper Elk, and, soon after, O'Brien. They had not been there long when Ben Carpenter and wife were killed, and their house burned; the others, being warned by the burning of Ben Carpenter's house, fled, secreted themselves, and escaped.

Thomas Lewis established the first ferries, at Point Pleasant, across both rivers, December 9th.

In May, a party of eighteen whites were attacked by about thirty Indians, about half a mile up the Ohio from the Point Pleasant Fort. Michael See and Robert Sinclair were killed; Hampton and Thomas Northup, and a black boy belonging to See, were made prisoners. The boy was the son of Dick Pointer, who fought so bravely to defend Donnally's Fort, in 1782. He became an Indian (?) Chief, and fought with the friendly Indians on the side of the Americans, against the English, in the war of 1812.

Mr. Atkinson, in his "History of Kanawha," gives an interesting account of the sad fate of a Mr. Strange. He came over on to the upper waters of Elk with a surveying party. He was not an experienced woodsman, and, becoming separated from the party, soon got lost. His companions fired guns to indicate where they were, but it is supposed he thought the Indians were after him, and he fled for life. He was never seen alive again; but, some years after, his skeleton, portions of his shot-pouch, and the remains of his rusted rifle were found, forty miles distant from where he was lost, at the foot of a beech tree, at the mouth of a creek emptying into Elk, which, from that time, has been called "Strange Creek." Before he finally succumbed to hunger and exhaustion, he cut, with his penknife, in the bark of the tree, the following lines:

> "Strange is my name, and I'm on strange ground,
> And strange it is that I can't be found."

Two daughters of Henry Morris, who lived on Peters' Creek of Gauley, were murdered by Indians. Morris made the Indians suffer dearly for it afterwards.

George Clendenin and Daniel Boone were elected to the Legislature of Virginia.

By a ruse with cow bells, the Indians captured the Misses Tyler, near the Fort at Point Pleasant.

1792. Kentucky County was made a State and admitted into the Union. This was the first child of Virginia, the "Mother of States," and the first addition to the original thirteen.

John Wheeler, with wife and four children, lived opposite the mouth of Cabin Creek. They were attacked by Indians, all killed but one boy, Nat, and their house and the bodies burned.

Christiansburg, Montgomery County, Virginia, was established (October 10th), and the following named gentlemen appointed trustees: Christian Snydow, Byrd Smith, James Barnett, Hugh Crockett, Samuel Eason, Joseph Cloyd, John Preston, James Charlton and James Craig.

1793. The *last* Indian raid on the Kentucky border, says Collins, was by about twenty Indians. Simon

Kenton was the right man in the right place. He and his party waylaid them at the mouth of Holt's Creek, a few miles below Limestone, now Maysville, killed six, stampeded the rest, and recovered a lot of stolen horses.

Collins says the *first* line of packet boats established on the Ohio were keel and flat-bottomed, making one round trip between Cincinnati and Pittsburg per month. Passengers were allowed to work their passage, if short of cash. There was one boat fortnightly, soon increased to one weekly; they each carried six one-pound guns. The cabins were bullet-proof, and had port holes to fire from. There was a separate cabin for ladies.

1794. Shaderick Harriman, then living at the mouth of Lower Vanable Branch, two miles above Charleston, on the south side, was the *last* person killed by Indians in the Kanawha Valley.

General Wayne's crushing defeat of the Indians, at "Fallen Timbers," August 20th, gave after peace and security to this region.

December 19th, the Legislature of Virginia established the town of "Charlestown." (See chapter on Charleston.)

The Legislature enacted "that forty acres of land, the property of Thomas Lewis, at the mouth of Kenhawa, and in the said county of Kenhawa, as they are already laid off into lots and streets, shall be established a town by the name of Point Pleasant, and Leonard Cooper, John Van Bibber, Isaac Tyler, William Owens, William Allyn, Allyn Pryor, John Reynolds, George Clendenin and William Morris, gentlemen, appointed trustees thereof, December 19, 1794."

1795. Treaty of peace with the Indian tribes, at Greenville, Ohio, August 3d.

1796. Volney, the distinguished French author and infidel, was in the valley.

Thomas Hannon, the first settler on the Ohio River, from Kanawha to Big Sandy, settled at Green Bottom, above Guyandotte.

1797. The late General Lewis Ruffner was born, October 1st, in the Clendenin blockhouse, probably the first white child born within the present limits of Charleston.

Elisha Brooks erected a small kettle furnace and commenced the manufacture of salt, above Campbell's Creek.

1798. Peter Bowyer, father of the late Colonel John Bowyer, of Putnam County, made the *first* settlement in the New River gorge, and established a ferry at Sewell.

Daniel Boone made his *last* survey in Kanawha (September 8th), and probably the *last* he ever made.

1799. He left Kanawha for the Spanish Missouri Territory.

1802. Ohio was made a State and admitted into the Union.

1805–6–7. Eight thousand bear skins shipped from the mouths of Guyandotte and Big Sandy, according to J. P. Hildreth.

1808. David and Tobias Ruffner bored the *first* salt well and erected a larger furnace for the manufacture of salt.

1809. William Whitteker bored the *first* salt well and built the first salt furnace on the south side of Kanawha.

1810–12.   Audubon, the naturalist, was here.

Hon. Thomas Ewing, the elder, boiled salt and studied law and Latin here.

1815.   Captain James Wilson, boring for salt water, struck the *first* natural gas well of America.

Last buffalo killed in the Kanawha Valley.

1817.   David and Tobias Ruffner *first* discovered and used coal here.

1819.   The steamboat Robert Thompson, the first ever in the river, came as far as Red-House, but could not get farther up.

1820.   The failure of the Thompson to get up induced the State of Virginia to direct the James River and Kanawha Company to improve the navigation of Kanawha River so as to give three feet of water from the mouth to Kanawha Falls, all the year, and to construct a turnpike road across the mountains to the Kanawha Falls.

Last elk killed in the Kanawha Valley.

1823.   The Eliza was the *first* steamer to ascend the river as high as Charleston.

1831.   Billy Morris invented the "slips," or "jars," a simple tool which made deep well boring possible. It is now used wherever deep well boring is done, and its great utility and value entitle him to be ranked, among inventors, as a great public benefactor.

1838.   Ingles' Bridge built; the *first* bridge across New River or Kanawha.

1841.   William Tompkins "struck" natural gas near the Burning Spring, and used it for boiling salt. He was the first person in America to utilize natural gas for manufacturing.

1843. Dickinson & Shrewsberry got natural gas on the Burning Spring tract originally taken up by Generals Washington and Lewis. Messrs. D. & S. also used the gas in the manufacture of salt, as did several others in the neighborhood soon after.

1845. McAdam turnpike constructed from Buchanan, on James River, to the Tennessee line.

1846. Sutton Matthews discovered, on Falling Rock Creek of Elk, the first cannel coal known in the Kanawha Valley; perhaps the first in America.

1855. The Virginia & Tennessee, now Norfolk & Western Railroad, was opened—the *first* railroad to cross the New River-Kanawha.

1855–56. The *first* commercial shipments of coal from Kanawha commenced.

The *first* coal oil works (Cannelton) erected in this valley.

1861. The battle of Scary, one of the first during the late Civil War, was fought, July 17th.

The highest water in Kanawha since the settlement of the valley.

The Southern forces, under General Henry A. Wise, retired from the valley, and it was occupied by the Federals, under General J. D. Cox, July 24th.

Battle of Cross Lanes and Carnifax's Ferry, on the Gauley. General Lytle wounded, but not killed, as generally stated—September.

General Floyd wintered his army at Dublin. (See chapter on Dublin.)

1862. The Confederates, under General Loring, re-entered the Kanawha Valley; the Federals, under General Lightburn, retiring—September.

General Loring retired from the valley, and General Cox again came in—October.

1863. Virginia divided, and West Virginia established as a separate State—June 20th.

1864. Battle of Cloyd's Mountain, Pulaski County, May 9th; General A. G. Jenkins, killed; Colonel T. L. Broun, wounded.

1873. Chesapeake & Ohio Railroad opened.

United States Government commenced improving Kanawha River.

The Quinnemont Company established the first iron furnace and the first coke works on New River.

1874. Centennial celebration of the battle of Point Pleasant, at the Point.

1878. William Wyant established the first coke works on Kanawha River.

1883. The New River branch of the Norfolk & Western Railroad opened to Pocahontas.

1883–84. The late Colonel P. W. Norris, who, it is claimed, was the original suggestor of the Yellowstone National Park, and through whose efforts, largely, the Government was induced to reserve and set apart that Wonderland as a National pleasure park, and who was, for several years, the Government Superintendent of the park, made several visits to this (Kanawha) valley, under the auspices of the Smithsonian Institution, to examine and explore the numerous and extensive earthworks, stone cairns and other interesting remains of the prehistoric mound-builder race, which, at some early period, seems to have been very populous in this valley. Colonel Norris opened and explored many of the mounds, cairns, graves, fortifications, etc., and collected and forwarded from here to the Smithsonian Institntion several thousand relics of this ancient, interesting and mysterious people.

The Bettie Black Band Iron Furnace, the first in the immediate Kanawha Valley, and the Davis' Creek Railroad, were constructed.

1884. The most disastrous mine explosion at Pocahontas (in March) that has ever occurred in America, causing the loss of about two hundred lives.

The Ohio Central, now Kanawha & Ohio Railroad, opened to Charleston.

1885. The railroad bridge across the Ohio River, at Point Pleasant, completed.

The State capital of West Virginia permanently established at Charleston, and the new capitol building occupied.

1886. Peace, health, plenty, and a fair degree of prosperity prevail in the New River-Kanawha Valley, and throughout the borders of West Virginia generally.

J. W. McLaughlin Archt. & Del. Cincinnati. O.

CHAPTER XXXVII.

CHARLESTON, WEST VIRGINIA.

IT is not my purpose to attempt a full history of Charleston; that would far exceed the intended limits of this little volume; but as there is very little of its early history recorded—our older citizens knowing it chiefly by tradition, and our later population scarcely at all—it may be well to give here a brief outline sketch of its early settlement and after-progress; though such a sketch can be expected to have but a local interest.

Previous to 1755, so far as I know, no white person had ever trodden upon the site where Charleston now stands.

In July of that year, as elsewhere stated, Mrs. Mary Ingles and Mrs. Bettie Draper passed over it, as captives, on their way to the Indian towns north of the Ohio.

The next white person here was Matthew Arbuckle, an enterprising frontier hunter and trapper from the Greenbriar country, who passed down the valley in 1764, to a French trading post at the mouth of the Kanawha, to barter his peltries, and returned.

The next we hear of were Simon Kenton and his companions, Yeager and Strader, in 1771, when they passed over it and built a camp at or near the mouth of Two-mile Creek of Elk, and occupied it, and hunted and trapped until the Spring of 1773, when they were attacked by Indians, Yeager killed, and Kenton and Strader both wounded, but succeeded in making their escape to the mouth of Kanawha, where they were cared for by the traders.

In 1773, Colonel Thomas Bullitt, who had distinguished himself for bravery and efficient service in the Braddock war, and in the expedition against Fort Du Quesne, under General Forbes, in 1758, came here to locate his military lands. He was attracted by this fine bottom, and "took up" 1,030 acres lying along the Kanawha, from Elk River up to Wilson's Branch. Later, Colonel Bullitt sold this tract to his brother, Cuthbert Bullitt, a distinguished Judge, and President of the Court of Appeals of Virginia.

His son, Cuthbert Bullitt, Jr., was a Judge in Maryland; and another son, Alexander Scott Bullitt, was member of the Legislature, President of the Senate, President of the State Convention, and Lieutentant Governor of Kentucky.

After the battle of Point Pleasant, in 1774, this valley began to fill up rapidly; but as this tract was held by non-residents, no settlement was made on it, and nothing done with it until some thirteen or fourteen years later.

In December, 1787, a Mr. Clendenin, who had seen the land in 1774, when going to, and returning from, the battle of the Point, and again in 1785–86, when he was one of the State Commissioners for laying out and constructing the first wagon road from Lewisburg to the Kanawha, met Judge Bullitt in Richmond, purchased the tract, and at once began his preparations to settle on it.

There seems to be no record of the exact date of his commencing his settlement; but it is known that he and his party reached the locality on the last of April, and as they were not persons to waste time, I think it safe to assume that the settlement of Charleston dates from the 1st day of May, 1788. Tackett's Fort, at the mouth of Coal River, was built a little later, during the same year. Clendenin built the first house on this bottom, near the river, at the northeast corner of what are now Kanawha and Brooks streets. It was a two-story, double, hewed, bullet-proof, log house, with two rooms below and two above.

Immediately in front of this was also built a stockade fort. Both were used, as occasion required, for protection.

Several other settlers came out with Clendenin. These were: His brothers, William, Robert and Alexander, Josiah Harrison, Francis Watkins, Shaderick Harriman, Charles McClung, John Edwards, Lewis Tackett, and, perhaps, others; and it was probably they, or some of them, who immediately, or very soon after, built the first six or seven houses.

This was then Greenbriar County, and Clendenin got the then surveyor of the county, Mr. Alexander Welch, who lived at Lewisburg, to come down and lay off a town for him. A block of forty acres was divided and laid off into as many one-acre lots. There were two streets, called "Front" and "Main," now Kanawha and Virginia streets. The cross streets were numbered, not named.

This town extended from Elk River up to now Capital street. A plat was made of it by the surveyor; but, from some neglect, was never recorded. According to tradition, the first half dozen houses built here, after Clendenin's, were: One at the upper corner of now Truslow and Kanawha streets, where Mr. C. J. Bodkin now resides; one at the northeast corner of Kanawha and Court streets, where the Barlow building now stands; one between Alderson and Summers streets, where Dr. Rogers' drug-store now stands; one at the northeast corner of Kanawha and Summers streets, where the Frankenberger block now stands; one at the northwest corner of Capital and Kanawha streets, where the Kanawha Valley Bank now stands, and one at the northeast corner of Kanawha and Hale streets, where J. P. Hale now resides. In 1789, when Kanawha County was formed, there were but seven houses. In 1798, these had increased to twelve, and in 1803 to 1810, to about twenty.

No name was given to the town for several years after it was laid out. It was called, indiscriminately, "Clendenin's Settlement," or "The Town at the Mouth of Elk."

After the formation of the county, Mr. Reuben Slaughter, the County Surveyor, made another plat of the town, following substantially, if not exactly, the plat of Surveyor Welch, up to Capital street; but extended it up to Dunbar street. This plat is on record in the Clerk's office of this county.

Some years ago, the late Mr. John Dryden, then Clerk of this county, through some friend in Lewisburg, found among the old private papers of Mr. Welch, in possession of some of his descendants, the original plat of the town. Though never recorded, it is, fortunately, preserved, and is now before me. It is an interesting historical relic.

On the 19th of December, 1794, the Legislature of Virginia formally established the town, and fixed its name as " Charlestown."

It is a curious fact that, although the Legislature had officially established the county, in 1789, as " Kenhawa," and now the town, in 1794, as " Charlestown," both names, by common consent, became changed—one to Kanawha and the other to Charleston. How, why or when, no body knows.

Some years ago there was much trouble and annoyance about our mail matter, growing out of the confusion of the post-office names of our Charleston and Charlestown, Jefferson County. With a view to remedy this, a public meeting was called here to discuss the propriety of changing the name of our town from Charleston to " Kanawha City." It was warmly discussed, but defeated, mainly on the sentimental ground that it would be sacrilege to abolish the name of the dear old pioneer who had shed his blood and risked his life here, "in an early day," among the Indians; had founded the town, given it his own name, and built a Fort to protect and defend his neighbors as well as himself, etc.

Sentiment prevailed, and the name remained unchanged; but the writer took some pains to look up the early history of the settling and naming of the town. It was soon discovered that the founder's name was George, not Charles. This somewhat staggered the sentimentalists, but they recovered, saying that George was a very modest gentleman, and, instead of taking it himself, he had conceded

19

the honor of the name to his brother, whose name
was Charles; and they clinched this by quoting
Howe, who, in his History of Virginia, so states; and
other historians all follow Howe. But a further investigation of the family records showed that George
had no brother Charles; then it was conjectured that
the name was probably given in honor of his son
Charles, but a still further investigation of the family
genealogies proved that he had no son.

After much search of records, and tracing of traditions among the old timers, I have but recently
arrived at the facts of this case through Mr. C. C.
Miller, of Mason County, a descendant of the Clen-
denins. He says the town was named by George
Clendenin, the founder, in honor of his *father*, whose
name was Charles. He was an elderly gentleman,
who came here with his sons, died in the Clendenin
block house, and was buried near the upper end of
the garden, and near the front fence. The fences
have been somewhat changed here within recent
years; but from Mr. Miller's description of the place,
and my knowledge of the lines, I conclude that the
grave of Charles Clendenin, whose name the town
bears, lies between the present sidewalk on Kanawha street and the roadway, about thirty feet above,
midway between Brooks and Morris streets, and
at a right angle from the river, about opposite the
gum of the old gas well. It would be a graceful act
for the city to mark the spot with a durable monument and suitable inscription.

Shortly after the Clendenin Fort was built, a
smaller block house was built about a mile above,
and just in front of the present residence of Mr.

Silas Ruffner. This small block house was probably built by Clendenin as a protection to his tenants and farm hands, as it was before he had sold all the bottom above the town, as he afterwards did, in 1796, to Mr. Joseph Ruffner.

In 1793, at a time when the Indians were quite numerous hereabout, and hostile, a Mr. James Van Bibber, passing early one morning from the lower Fort to the little block house above, saw an Indian in war paint suddenly rise up from behind a log in front of him. Each raised his gun and fired as quickly as possible, the shots being so nearly simultaneous as to make but one report. The Indian fell, and his ball had grazed the body of his opponent. Van Bibber, not knowing how many more there might be, made all possible speed toward the upper Fort, and met some of the inmates coming to the scene of danger, being warned by what they supposed a single shot, which was an agreed danger signal. Van Bibber exclaimed that he had just "fought a duel," and related the circumstances. Upon repairing to the scene of the conflict, they found the blood of the victim, but the enemy had disappeared. Some days after, the weather being quite warm, the vultures were observed hovering about the base of the hill back of the bottom, and, upon examining into the cause, the remains of the dead Indian were found in a crevice of the rock in the ravine which leads from the present Piedmont road to Spring Hill Cemetery, where they had been conveyed and secreted by his companions.

I find this incident contributed by our worthy citizen, Dr. E. A. Summers to the "American Pioneer," a periodical published in Cincinnati, in 1843.

In 1790, an interesting, but tragical, incident occurred at the Clendenin Fort. As related by the old
traditions, it is as follows: The neighboring families
were all gathered in the Fort for safety, as the Indians were known to be prowling about the neighborhood. One of the inmates, a beautiful young
lady, was very ill with a fever. It so happened—and
it always so happens—that this fair young lady had
a gallant young lover, also in the Fort, and whose
name was James Hale. As there were no ice houses,
nor ice machines, in those days, the gallant young
lover determined, at the risk of his life, to go to a
fine spring across the river, for a bucket of fresh
water to cool the parched tongue and fevered brow
of his fair lady-love; so he took his life in one hand
and a bucket in the other, and crossed over, but just
as he was in the act of dipping up the cool, sparkling
water, he was pierced by several shots from the Indians, and fell dead in the spring; upon hearing of
which, his fair sweetheart was so shocked that she
swooned, and sank, and died. How could she have
done less in recognition of the brave and generous
act of her daring lover, who had risked his own life
in endeavoring to save hers?

Unfortunately—or, perhaps fortunately—there is
another version of this highly romantic story. As
there may be matter-of-fact, commonplace readers as
well as sentimental ones, I shall give both versions,
that persons may choose according to their tastes
and mental idiosyncracies.

The reverse of the picture above given is as follows: Mr. Clendenin had in his household employ-
ment a buxom country lass who cooked the frugal

fare, milked the cows and washed the dishes. She was, probably, never sick in her life, and if she ever loved anybody, she probably did not know it, or " let concealment, like a worm in the bud," etc. Mr. Clendenin also had as farm hands, one James Hale, and another, whose name may have been—Smith. These were strapping young fellows, who plowed the corn, fed the stock, and did other farm work, and would, sometimes, "while resting," go over to the spring for some fresh water.

On one occasion, when they were both over, they were fired on by Indians; Hale was killed and Smith made his escape by jumping into and swimming across the river, diving, from time to time, to avoid the bullets fired after him.

Whichever version of this story is accepted, the central historical fact remains—that James Hale, while at the spring opposite the Fort, for water, was shot and killed by the Indians, and the branch, hitherto nameless, was called after him, and still bears the name of " Hale's Branch."

It is generally claimed for Mr. Norris Whittaker, one of our oldest citizens, who was born in 1807, on the lot where I now write, was the first white child born within the present limits of the city of Charleston; this, however, is a mistake, as I remember frequently to have heard the late General Lewis Ruffner relate that he was born in the Clendenin Fort, on the 1st of October, 1797, ten years before Mr. Whittaker, but Mr. Whittaker is now, doubtless, the oldest surviving person born within the limits of Charleston.

It may be as well here to correct an error of fact in regard to the old Fort, fallen into by Mr. Atkinson, in his valuable history of Kanawha County. He says: " The Clendenin Fort was *torn down* by Mr. C. C. Lewis, in 1874, to make room for the elegant mansion in which he now resides."

The facts are as follows: The old stockade fort proper, being nearly rotted down, was torn away and removed about 1815, but the Clendenin block house, or resident fort, continued to be used as a family residence.

After the death or removal of George Clendenin the property passed into the possession of Colonel David Ruffner; next into that of Captain James Wilson; after his death into that of Mr. Frederick Brooks, who long resided there, and after him of Mr. John A. Truslow, from whom the writer purchased it in 1872. Wishing to make room for more modern buildings, and being unwilling to sacrifice so interesting a historical land-mark, I went to great expense and trouble to move the building bodily, about five hundred feet, to a vacant lot on the northeast corner of Brooks and Virginia streets, where it was located, thoroughly repaired, painted, and made sightly and comfortable. Having long been a weather-boarded house, the logs are not visible, and it has every appearance of a frame house. It is at present owned and occupied by Major Delafield DuBois.

It was, as stated, the first house built within the limits of Charleston, is now nearly one hundred years old, is in excellent repair and good for another century.

I am glad to.say that it was *not* pulled down and destroyed, and proud to say that I was instrumental in preserving it. The lot from which it was removed was sold to Mr. C. C. Lewis, who built upon it his present elegant residence.

In about 1789–90, when Indians were troublesome and threatening, the famous female spy, scout, messenger, etc., "Mad Ann Bailey," made her daring ride, alone, through the wilderness, from here to Fort Union (Lewisburg), and brought back a supply of powder and lead for the Fort. Ann was English by birth and never got rid of her cockney dialect. She was a first rate rifle shot, and, in telling some of her friends, at one time, of one of her recent feats she said she had just "killed a howl hoff a helm tree across Helk River."

At another time, about 1790–91, the Clendenin Fort was short of ammunition, and Fleming Cobb, an expert woodsman and waterman, was detailed to go to Point Pleasant for a supply. He started by canoe with his ready rifle and enough cooked food for the trip. He floated down by night to avoid being seen by Indians along shore. By daylight, next morning, he had made fifty miles of the sixty miles distance. He drew his canoe into the mouth of Ten Mile Creek, and secreted it and himself under overhanging boughs, and took a refreshing sleep in the bottom of the canoe.

During the day, while he was waiting the darkness of another night, to complete his journey, he saw, passing up on the opposite side of the river, about twenty Indians; they did not discover him, but the sight at once suggested to him the danger he should have to encounter on his up trip.

When night came, he went on safely to the Fort at the Point. Next day he got his powder, lead and flints, and, at dark, set out on his perilous return. After a few hours travel, poling his canoe up stream, he was discovered and pursued by a party of three Indians, but, as they were on the opposite side of the river, and as he kept his canoe close to his shore, he managed, during the night, to escape harm.

Next morning, being about the mouth of Coal River, one of the Indians undertook to swim the Kanawha, so that if he (Cobb) escaped the two on one side, he would inevitably fall within reach of the one on the opposite side. Cobb at once saw the danger that threatened him, and started his canoe full speed for the crossing Indian, being determined to kill him if possible. When within good range he fired and wounded his man. He did not wait to see results, as the other two were firing upon him, but started his canoe up stream with all energy he could command; and while the two Indians were rescuing the wounded one from the water and taking care of him, he (Cobb) had gotten out of sight; and, about ten o'clock, reached the Clendenin Fort safely, having made sixty miles by canoe, up stream, without food, sleep, or rest, most of the way by night, and most of the way pursued by three armed Indians, one of whom he succeeded in killing or wounding, and thereby escaping them all.

What wonderful powers of physical endurance these early frontiersmen had! Without it they could not, with all their nerve and pluck, have executed such daring, dangerous and desperate undertakings.

The bottom on which Charleston stands was, originally, largely covered by beech timber. Bears and turkeys are very fond of beech mast, and used to con-

gregate here in great numbers in the Fall and fatten
on it. The early settlers used to kill and "put up"
bear meat for their winter's bacon. Tradition says
that Ben. Morris, a noted hunter, killed thirteen bears
near here in one afternoon. It is not stated whether
it was an extra good day for bears.

Mr. John L. Cole, whose memory is well stored
with the early traditions of the valley, tells me of an
interesting one in the Price family, to the effect that
Archibald Price, "in an early day," was making
sugar at a sugar camp across the river, probably about
where the C. & O. Depot now stands, when he discovered that there were Indians in very dangerous prox-
imity, and that his canoe was on the wrong side of
the river; but, "Necessity is the mother of invention." He gathered up his sugar kettle, inverted it
over his head, thus making a diving bell of it, and
walked into and waded through the river on the bottom, saving his life and saving his—kettle.

It is well known to hunters and woodsmen that
buffalo, deer, bears, etc., have regular trails of travel
through the forests, and especially regular crossing
places along the streams. It is said that there was a
regular bear crossing just in front of the present
court house; and a deer crossing opposite the Fort
and mouth of Hale's Branch.

The year that Kanawha County was established
(1789) was an eventful one. In this year the first
United States Congress met, the United States Constitution became operative, and George Washington
took his seat as first President of the United States.

When the county was organized, it extended from
the mouth of Pond Creek, five miles below the mouth

of Little Kanawha, to the mouth of Big Sandy River, up Big Sandy to Cumberland Mountains, and across by Sewell's, etc., containing about ten thousand square miles.

Charleston, although it then had but seven houses, was the capital and county seat of this vast territory. Until the county buildings were erected the courts were held in the Clendenin blockhouse. The first public building erected was a jail, in 1792; it was built of logs, stood on and partly in the bank near the Fort, was twelve by twelve feet square, and seven feet high. The next jail built was on part of the present court house lot, on the corner of Kanawha and Court streets. The first court house built was of logs, in 1796, on the lot where the present court house stands. It was forty by thirty feet, one story, with two jury rooms fourteen by fourteen feet.

The first clerk's office was about fourteen by fourteen feet, built in 1802, of stone, on the present Hale House lot. It was the first stone building in the valley. The present court house was built in 1817. The present county clerk's office and the stone jail in 1829, and the circuit court office in 1873.

The lot upon which the county public buildings stand was acquired from George Alderson, in settlement of an unpaid balance of about one hundred dollars due from Alderson to the county.

In front of the court house lot there was an open, covered, public market house. This stood until about 1845. There were no special meat markets then as now.

In the early years of Kanawha County there was but one voting precinct, and that was at the Clendenin Fort. The polls were then kept open three days. At the first election held, there were but thirteen votes polled. Of course, the candidates were elected by " overwhelming majorities."

In 1790, George Clendenin and Andrew Donnally, Sr., were the first members elected to represent the county in the Legislature. In 1791, George Clendenin and Daniel Boone were elected.

While on the subject, I will give here, as a valuable table for reference, a complete list of all the delegates from Kanawha, from the organization of the county in 1789 until the division of the State in 1863. This list is the more valuable from the fact that the poll-books in our clerk's office, which contained these early records, were destroyed during the late war. The list, from 1789 to 1847, inclusive, I cut from the " Kanawha Republican," in 1847, and it is probably the only complete list extant:

1790.　George Clendenin, Andrew Donnally.
1791.　George Clendenin, Daniel Boone.
1792.　Henry Banks, Wm. Morriss.
1792.　George Clendenin, Wm. Morriss.
1794.　Wm. Morriss, George Clendenin.
1795.　Thos. Lewis, George Clendenin.
1796.　William Clendenin, William Morriss.
1797.　Edward Graham, William Morriss.
1798.　William Morriss, Thomas Lewis.
1799.　Thomas Lewis, David Ruffner.
1800.　William Morriss, Thomas Lewis.
1801.　William Clendenin, David Ruffner.
1802.　R. McKee, D. Ruffner.
1803.　William Clendenin, Andrew Donnally.
1804.　D. Ruffner, Carroll Morriss.
1805.　Nehemiah Wood, William Morriss.
1806.　John Reynolds, William Morriss.
1807.　John Reynolds, William Morriss.

1808. John Reynolds, Edmund Morriss.
1809. John Reynolds, David Cartmill.
1810. John Reynolds, Claudius Buster.
1811. John Hansford, David Ruffner.
1812. David Cartmill, John Hansford.
1813. John Wilson, John Hansford.
1814. John Wilson, John Hansford.
1815. John Wilson, John Hansford.
1816. John Wilson, Thomas S. Buster.
1817. John Hansford, Lewis Summers.
1818. John Hansford, P. R. Thompson.
1819. Joseph Lovell, Claudius Buster.
1820. Joseph Lovell, N. W. Thompson.
1821. Joseph Lovell, Lewis Ruffner.
1822. Matthew Dunbar, James Wilson.
1823. James Wilson, Van B. Reynolds.
1824. Joseph Lovell, John Welch.
1825. Lewis Ruffner, Van B. Reynolds.
1826. James H. Fry, Lewis Ruffner.
1827. James C. McFarland, Daniel Smith.
1828. Daniel Smith, Matthew Dunbar.
1829. Daniel Smith, Matthew Dunbar.
1830. George W. Summers.
1831. George W. Summers.
1832. James H. Fry.
1833. James H. Fry.
1834. George W. Summers.
1835. George W. Summers.
1836. A. Donnally.
1837. Daniel Smith.
1838. Daniel Smith.
1839. Van B. Reynolds.
1840. Andrew Donnally.
1841. Daniel Smith.
1842. Andrew Parks.
1843. John Lewis.
1844. Daniel Smith.
1845. Spicer Patrick.
1846. Spicer Patrick.
1847. Andrew Parks.
1848. James M. Laidley.

1849.   Dr. Spicer Patrick.

1850.   General Daniel Smith.

1851.   Major Andrew Parks.

Two delegates were now again allowed and the sessions made biennial.

1853.   A. P. Fry, Dr. S. Patrick.

1855.   Colonel B. H. Smith, Colonel Charles Ruffner.

1857.   Colonel Charles Ruffner, Major N. Fitzhugh.

1859.   Isaac N. Smith, Isaiah A. Welch.

1861.   I. A. Welch represented the State in Richmond and General Lewis Ruffner and Greenbery Slack in Wheeling.

1863.   I. A. Welch re-elected by the Confederates to represent the State at Richmond.

1863.   June 20th, the State was divided and West Virginia organized as a separate State.

At the first court for Kanawha County, held at the Clendenin Fort, in Charleston, Virginia, October 6, 1789, the following "Gentlemen Justices" were severally sworn‑ and qualified as members of the court:

Thomas Lewis, Robert Clendenin, Francis Watkins, Charles McClung, Benjamin Strother, William Clendenin, David Robinson, George Alderson, Leonard Morris and James Van Bibber.

Thomas Lewis, being the oldest member of the court, was, by the law of the State, entitled to the sheriffalty of the county. He was duly commissioned, and he appointed John Lewis his deputy.

William H. Cavendish was appointed clerk and Francis Watkins his deputy. The first "will" he recorded was the last will and testament of William Morris, the first permanent settler at Kelly's Creek.

Reuben Slaughter was appointed County Surveyor. The first survey he entered was one for 1,000 acres, lying about the mouth of Coal River, made for Phineas Taylor, grandfather of the great showman, Phineas Taylor Barnum.

David Robinson and John Van Bibber were appointed Commissioners of the Revenue, and William Drowdy and William Boggs, Coroners.

In those days counties had military organizations. For Kanawha, George Clendenin was County Lieutenant; Thomas Lewis, Colonel; Daniel Boone, Lieutenant-Colonel; William Clendenin, Major; Leonard Cooper and John Morris, Captains; James Van Bibber and John Young, Lieutenants, and William Owens and Alexander Clendenin, Ensigns.

It was six years after the beginning of the Clendenin settlement; and five years after it had become the county seat of Kanawha, before it was formally incorporated as a town. The Legislature then (December 19, 1794,) enacted that "Forty acres of land, the property of George Clendenin, at the mouth of Elk River, in the County of 'Kenhawa,' as the same are already laid off into lots and streets, shall be established as a town, by the name of 'Charlestown; and Reuben Slaughter, Andrew Donnally, Sr., William Clendenin, John Morris, Sr., Leonard Morris, George Alderson, Abraham Baker, John Young and William Morris, gentlemen, are appointed trustees." Surely no set of men ever had such a "corner" on public offices as these few gentlemen who first settled about Charleston.

Up to about 1805, there was no grist mill at or very near Charleston. Tin graters, not yet quite obsolete in the rural districts, were then largely used. Thomas Alsbury had, "in an early day," built a little

water-power tub mill at the falls of Coal River, about
twelve miles distant, and to this the few settlers had
to send their grists of wheat and corn to be ground,.
and wait their respective turns, according to millers'
rule. No flour or meal was kept on sale here at that
day. The first mill built near the town was a little
floating tub mill in Elk Shoal, below the mouth of
Elk River, in 1805. The Ruffners had built a little
corn-cracker at the mouth of Campbell's Creek, five
miles above town, two years before (in 1803) and,.
later, William Blaine one at Blaine's Island.

The first sawed lumber used here was all whip-
sawed, by hand. The first saw mills established were
about 1815 to 1820, on Two-Mile Creek of Elk..
There were three of them, and two of them had
corn-cracker attachments.

The first steam flour mill and steam saw mill
erected in the town, were by David and Daniel
Ruffner, in 1832.

Mr. Joseph Bibby, then just arrived from England,.
and who had learned milling there, engaged with
the Messrs. Ruffner to operate the flour mill, and, in
1837, he became the purchaser of it. This mill is
still in successful operation; Mr. Bibby is still living,.
and a well preserved man, and has now been connected with this mill, as operator and owner, for
fifty-four years.

The first sermon ever preached in Charleston, according to Mr. Atkinson, was by Rev. William Steele,.
January 1, 1804, at the house of Mr. Williams, who
lived at the upper corner of Hale and Kanawha.
streets. He came from the Little Kanawha Methodist
Circuit, and, for some time after, preached here once.

a month.   Rev. Asa Shinn, a Methodist, was the first minister to be regularly appointed to this circuit, a few months later.

Rev. Henry Bascom, the afterwards distinguished and eloquent Bishop Bascom, preached here for a while, in 1813.

The first Methodist brick church was erected on Virginia street, between Summers and Alderson streets, in 1833.

Rev. Dr. Henry Ruffner was the first Presbyterian preacher here, about 1816, and was the father of Presbyterianism in the valley.   He organized the first Presbyterian congregation in Mercer Academy, in March, 1819.   After him, Rev. Francis Crutchfield was the first ordained minister to locate here, later in 1819; and he was followed, in 1820, by Rev. Calvin Chadwick.   The first Presbyterian church building was erected on Virginia street, between Hale and Capital, in 1828.   The Kanawha Presbyterian Church, on Virginia, between McFarland and Dunbar streets, was completed in 1885.

The first Episcopal minister was Rev. Joseph Willard, in 1816, followed by Rev. Charles Page, in 1821. This church, corner of Virginia and McFarland streets, was built in 1834.

The first Catholic congregation and St. Mary's Academy were organized in 1866, by Rev. Father Joseph W. Stenger.   Their church building was completed in 1869, and the convent in 1872.

The first Baptist congregation was organized by Rev. P. H. Murry, in 1869, and a church was built on the corner of Donnally and Laidly streets.

The first Jewish congregation was organized in

1873. Rabbi Sched was their first teacher, followed by Rabbi Strauss. Their synagogue was built on State street, near Court, in 1876.

The colored Methodists erected a church at the corner of Quarrier and Dickinson streets, in 1867. Rev. Charles Fisher was the first colored minister.

The colored Baptists erected a church on Washington street, near Dickinson, in 1873, Rev. Frank James being their first colored minister.

The first colored free school was established in 1867, Miss Lucy James being their first teacher.

The first attorney admitted to practice in our courts was Mr. Edward Graham, August 1, 1796. He was appointed Commonwealth's Attorney, at a salary of forty dollars a year. Captain Cartmill and Scotch Jamie Wilson were among the earliest lawyers. A little later came Charles Baldwin, Judge Matthew Dunbar, Colonel B. H. Smith, Colonel Joseph Lovel, Major Andrew Parks, etc.

As evidence that the early courts had due regard for the moralities and proprieties, the records show that they fined one Ben Lemasters fifteen shillings, at a court in 1792, for "saying cuss words" in the presence of a member of the court. He could, probably, have sworn in the presence of common mortals for half price. In 1796, the grand jury indicted Joseph Burwell for hunting on Sunday, and William Jones for "taking the name of the Lord in vain."

Tobacco was an important crop, and was largely raised by the early settlers. It was used as a "legal tender," in place of money.

At the May term of court for 1792 it was "Ordered that 4,800 weight of tobacco be levied upon the

20

tithables of this county for the extra services of the clerk for four years last past;" also, "that 3,300 weight of tobacco be levied on the tithables of this county for extra services performed by Thomas Lewis, as Sheriff, from the 5th of October, 1789, until the 2d day of July, 1792;" also, "that William Clendenin be allowed 1,300 pounds of tobacco for his services as Sheriff from the 2d day of July, 1792, until the 6th day of August, 1793;" also, "that George Clendenin be allowed 1,920 pounds of tobacco for books furnished for the use of this county;" also, "that a deposit of 10,000 pounds of tobacco be applied to the use of the county; and, further, it is ordered that the Sheriff proceed to collect the above quantity of tobacco, and settle with the county at the February court, next."

November term, 1793: "Judgment for 1,525 pounds of tobacco in favor of John Stewart, clerk of Greenbriar, against John Edwards, of Kanawha."

The first resident physician here was Dr. Eoff, who came in 1811 or 1812, and was followed by Dr. N. W. Thompson. The late venerable Dr. Spicer Patrick came in 1816, and after a long, active, useful and honorable career, recently went to his rest at but little short of one hundred years of age.

The first taverns, or inns, as they were then called, so far as I can learn, were the Buster Tavern, at the northeast corner of Court and Kanawha streets, and the Griffin Tavern, at the northeast corner of Summers and Kanawha streets.

The prices of accommodations at such places of public entertainment were prescribed by the courts. The following is a list of prices established at a court in 1820:

Breakfast, dinner, or supper, each............ 25c.
Lodging, per night........................... 12½c.
Horse at hay, per night...................... 25c.
Horse at pasture, per night................... 12½c.
Jamaica Spirits, Cogniac Brandy, and Madeira
    Wine, per gallon........................600c.
Cherry Bounce and Country Gin, per gal.......300c.
Whisky and Peach Brandy, per gal............200c.
Beer and Cider, per gal...................... 50c.

Clearly, they were not Prohibitionists.

Colonel Joel Ruffner (in "Atkinson's Kanawha") says that John Greenlee, who came here from Rockbridge, "in a very early day," was the first blacksmith.

Probably the next was the negro, Jack Neal, who had such an eventful history. He was captured near Georgetown, though a free man, and was attempted to be carried South, into slavery. He got loose, killed his captor, escaped, was recaptured near Gallipolis, brought here for trial, confessed, was convicted and pardoned.

He was the first criminal ever in our little twelve by twelve jail, and the first tried before the courts. He opened his blacksmith shop soon after his pardon, in 1804 or 1805.

Among school teachers Herbert P. Gaines is said to have been the first, with Levi Welch a good second. Jacob Rand, James A. Lewis, Lewis Ruffner and Ezra Walker were all very early.

Mercer Academy was built in 1818. The lot on which it and the First Presbyterian Church are built was donated by Colonel David Ruffner.

The first drug store was established by Dr. Henry Rogers, father of Dr. J. H. Rogers, about 1825. The first cabinet and furniture maker was James G. Taylor, about 1833. The first regular undertaker and furniture dealer was S. A. Skees, in 1867, succeeded by R. R. Skees.

The first tan-yard was started by William Blaine, below Elk, " in an early day."

Fleming Cobb, of canoe memory, brought out from old Virginia the first fruit trees. Ann Bailey brought out the first pair of geese, and also brought, on horseback, from Lewisburg, the first copper worm still.

The first clock and watch maker was the elder Thomas Matthews, who came from Eastern Virginia in 1808. He was a most ingenious and skillful workman. He made many of the old eight feet high eight-day clocks for those who were able to buy them. Some of them are still extant.

Mr. Matthews was an eccentric, as well as ingenious man. He used to say that the primitive settlers here were as healthy, peaceable, moral and happy a people as he ever saw, until the doctors, lawyers and preachers came in; then, he said, they began to get sick, to quarrel and law each other, and to develop all sorts of meanness.

I don't know whether he claimed to have established the relation of cause and effect between these phenoména, or whether he regarded them as merely curious coincidences.

The first post-office established here was April 1, 1801, and called " Kanawha C. H." The first postmaster was Edward Graham; the second was Francis A. Dubois, January 1, 1803, followed by William Whitteker, October 1, 1808. The post-office was in the old log house that stood on the north-east corner of Kanawha and Hale streets. The official name of the post-office remained Kanawha C. H. until September 30, 1879, when it was changed by the Post-Office Department to Charleston.

Up to as late as 1810, and probably later, there was only a fortnightly mail here, brought from Lewisburg on horseback.

The first newspapers established here were the " Kanawha Patriot," by Herbert P. Gaines, in 1819, followed by the "Western Courier," by Mason Campbell, in 1820, and by the "Western Register," by Messrs. J. M. & A. T. Laidley, in 1829. Mr. Mason Campbell is but recently deceased, and Messrs. J. M. & A. T. Laidley both still survive.

The first bank established here was a branch of the Bank of Virginia, in 1832—J. C. McFarland, president; Samuel Hannah, cashier; John M. Doddridge, teller. The first local brass-band was organized and instructed by Prof. Carl Fine, a German music teacher, in 1858.

The first ferry was a sort of double-barreled affair, crossing both Kanawha and Elk Rivers from the point at the junction. The Legislature granted the franchise to George Clendenin, December 19, 1794. Later, there was an opposition ferry, crossing Kanawha from the mouth of Ferry Branch, landing on the upper or lower side of Elk, as desired. It was started, in 1809, by John and Langston Ward, but not officially established until 1812. The Wards lived on the south side of Kanawha, at the mouth of Ferry Branch, which took its name from their ferry.

The Alexander Quarrier Ferry and the James

Wilson Ferry, afterward the Goshorn and Hale Ferries, now owned by Ruffner Bros., or the "Charleston Ferry Company," were established in 1820.

The wire suspension bridge, over Elk River, was built by a stock company in 1852.

The Keystone Bridge was built, chiefly by Mr. J. Brisbin Walker in the interest of his "West End" extension, in 1873; was destroyed by an ice gorge in 1879, and rebuilt by the city in 1886, when the suspension bridge was purchased and both made free bridges.

The Elk Log Boom was constructed about 1869 by Messrs. Huling and Brokerhoff.

The first Circuit Court held here was on the 24th of April, 1809, Judge John Coulter presiding, about whom the following anecdote is told: Having, at this first sitting, fined some transgressor for some infraction of law, the victim, probably not a prohibitionist, got up in court and addressing the court said: "See here, Mr. Judge, aint you a settin' of your Coulter a leetle too deep for new ground?"

Judge James Allen followed Judge Coulter in September, 1811, and Judge Lewis Summers succeeded Judge Allen on the bench, in 1819, and held the position until 1843, about a quarter of a century.

The first steamboat ever at Charleston was the "Eliza," in 1823. She was built at Wheeling for Andrew Donnally and Isaac Noyes. She went to Cincinnati, but never returned. She was a failure.

The next was the "Fairy Queen," built at Cincinnati in 1824, by Andrew Donnally and A. M. Henderson. She ran for some time as a Charleston and Cincinnati packet.

The next was the "Paul Pry," in 1826, built and owned by Joel Shrewsbury, Jr., and Captain John Rogers. She ran in the trade for two years, when she "blew up" at Guyandotte.

In 1830, Armstrong, Grant & Co. bought the "O. H. Perry" and put her in the Kanawha trade. Her name was afterwards changed to the "Daniel Webster."

In 1830, the "Enterprise," built at Pittsburgh, and commanded by Captain James Payne, was the first towboat ever in Kanawha. Her machinery was afterwards put on the "Hope," built by Messrs. Payne and Hall.

Captain Payne next built the "Salem," at Red House. She is said to have carried the first steam whistle ever in the Kanawha, and was the first steamer ever to reach the Kanawha Falls.

In 1832, Captain Andrew Ruffner built the steamer "Tiskelwah," at the mouth of Elk, and ran her for a while in the Charleston and Cincinnati trade. She was the first steamer ever built at Charleston.

About this time Captain Payne built the "Jim," at Red House, putting on her the "Hope's" machinery.

In 1837, the Summers Bros. built the "Texas" and ran her for a time.

In 1838, Dr. Putney, William Atkinson and Samuel Summers built the "Oceola," at Buffalo, on the Kanawha River.

In 1839, James M. Laidley built the steamer "Elk."

In 1843, Captain Payne built the "Ark" and put on her the machinery of the "Julia Gratiot."

In 1846, Captain B. J. Caffrey built and ran the "Triumph."

In the same year, Warth & English built the "Blue

Ridge" and sold her to Captain Payne. She exploded her boilers in 1848, killing half a dozen or more persons.

After this, Kanawha packets and towboats became too numerous even to be mentioned.

The first little up-river packet, Charleston and above, was the " Here's Your Mule," in 1864. The next two built here expressly for the upper trade were the " Wild Goose" and " Lame Duck " in 1878.

In the early days of steamboating here, about 1833, there was a very exciting and long famous steamboat–canoe race. Mr. Sutton Matthews got up the race and backed the canoe for $500, against the steamer Daniel Webster, Captain N. B. Coleman, commander. The canoe keel was polished and varnished to lessen friction, and she was manned by six vigorous, young, athletic rowers, of whom Mr. J. H. Goshorn was one, and the shores were lined with people to witness the race. The canoe soon came to grief, was upset by the steamer's waves, and the rowers got an unexpected and involuntary bath. Although the original bet between the steamer and the canoe was but $500, it is said that $5,000 to $8,000 changed hands on the result. Several gentlemen won or lost several hundred dollars each, and the smaller bets were innumerable. Opinions were about equally divided, and nearly everybody backed his judgment with a bet, from staid, sober-sided citizens to the deck hands on the steamboats and the salt packers about the furnaces. Clerks and laborers drew their wages, up to date, and bet every dollar they could raise. A sensational account of the race was published in the papers, at the time, throughout the West.

The two gentlemen above named (Captain Coleman and Mr. J. H. Goshorn) are the only two survivors I know of, who participated in the exciting race.

In 1822 occurred one of the highest rises known in the Kanawha River. The water was around the Court House.

In 1832, and again in 1849, Charleston had severe visitations of the cholera.

In May, 1844, a very narrow, but very violent hurricane passed over the lower end of the town. Mr. Joseph Caldwell lived in a two-story brick house, just above the present Farley House. After uprooting trees on both banks of the river, the hurricane, or cyclone, struck this house, taking off the upper story evenly, and took a bed, with two children sleeping in it, and landed them "right side up with care" in the garden, in the rear of the house, unhurt and unharmed. The course of the cyclone was southwest to northeast. It passed up Elk, up Two-Mile, over to Blue Creek, and on. Its path was easily traceable from Central Kentucky to Central Pennsylvania, and how much farther I don't know.

In 1861, Charleston was mostly inundated by the greatest "flood" that has occurred in the Kanawha since the valley was settled. Its extreme height above the present Government standard low water gauge was 46 feet 10½ inches.

The next highest water was in September, 1878, when the gauge marked 41 feet, 7 inches.

The first frame house was on Kanawha street, immediately below the Court House lot. The next, on the south side of Kanawha, above Alderson street; and, about the same time, the old Central House, or Hoge building, on the northwest corner of Kanawha and Alderson streets. The date of these was 1812 to 1815. The first brick house was the Gabriel Garrou hatter's shop, on the bank, between Truslow and Alderson streets.

The first regular merchants were Henning & McFarland, in 1813; followed closely by Bureau, Scales & Summers, on the northwest corner of Summers and Kanawha streets.

In 1871, the street nomenclature of the city, which was in a very confused and unsatisfactory condition, was entirely reconstructed and officially recorded.

In the same year the Spring Hill Cemetery was established and laid out. It was named from the Chalybeate Spring, on the hillside, near the Cemetery road.

The same year the Piedmont road was constructed.

In May, 1871, Charleston was first lighted with gas.

In 1871, the first steam ferry was established here.

In January, 1872, the Hale House, the finest hotel in West Virginia, was opened. It was destroyed by fire in 1885. To meet the growing wants of the rapidly growing city, a still larger and finer hotel building is now being erected on the site of the old one, by Messrs. Ruffner Bros. The accompanying view of it is from the architect's drawings.

In January, 1872, the West Virginia Legislature met here.

In 1873, the Chesapeake & Ohio Railroad was opened to travel.

HALE HOUSE

In 1873, Summers street was paved with a combination pavement of hard-burned brick, with sand and board floor foundation, which has proved so satisfactory that no other street paving has since been used in the city.

In 1873, the United States Government began the improvement of the navigation of the Kanawha River, and established the Engineer's office in this city.

In 1875, Judge Lynch held his first court here. On the night of the 24th of December, some two or three hundred men marched orderly into town, took from the jail three murderers, Estep, Dawson and Hines, marched them up to the Campbell's Creek bridge, swung them up by their necks and quietly dispersed to their several homes.

In 1875, the "State Capitol on Wheels" was removed from Charleston to Wheeling.

In 1885, it was again returned to Charleston, its now "permanent location."

In 1884, the Government Post-Office building was completed and occupied.

In the same year, the O. C. R. R., now K. & O., was completed to Charleston.

In 1880, the Kanawha Military Academy was established by Major Thomas Snyder.

In the same year, the Eureka Detective Agency was established by Captain A. W. Burnett.

About 1883, the Ward patent water-tube boiler was perfected, and a manufactory established here by Mr. Charles Ward, the patentee.

Table of approximate population of Charleston at different periods since its first settlement:

1788 to 1790, seven houses.........say..	35	persons
1798 to 1800, twelve houses.........say..	60	"
1805 to 1810, twenty houses........say..	100	"
1820.................................say..	500	"
1830.................................say..	750	"
1840.................................say..	1,200	"
1850.................................say..	1,500	"
1860.................................say..	1,800	"
1870.................................say..	4,000	"
1880.................................say..	4,500	"
1886.................................say..	6,500	"

About twenty per cent. of the population is col-ored.

In 1852, a young lady from one of the Northern cities, who had been reared amid all the conveniences and luxuries of city life, came to Charleston to visit one of her "country cousins." Upon her return home, she reported that the Charlestonians were a charmingly simple-minded and worthy sort of people, but with, oh, such primitive ways! "Would you be-lieve," said she, "that they still preach hell fire down there, and haul their water in barrels?"

A Water Works Company is now "laying pipe" and erecting machinery, under the direction of Colonel E. L. Davenport, and we are promised, by July next (1886), an abundant supply of the whole-some beverage that "refreshes, but not inebriates."

Last year (1885), the first ice machinery was erected here, by Lieutenant M. Staunton, so that, henceforth, our citizens will be enabled to keep cool, independ-ently of Jack Frost, who, in this latitude, is capri-cious and unreliable.

In 1884, the City Hall, including the Mayor's office, etc., was erected.

THE NEW GOVERNMENT BUILDING.

The first Mayor of the city, under the organized city government, in 1861, was Mr. Jacob Goshorn.

The first building here for theatrical purposes was a temporary wooden structure, with seating capacity for eight hundred persons, erected by the Hale House proprietor in 1872.

In 1873, the first substantial Opera House was built by Dr. J. T. Cotton, Colonel T. B. Swann and Mr. Joseph Shields, and called the Cotton Opera House; when the temporary structure above mentioned was converted into the first regular livery stable of the city, by W L. Moffitt, S. M. Smith, and others.

The first dry docks were established at the mouth of Elk, in 1873, by J. J. Thaxton & Co.

The first machine barrel factory (with capacity for one thousand barrels per day) was started by Morgan & Hale, in 1872.

The first foundry and machine shop was erected by O. A. & W. T. Thayer, on the south side, in 1871. The first woolen mill had a small beginning by Messrs. Rand & Minsker about 1866, increased in 1868 by Messrs. Parsons, Appleton & Co., and largely extended in 1875 by Mr. Frank Woodman.

The first wharf-boat was established by H. W. Goodwin, in 1865.

The temporary capitol building was erected in 1871; the permanent capitol was partly occupied in 1885, but only completed in 1886.

The first public school building was put up in 1870.

The first steam-power brick machinery was introduced in 1870.

In 1815, Captain James Wilson, who then owned and occupied the Clendenin blockhouse, bored a well near it, for salt water; he struck, at a few hundred feet, a large yield of natural gas. This is believed to have been the first natural gas well in America.

In 1859, the Clendenin blockhouse property, which had then but recently been occupied by Mr. F. Brooks, and known as the Brooks farm, lying between the present Brooks and Morris streets, and back to the hills, was cut up into building lots and sold out.

In 1862, a company, called the "Charleston Extension Company," bought the Cox farm, or, as then more recently called, the Clarkson farm, and cut it up and sold it out for building purposes.

Within a few years after, all the property lying

back of the original town, and from Elk up to Bradford street, hitherto farms and orchards, were subdi-
vided into building lots and put upon the market,
and much of it is now built over.

In 1871, Mr. J. Brisbin Walker bought land on
the lower side of Elk, had it laid out in a town plat,
calling it "West Charleston," and sold lots.

In 1884, the "Glen Elk Company" purchased the
land extending from the suspension bridge up Elk,
on the lower side, laid it out in building lots for still
another "annex" to the town, called it Glen Elk,
and are rapidly selling lots. So that, altogether,
enough space is now appropriated for building purposes to make quite a large city when it shall all be
occupied; and it has been growing more rapidly
recently than at any former period of its history.

Upon the inauguration of the Civil War in
1861, the following military companies were raised
in Charleston and vicinity, in the interest of the
Southern cause: The Kanawha Riflemen, by Captain,
afterwards Colonel, George S. Patton; the Elk River
Tigers, by Captain, afterwards Colonel, T. B. Swann;
the Charleston Sharp-shooters, by Captain John S.
Swann; the Hale Artillery, by Dr. J. P. Hale; and a
Cavalry Company, mostly from the upper end of the
valley, by Dr. Ervin Lewis. These companies formed
parts of the Twenty-second and Thirty-sixth Virginia
Regiments.

Later, several Federal companies were gotten up
in the country round about Charleston, by Captain
Wood Blake, Major L. Martin, Major H. Slack, Dr.
R. H. Lee, Captain Green Slack, Jr., Major Gramm,
etc. These companies were united with the Fourth,
Seventh, Eighth, and Thirteenth Regiments.

In July, 1861, General Wise, then in command of the Southern forces here, evacuated the valley, and it was occupied by the Federals, under General J. D. Cox.

In September, 1862, the Southern army, under General Loring, re-entered the valley, and General Lightburn, then in command, retired. There was a slight skirmish in and about Charleston, and a few killed on each side, eight or ten in all. The Federals, before retreating, burned several of our prominent buildings, among them the Bank of Virginia, the Kanawha House, the Southern Methodist Church, the Brooks Store and Warehouse, etc.

In October following, General Loring, and a few days later, General Echols, again retired, and the town was re-occupied by the Federals, under General Cox; and remained in Federal possession, under several successive commanders, until the termination of the war. I shall not attempt a history of the military campaigns of the valley during the late war. This is being done, or about to be done, by more competent hands.

The first dray and hearse were introduced here by Noah Colley, an enterprising colored man, early in the thirties, and for a long time he had a practical monopoly of the town transportation, *for* the living and *of* the dead. Previous to that time the transportation to and from the river and steamboats and elsewhere was chiefly by sleds and carts, drawn by oxen, and the country transportation was by pack-horses, on pack-saddles.

The first pottery-ware establishment for manufacturing milk crocks, whisky jugs, etc., was by Stephen Shepherd, about 1818.

The first to carry on the hatter's trade was Gabriel Garrou, about 1816.

The first tailor was James Truslow, about 1815.

The first regularly established shoemaker was, probably, George Mitchell, about 1815.

The wagon and cart makers were not established in town, but up among the salt furnaces.

Up to 1840, and after, there were few or no mosquitoes here, and, consequently, mosquito bars were unknown.

The first wholesale grocery established here was by Messrs. Ruby & Hale, in 1872, followed by Messrs. Ruffner Brothers, in 1876, and Messrs. P. H. Noyes & Co., in 1883.

The first wholesale dry goods house was by Messrs. Jelenko Brothers, in 1874, followed by Messrs. Arnold & Abney, in 1882.

The first wholesale hardware dealers were Messrs. W. F. & J. H. Goshorn, in 1875, followed by Messrs. N. Berlew & Co., in 1883.

The first liquor wholesalers were Messrs. S. Strauss & Co., in 1876, followed by Charles Capito, in 1885.

The first wholesale shoe house was by Messrs. Jelenko & Loeb, in 1877, followed by Mr. John Anderson, in 1878.

Near the intersection of Kanawha and Goshorn streets there seems to have been an ancient burying ground of some primitive race. The caving of the bank and occasional excavations expose the remains and relics of this departed people. I have a handsome celt dug up there about six feet below the surface.

Charleston was visited, in 1796, by Volney, the dis-

21

tinguished French historian, philosopher and free thinker; and, in 1812, by the great naturalist, Audubon.

Albert Gallatin and DeWitt Clinton were extensive land locators here " in an early day."

In the early salt, flat-boating times, here, the boat-men gave the Kanawha the nick-name of " Old Greasy," on account of the petroleum that then flowed in greater or less quantities from the salt-wells, and covered the surface of the water with its beautiful iridescent hues.

Charleston and Cincinnati were both settled in the same year (1788), the former in May and the latter in December, so that Charleston is the older by several months, and is nearly one hundred years old. (Ninety-eight.)

To go back to the semi-centennial of Charleston, or half a century ago, and half a century after the first settlement—say to 1836 to '38—and give the names and occupations of the then citizens, who were worrying themselves over the same social, political, financial and bread and butter problems that are ex-ercising us now, may interest some readers, and serve to pleasurably revive the recollections of those whose memories go back that far. I therefore give the fol-lowing approximate list for such as may feel an in-terest in it:

> " Charley " Brown, ferryman and farmer.
> (Scotch) James Wilson, lawyer.
> Joseph Caldwell, merchant.
> Charles Neal, carpenter.
> Gabriel Garrou, hatter.
> John Hull, blacksmith.
> James Mays, boatman.

Judy Grinnan, colored, washerwoman.
Nancy Gibson, colored, washerwoman.
Henry B. Saunders, hotel keeper and stage runner.
John Snyder, preacher.
George Goshorn, hotel and ferry keeper.
Justin White, baker.
William Hutt, constable.
Silas Cobb, carpenter.
Matthew Dunbar, lawyer.
Crockett Ingles, merchant and salt maker.
John Mays, hotel keeper and builder.
Andrew Beach, shoemaker.
John Wilson, carpenter.
George W. Summers, lawyer.
John and Charles Allen, grocers and bakers.
Aaron Whittaker, hotel keeper and merchant.
Franklin Reynolds, salt inspector.
Samuel Hannah, bank cashier.
Captain James Wilson, hotel and ferry keeper.
Lewis D. Wilson, hotel and ferry keeper.
Mrs. Aletha Brigham, young ladies' school teacher.
Benj. H. Smith, lawyer.
William Whittaker, Sr., river toll collector.
Thomas Whittaker, merchant and saw miller.
Norris Whittaker, brick maker and builder.
Dr. Caruthers, physcian and author.
John Hall, blacksmith.
William Honeyman, silversmith and watchmaker.
Garrett Kelley, tailor.
Gilbert Adams, merchant.
James C. McFarland, bank president.
Dr. Spicer Patrick, physician.
Mason Campbell, editor and merchant.
John Truejohn, carpenter and builder.
Rev. James M. Brown, preacher.
Henry Fitzhugh, Sr.
Rev. James Craik, preacher.
Joseph Friend, salt maker and merchant.
Dr. Thompson C. Watkins, physician.
Isaac Noyes, salt maker.
Frederick Brooks, salt maker.

C. E. Doddridge, lawyer.

William J. Rand, merchant and salt maker.

Henry McFarland, merchant.

James H. Fry, sheriff and salt maker.

Bradford Noyes, farmer.

James Y. Querrier, deputy sheriff.

Ezra Walker, superintendent James River and Kanawha improvement.

James L. Carr, lawyer.

James Hendricks, lawyer.

Noah Colley, colored, dray and hearse runner.

Dock & Gabe, colored, coal haulers.

Andrew Cunningham, brickmason.

Thomas C. Thomas, carpenter and builder.

Mrs. Snyder, widow.

William W. Kelley, saddle and harness maker.

William A. Kelley, jailer.

Thomas R. Fife, carpenter and builder.

Alexander W. Quarrier, county clerk.

Mrs. Todd, widow.

James A. Lewis, merchant and postmaster.

Franklin Noyes, merchant and salt maker.

William R. Cox, salt maker and farmer.

Mrs. Chilten, widow.

James G. Taylor, cabinet maker.

John M. Doddridge, bank teller.

James M. Laidley, lawyer.

John Welch, merchant.

Joel Shrewsberry, Jr., merchant and salt maker.

Snelling C. Farley, tailor and steamboat captain.

Dr. Henry Rogers, druggist and physcian.

Jacob Rand, teacher.

John A. Truslow, tailor.

James Truslow, tailor.

John F. Faure, merchant and salt maker.

Joseph Lovell, lawyer and salt maker.

Stephen Shepherd, crockeryware maker.

John Starks, carpenter.

Nelson B. Coleman, merchant, salt maker and steamboat captain.

Joseph Bibby, miller.

Rev. James R. Baldwin, preacher.

John G. M. Spriggle, butcher.

Dr. Noah Cushman, physician.

William Hatcher, deputy clerk and jailer.

William Gillison, magistrate.

Mrs. S. Cook, widow.

Just above the town, to the head of the bottom, lived Black-wood Chilton, Mrs. Harshbarger, Daniel Ruffner, and the several sons of the latter: Charles, Joel, Augustus, Andrew and James.

The early settlers of a new locality are generally an. enterprising, wide-awake, progressive people. It is such people who have the pluck and energy to sever their relations with an old community and go to a new; to "go West and grow up with the country;" or go West and build up a country. From all the accounts we have of them, the earlier settlers of Charleston and vicinity were no exception to this rule. On the contrary, these characteristics were probably exceptionally emphasized in their cases; and for racy, sprightly wit and fresh originality, in addition to their general intellectual developments, I doubt if they were excelled by the builders of any other Western town.

There is still afloat here, handed down traditionally, a fund of humorous and racy anecdote in relation to the smart sayings, doings, and practical jokings of these old worthies that would fill a volume, if gathered together; and there are still surviving a few connecting links between the past and the present, who still delight to tell over, and their listeners are delighted to hear, the oft told stories of these lingering remnants of the rear-guard of the long-ago.

> "They were such men, take them for all in all,
> We shall not look upon their like again."

CHAPTER XXXVIII.

IT may interest the citizens of Dublin, the thriving railroad town of Pulaski County, Virginia, and their neighbors, to know something of its history, and by what steps of evolution the place acquired its name.

"In a very early day" a Dublin Irishman, named Reed, settled about two miles west of Ingles' Ferry, on the road laid out by William Ingles, leading westward. Reed kept a place of entertainment, a blacksmith's shop, etc., for the accommodation of the early emigrants, then just beginning to "Go West." Being a patriotic Irishman, from old Dublin, he called his place "New Dublin;" but all new things in time become old, and this New Dublin in time became "Old Dublin," in name and in fact. Its founder died or moved West, and the place was abandoned. I remember the old buildings, still standing, in a tumble-down condition, fifty years ago, but now entirely disappeared. About 1833, a number of families, among them the Ingleses, Cloyds, Kents, Wygals, Wysors, Trolingers, Hudsons, Morgans, and others, wanting a place of worship, each contributed to a fund and built a frame church in the forest, by a fine cold spring, a few miles from Old Dublin, located to suit the common convenience of the contributors and the neighborhood, and called it "New

Dublin Church." In time, this also became old, and they left off the prefix and called it "Dublin Church." The frame building becoming dilapidated, it was in time replaced by a more substantial brick structure.

About 1855, when the Virginia & Tennessee Railroad—now Norfolk & Western—was constructed, it passed near this church. A station was located here for the accommodation of this neighborhood; and as Dublin Church was the only thing in the immediate neighborhood that had a name, and as the railroad people seemed unequal to the effort of inventing a new name, they called it "Dublin Depot;" and being the nearest station to Newburn, the county seat of Pulaski County, it was, for a long time, indiscriminately called Dublin Depot, or Newbern Station. The name of Dublin, having better sticking qualities, at last prevailed, however, and, having sloughed off the suffix of Depot, now stands out as "Dublin," pure and simple; and though now the largest town in the county, I doubt if one of its citizens knows the history of its name, or that it dates back to the Irishman's log house, one of the first west of New River.

CHAPTER XXXIX.

IN 1734, Virginia organized the county of Orange, so called from the color of the soil of that portion lying east of the Blue Ridge. Orange County embraced not only the area east of the Blue Ridge, but all the indefinite territorial claims of the colony from the Blue Ridge to the Pacific Ocean.

In 1738, the bounds of Orange were curtailed by the formation of Augusta and Frederick Counties, covering all Virginia territory west of the Blue Ridge, and limiting Orange to the small area lying east of the Ridge.

In 1748, when settlements were begun west of the Alleghenies, Augusta County (excepting the comparatively small area in the lower part of the Valley of Virginia covered by Frederick County) included the same great scope of Western country lately Orange County.

By the treaty of Paris, in 1763, its western bounds were limited by the Mississippi River; but, even then, it covered (excepting Frederick, as above,) the vast territory now embracing all of the present State of Virginia west of the Blue Ridge, West Virginia, Kentucky, Ohio, Indiana, Illinois, Michigan and Wisconsin.

In 1748, the entire white population of this vast area was but a few hundred souls, all within the

Valley of Virginia, between the Blue Ridge and the Alleghenies; now, the aggregate population is about 17,000,000.

It may be a matter of curious interest to some, and valuable as a table of reference to others, to give a list of the progressive subdivisions into smaller counties, and the dates thereof, of that portion of this vast county (and of Frederick) still within the limits of Virginia and West Virginia, and between the Blue Ridge and the Ohio River:

AUGUSTA COUNTY AND ITS SUBDIVISIONS.
(INCLUDING FREDERICK.)

Augusta and Frederick formed	1738	Russell	1786
		Randolph	1787
Hampshire	1754	Pendleton	1788
Bottetourt	1770	Kanawha	1789
Berkely	1772	Wythe	1790
Dunmore	1772	Bath	1791
Fincastle	1772	Lee	1792
Montgomery		Grayson	1793
Washington		Brooke	1797
Kentucky	1776	Monroe	1799
Fincastle abolished		Tazewell	1799
Bounds of West Augusta defined	1776	Wood	1799
Ohio County formed	1776	Jefferson	1801
Monongalia	1776	Mason	1804
Youghiogheny*	1776	Giles	1806
Shenandoah†	1777	Cabell	1809
Greenbriar	1777	Scott	1814
Rockbridge	1777	Tyler	1814
Rockingham	1778	Lewis	1816
Harrison	1778	Preston	1818
Hardy	1786	Nicholas	1818
		Morgan	1820

* Youghiogheny abolished when the State line between Virginia and Pennsylvania was settled.

† Instead of Dunmore, and Dunmore abolished.

22

>|-|<

INDEX

COULTER, John 310
COWARD, 183
COX, Gen 320 J D 281 320 William R 324
CRAIG, Daniel 232 James 277
CRAIK, James 323
CRAWFARD, Col 270
CRAWFORD, Col 8 64 132 261 Maj 223
CRESAP, 265 Capt 180 264 Col 226 Michael 179 259
CRITTENDEN, 101
CROCKETT, 139 Davy 148 Hugh 277 Jane 106 Margaret 147
CROGHAM, Col 62
CRUTCHFIELD, Francis 304
CULL, James 29
CUMBERLAND, Duke of 15 Louisa Duchess of 15
CUNNINGHAM, Andrew 324 Robert 262
CUSHMAN, Noah 325
DAVENPORT, E L 316
DAVIDSON, Andrew 137–139 Daniel 262 John 176 Mrs 138 139 Rebecca 8 137
DAWSON, 315 Charles 233 Susan 233
DECELERON, 53 Capt 47 250
DECKER, 260 Thomas 255
DEHASS, 194
DENNIS, Hannah 8 243 244 246 257 258 Thomas 243
DESOTO, Hernando 109 110
DICK, 237 238
DICKINSON, 281 Capt 187 John 181 189 219 271 Mr 68
DINWIDDIE, Gov 176
DIXON, 190 270
DOCK, 324
DODDRIDGE, 207 C E 324 Dr 63 193 John 262 John M 309 324 Joseph 128
DONNALLY, 240 A 300 Andrew 221 236 261 270 299 300 310 Andrew Sr 299 302 Col 237
DONNELLY, Andrew 170
DOUGLAS, 103 111
DRAPER, 7 10 18 25 33 139 146 154 Alice 106 Bettie 8 28 37 99 105 106 254 285 Elenor 13 George 13 14 39 105 James

DRAPER (continued)
105 Jane 105 106 John 13 28 29 92 99 100 105 106 109 144 182 219 John S 105 106 L C 169 Mary 13 27 148 250 Mrs 16 34 39 115 Mrs George 29 Mrs John 29 Rhoda 106 Silas 105 106
DRENNON, Lawrence 240 Mr 241 Mrs 242 Thomas 242 269
DROWDY, William 302
DRYDEN, John 288
DUBOIS, Delafield 294 Francis A 308
DUFF, 17
DUNBAR, Matthew 300 305 323
DUNKLEBERRY, 26
DUNLAP, Capt 95
DUNMORE, 209 223 Gov 104 106 136 180 181 186 189 192 200 202–204 265 Lord 136 180 182 184–186 200 204–208 210 222 226 227 266 267
EASON, Samuel 277
EASTHAM, A G 223 William 223
ECHOLS, Gen 320 John 26
ECKERLY, 255 Dr 255 Thomas 254
EDGAR, Thomas 270
EDMUNSTON, 101
EDWARDS, John 287 306
ELINIPSICO, 186 230 249 267
ENGLISH, 311
EOFF, Dr 306
ESTEP, 315
EULIN, Ben 273
EVANS, Martha 132 133
EWING, Thomas 280
FAIRFAX, Lord 31 176
FARLEY, Snelling C 324
FAURE, John F 324
FIELD, Col 182 183 188 197 216 217 265 John 181 189 215
FIFE, Thomas R 324
FILES, Mr 253
FILSON, 173 John 53
FINDLEY, John 15
FINE, Carl 309
FINK, Henry 262
FINLEY, John 260 267
FISHER, Charles 305
FITZHUGH, Henry Sr 323 N 301

HOGG, Peter 95
HOLLIS, John 240
HONEYMAN, William 323
HOOPAUGH, 29 George 25 26
HORTON, Joshua 259
HOTCHKISS, Jed 15
HOWE, 290
HUDDLESTONE, Jared 169 Paddy 169 170 273
HUDSON, 326
HUGHES, 259 Ellis 223 Robert 267 Thomas 259
HULING, Mr 310
HULL, John 322
HUTT, William 323
ICE, 261 Adam 259 Adam Jr 259
INGLES, 7 10 18 25 122 123 146 154 Crockett 38 145 323 Eleanor 123 George 39 115 John 12 93 94 130 142 144 147 149 153 Malinda 147 Margaret 147 Mary 8 27 92 105 114 115 126 144 147 153 250 254 285 Matthew 12 93 94 Mrs 34–44 54 56 58 60 61 67 73–77 80–93 96 99 117 119 127 128 139 145 Mrs William 29 Rhoda 130 147 Susan 147 Thomas 11–13 16 39 114 115 119 124–130 136 140– 142 153 218 251 267 269 270 Thomas Jr 142 William 12 13 27 32 33 53 92 93 96 97 105 109 114 115 117 119 124 126– 128 144 147 153 250 252 256 326
INGLIS, 12 Thomas 11
JACKSON, Edward 259 George 259 John 259
JAMES, Frank 305 Lucy 305
JAMES I, 11
JARRETT, Capt 261
JEFFERSON, 50 51 122 123 Mr 225 Peter 24 Thomas 24 209
JELENKO, 321
JENKINS, A G 282
JOHNSON, 101 172 Charles 111 274 275 William 178 259
JONES, William 305
JOUMONDVILLE, Capt 177
JOUMONVILLE, Capt 252
KELLEY, Garrett 323 William A 324 William W 324

KELLY, Walter 69 215 263 265
KENT, 326 Jacob 94
KENTON, 7 184 224 261 263 266 267 286 Simon 66 192 222 234 271 277 278 285
KERCHEVAL, 232
KISKEPILA, 256
KNOX, Col 129 261 Lt 102
LAIDLEY, A T 309 J M 309 James M 48 300 311 324
LARD, Lt 189
LASALLE, 45 175
LEE, 64 65 Arthur 64 260 Capt 187 F L 64 260 R H 64 203 260 319 Richard Henry 227
LEFLER, George 262
LEMASTERS, Ben 305
LENARD, Henry 16 25 29
LEWIS, 7 101 111 222 239 240 269 Andrew 8 47 50 51 68 95 170 180 181 184 187 191 192 194 201 205–207 211 214 227 251 254 267 C C 294 295 Charles 180 181 187–189 212 214 215 219 Col 217 238 Ervin 319 Gen 68 95 123 181–186 190 192 193 197 198 200 204 206 208 210 212 213 215 216 220 224 233 265–267 281 James A 307 324 John 17 51 181 187 219 249 251 300 Samuel 170 238 270 Thomas 276 278 299 301 302 306 Thos 299 V A 233 William 181
LIGHTBURN, Gen 281 320
LINSEY, Joseph 257
LITTLE EAGLE, 256
LOCKRIDGE, Capt 187
LOEB, 321
LOGAN 8 101 179 185 225 226 227 234 267 Benjamin 222
LOONEY, Absalom 131 261
LORING, Gen 281 320
LOVE, Capt 187
LOVEL, Joseph 305
LOVELL, Joseph 300 324
LYBROOK, John 33 264 Mrs 33 Philip 30 33
LYNCH, Judge 315
LYTLE, Gen 281
MADISON, 101 122 Elizabeth 95
MARLIN, 251 Jacob 250

POGUE, John 131
POINTER, Dick 276
PONTIAC, 8 227
PORTER, William 275
POWERS, John 262
PRESTON, 17 33 36 104 249 Capt
    95 Col 101 James 55 216 John
    277 Robert 16 Susanna 100
    William 30 51 55 95 100 216
PRICE, Archibald 62 297 Edmund
    170
PRICKETT, 261
PRINGLE, 258–260 John 257 258
    Samuel 257 258
PRITCHET, 240 John 237
PRYOR, 265 268 Allyn 278 John
    181 221 236 237 241 242 269
PURDIE, 190
QUARRIER, Alexander W 324
QUERRIER, James Y 324
RADCLIFF, 223
RADCLIFFE, 259
RAND, Jacob 307 324 Mr 318
    William J 324
RANDOLPH, Peyton 203
RED HAWK, 185 228 231 232 233
    267
REED, 326 Alexander 191 212
    James 253
REID, James 270
RENICK, William 229
RENIX, 257 Betsy 243 Joshua 243
    Mrs 243 Robert 243 Thomas
    243 William 243
RENNIX, Thomas 260
REYNOLDS, Franklin 323 John
    221 278 299 300 Van B 300
RIFFLE, 262
ROBERTSON, Bettie 28 John 181
    Mr 221
ROBINSON, 193 David 301 302 Lt
    189 Mr 234 Stuart 134
ROGERS, Dr 288 Henry 307 324 J
    H 307 John 311
RUBY, 321
RUFFNER, 310 314 321 Andrew
    311 325 Augustus 325 Charles
    301 325 Daniel 303 325 David
    279 280 294 299 300 303 307
    Henry 304 James 325 Joel 307
    325 Joseph 291 Lewis 279 293
    300 301 307 Robias 279 Silas

RUFFNER (continued)
    69 291 Tobias 280
RUMSEY, James 271 274
RUSSELL, 106 Capt 183 184 187
    193 William 182 218
SAINT PIERE, M de 176
SALLING, John 249
SANDUSKY, Jacob 264 James 264
SAUNDERS, Henry B 323 Mary
    147
SCALES, 314
SCHED, Rabbi 305
SCHOOLCRAFT, 7
SCOTT, Mollie 268 Walter 11
    William 11
SEE, Michael 276
SELIM, 256
SEWELL, Stephen 250
SHAKESPEARE, 225
SHELBY, 219 Capt 183 184 187
    193 198 217 Evan 182 217
    Isaac 218
SHEPHARD, 17 262
SHEPHERD, Stephen 320 324
SHIELDS, Joseph 317
SHILLING, John 97
SHINN, Asa 304
SHREWSBERRY, 281 Joel Jr 324
    Mr 68
SHREWSBURY, Joel Jr 311
SIMPSON, 135 John 131 258
SINCLAIR, Robert 276
SKEES, R R 308 S A 308
SKIDMAN, I 189
SKILLERN, Col 268 George 229
SKYLES, 172 Jacob 111 274
SLACK, Green Jr 319 Greenbery
    301 H 319 John Sr 62
SLAUGHTER, Goodrich 221
    Reuben 288 301 302
SMITH, 95 101 293 B H 199 219
    301 305 Benj H 323 Byrd 147
    277 Col 196 Daniel 219 300
    301 Isaac N 301 James 115
    195 259 Mr 242 269 Mrs 242
    Rhoda 147 S M 317 Susanna
    100
SMYTHE, Daniel 24 269
SNIDOW, 33 Jacob 34 264 John
    34 264 William 34
SNYDER, John 323 Mrs 324
    Thomas 315

WETZEL, 7 262
WHEELER, John 277 Nat 277
WHITE EYES, 206
WHITE, Justin 323 William 262
WHITEMAN, 262
WHITTAKER, Aaron 323 Norris
    293 323 Thomas 323 William
    323
WHITTEKER, William 279 308
WICKLIFF, 101
WILLARD, Joseph 304
WILLIAM, Col 216
WILLIAMS, Mr 303
WILLIAMSON, Rebecca 261
WILSON, Benjamin 227 Capt 187
    James 280 294 300 318 322
    323 John 300 323 Lewis D 323
    Samuel 181 189 Scotch Jamie
    305
WIRT, William 122
WISE, Gen 320 Henry A 65 281
WITHERS, 207 242

WOLF, 136
WOOD, Abraham 19 21 26 48 248
    Col 21-23 James 15 Joseph
    271 Nehemiah 299
WOODMAN, Frank 318
WOODSON, 95
WOODVILLE, 101
WOOLEY, 101
WRIGHT, Peter 77
WYANT, William 282
WYATT, William 274
WYGAL, 326
WYMAN, 49
WYSOR, 326
YEAGER, 66 261 263 286
YOLKUM, Conrad 245
YOUNG, 272 Billy 62 Jacob 273
    John 66 242 269 272 302
    Thomas 264
ZANE, 7 262 Bettie 8 268
    Ebenezer 260 Jonathan 260
    Silas 260